Acclaim for **Stanley Crouch**'s

Always in
Pursuit

"What is appealing about the views of Stanley Crouch . . . is that he fully acknowledges the worst about the contemporary American scene yet remains deeply optimistic about the country's future. . . . [Crouch] offers perspectives on the American scene that are often bracing."

—*The New York Times*

"When Stanley Crouch speaks, people get out of the way. But they listen."

—*The Washington Post*

"Crouch might well be the most elegant prose writer this side of James Baldwin. . . . *Always in Pursuit* might well be Crouch's best collection thus far, and it establishes him as a writer who must be read."

—*Washington City Paper*

"Stanley Crouch is the jazz virtuoso of the American essay. . . . He is also an American Orwell: a completely independent voice, free of all cant and ideological etiquette."

—Tom Wolfe

"Stanley Crouch is one of our most trustworthy generals in today's Culture Wars. . . . *Always in Pursuit* [is] an essential book for everyone concerned about the future of this country."

—Charles Johnson

"For independence of mind, keenness of insight and blitheness of wit, it is hard to match Stanley Crouch. *Always in Pursuit* is a brilliant commentary on the tensions and paradoxes of American culture and American life."

—Arthur Schlesinger, Jr.

Stanley Crouch

Always in Pursuit

Stanley Crouch is a contributing editor to *The New Republic*, a Sunday columnist for the New York *Daily News*, and a frequent panelist on *The Charlie Rose Show*. He is the author of *The All-American Skin Game* (which was nominated for a National Book Critics Circle Award) and *Notes of a Hanging Judge*. For years a jazz critic and staff writer for the *Village Voice*, he is Artistic Consultant to Jazz at Lincoln Center. He lives in New York City.

Always in Pursuit

Fresh American Perspectives

Stanley Crouch

Vintage Books
A Division of Random House, Inc.
New York

All rights reserved under International and Pan-American Copyright
Conventions. Published in the United States by Vintage Books, a division
of Random House, Inc., New York, and simultaneously in Canada by Random House of
Canada Limited, Toronto. Originally published in hardcover in slightly different form in the
United States by Pantheon Books, a division of Random House, Inc., New York, in 1998.

Vintage Books and colophon are registered trademarks of Random House, Inc.

Permissions Acknowledgments appear on page 356.

The Library of Congress has catalogued the Pantheon edition as follows:
Crouch, Stanley.
Always in pursuit: fresh American perspectives, 1995–1997 / Stanley Crouch.
p.   cm.
Includes index.
ISBN 0-375-40153-9
1. United States—Civilization—1970–   2. Popular culture—United States—History—
20th century.   I. Title.
E169. 12.C75   1998
973.92—dc21

Vintage ISBN: 9780-375-70168-9

Book design by Laura Hammond Hough

www.randomhouse.com/vintage

Just for You

This most recent book of essays is dedicated to my
wife, Gloria Nixon, who is not only a surprisingly fine
sculptor of the first order, but a woman who is able to
handle the varieties of unexpected experience that go
with being married to a writer of my sort. I met her in
Harlem at a party, where she floated through a room
so brown and beautiful she seemed incapable of
touching the floor. I was wrong. Gloria Nixon keeps
her mind on a star the other side of the heaven we all
know while her feet maintain traction on the earth.
She understands illumination and knows how to keep
from sinking down in the mud. I assume that most
of us wish for big spirits filled with light to enter our
personal lives. I got lucky and was able to retire from
the wishing business.

| Contents

Introduction: Blues to You, Part III   3

PART ONE.   To Throw an Arm Around Life and
            Move with It: An Overture in Themes   11

            Blues for Tomorrow: A Gathering
            of Commentaries on Our
            American Condition   13

PART TWO.   A Number One Himself: Reflections
            on a Master   41

            Duke Ellington: Transcontinental Swing   43

PART THREE. Celebrity Nudes: Bloodshed, Sex,
            and Narcissism   67

            Truth Crushed to Earth   69

            The Dardenilla Dilemma: Selling Hostile
            Chocolate and Vanilla Animus   78

            The Dream Was Not in Place   94

            Blues for Three Widows   97

            The Huffing and Puffing Military Blues   102

            The King of Narcissism   106

PART FOUR.   Regarding Books: Homeric or Not?   111

Two on the Money   114

Bible Belt Greco-Roman Blues: The Shadow
of the Negro   117

The Blues Is the Accompaniment   128

Some Words about Albert Murray: Universal
Counterpoint from the Bass Clef   132

Somebody Knew   179

PART FIVE.   Foreign Intrigue: Some Dateline
Ganders and Musings   189

Downstairs Blues Upstairs   191

World War II at Fifty   194

Hiroshima, Mon Amour   197

Who's Sorry Now?   200

Patty-Cake with Blood   203

Forgotten Girl-Slave Blues   206

Whose Business Is Our Business?   209

Trouble in the East   212

PART SIX.   Up from the Grim: Transitional
Speculation, Ron Brown, and a
Christmas Card   217

Who Will Enjoy the Shadow of Whom?   219

Meditation on Ron Brown, in Two Parts   227

Spirits Spun in Gold   232

PART SEVEN. Images of Light in Dark Rooms:
Some Cinematic Achievements   235

Two Out of Three:
Reinventing Americana   241

Blues at the Gallows Pole   250

John Henry Versus the Minstrel Machine   253

The Radio Play Goes Public as the Sit-down
Raises Up   259

The Nutty Professor   269

Bull Feeney Plays the Blues: John Ford
and the Meaning of Democracy   272

PART EIGHT. Coming From Strength   293

Miles Davis in the Fever of Spring, 1961   295

PART NINE. Shout-Chorus on the Way Out:
How Dare We Do All the Things
We Dare to Do?   325

Blues to Be Redefined   327

Index   345

Always in
Pursuit

Introduction:
Blues to You, Part III

I want to keep the velocity of my exchange with the world at a high pace because I am now at a point where I feel right in the middle of our time, our era, our age. I see myself becoming increasingly adept at recognizing, at least from my own perspective, the epic nature of our interconnections and our problems as Americans. It is the weight and complexity of those things—how profoundly, in every way, we exist as parts of each other, how many difficult triumphs we share, and how much trouble we all have to face—that draw most of my attention. Speaking to our common humanity is the case that I stay on. The clues are many.

In my last book, *The All-American Skin Game*, I expanded upon themes I had introduced in my first, *Notes of a Hanging Judge*. With *Always in Pursuit*, I am continuing to build and work on my ideas as I maintain a dialogue in motion, attempting to describe the sobering-togut-busting whopper of a tall tale the *facts* of American life would surely seem if all of us didn't experience the heat of their force on our own skins, see them for ourselves, and hear them with our own ears. That is one of the most exciting and bemusing things about living in our time. Reality outstrips itself over and over, on and on. We observe the lowest rise and the mightiest fall. Human and natural disasters periodically muscle everything else off the front pages of our newspapers and dominate our electronic communications media, horrifying or shocking or both. It is a concomitant fact that we witness things so hilarious that we can almost feel the need to draft a few legions of professional laughers, chucklers, and guffawers to help us adequately respond to the comedic surprises arriving with a verve that matches their surreal and mutating nature. There are also signal victories that snap the barbed-wire fences of race, class, sex, and religion. We can draw plenty of unsentimental inspiration from those triumphs, every one of them wet with tears, blood, and sweat. The scale of our national tale, with all kinds of players, climes, and motivations, is epic to the max. He or she who would assess this had better be fast and had better be ready.

In the longer pieces included here, the grand themes that dominate the collection are given variation. Certain ideas reappear in different essays, surfacing with another slant, an altered or deepened essence, according to the context. As is usual for me, I am taken by the meanings and implications of our American democracy as they so consistently show themselves across society and within our broad to intimate relationships, arriving in everything from our arts to our politics. In order to handle this demanding form of government and society, we work to recognize just what elements oppose or distort our understanding of ourselves. Since *Notes of a Hanging Judge*, I have been thinking and writing about what terrible influences came out of the 1966 arrival of Black Power, which kicked off the politics of narcissism. That theme arrives again but, as with the writing included here on jazz, popular culture, and social trends, it is used to say other things and is interpreted differently and takes on further meaning within the various subjects under scrutiny.

From my position the arts are as important to me as politics, even more so since they have the chance to last beyond almost anything else produced in a given era, sharing with the core facts of science the possibility of timeless information. Sometimes my point of view comes through focusing at length on an individual whose work sets up epic reverberations, which is why I have included what I hope are major essays about Duke Ellington, John Ford, William Faulkner, and Albert Murray (who, the reader will note, is an intellectual hero of this book). Far down the pecking order of the profound, the subject of Michael Jackson allows me to look at one sort of thing in our world, as does Tupac Shakur, or O.J. Simpson, or Christopher Darden. Mountain ranges and ticks are equally real; one group stands up next to heaven; the other swells itself on our blood.

The longer pieces, whether written to be read or initially created for public addresses, are almost always experiments with the form of the essay. I find myself looking for fresh ways to organize the material, to set up ideas, to work on thematic variations, to shift and play with rhythms. All of this leads back to what I first recognized when I stuck my nose between the covers of *In the American Grain* more than thirty years ago. Reading that book and examining the way William Carlos Williams handled his writing voice excited me as much as the experience of slowly going through *Moby Dick*, the novel I later saw, given its labyrinth of styles, as the major, unacknowledged bridge between *Tristram Shandy* and *Ulysses*. Williams turned me away from the Norman Mailer of *Advertisements for Myself*, which was so bold and combative and possessed of such an original sound, regardless of its bumpy and uneven ride. Mailer had provided an antidote to James Baldwin, whom I was taken by in terms of his eloquence but never found extremely convincing in a visceral manner because I wasn't—and am not—a Henry James enthusiast. Yet anyone should be impressed by how brilliantly Baldwin used the rhythms of Negro church rhetoric and music to adapt the old master for his own purposes.

Like the exceptional essayist Gerald Early, I remember reading *Home* by LeRoi Jones over and over. I had discovered Jones as an essayist in the liner notes of *Coltrane Live at Birdland*, which was the first time I had seen that kind of poetic sensibility brought to the discussion of jazz. It was as new to me as the way Coltrane and his band were reinventing the

4/4 swing, blues, ballads, and Afro-Hispanic rhythms that are the four elements essential to jazz. Jones was then influenced by Williams, Pound, and Charles Olson but had done the same thing with them that Baldwin had with Henry James. His was the first Negro voice that sailed to the center of my taste by combining the spunk and the raw horrors of the sidewalk with the library, then shooting for an elegant manhandling of the form. Few of those essays in *Home* now touch me the way they did then but I will never lose the memory of how it felt when I carried them as an auxiliary part of my wardrobe and read the book into the night, progressing from the sound of voices and automobiles out the window all the way to that point when there was only silence, no world other than me and those words.

In many places I have written about the central significance of Ralph Ellison and Albert Murray to what I do, though I don't think that the structural concerns of either in the essay form have been particularly important to my work. (Nor has the writing sound of either, though I now and again will make private jokes through affectionate allusions to their styles or Murray's clichés.) I was indelibly taken by their intellectual range within the context of the social progress since World War II and what we almost all recognize as the decay of the common values that once transcended race, class, and religion. (Perhaps the central question of our moment is whether or not we can actually redefine ourselves beyond the narrows of traditional prejudices while maintaining—or regenerating—the common values that once made possible civilized communities across our remarkably varied social spectrum.) Though fundamentally literary men, Ellison and Murray so brilliantly pulled out the best of Negro American life, the American scene at large, and the thinking of the European masters, whether literary or not, that their work could mightily help this democratic society learn how to appropriately oppose the Balkanizing elements that have dug themselves in, holding their fragmentations in place over the last thirty years. The presence of disease in the oyster doesn't change the fact of the pearl and the presence of the pearl doesn't change the fact of the disease. Learning how to avoid confusing the two in our world of so many increasing choices would help us get beyond the tendency to so desperately sentimentalize or demonize. Over the last three decades, since we became, in too many cases, so smugly "nonjudg-mental," our batting average is now just as high when it comes to either making an argument for keeping the baby *and* the bath water or chucking out both.

Probably the single event of prose writing that has most impressed me over the last decade or so is what Evan Connell did in *Son of the Morn-ing Star,* where he used a digressive, Melvillian technique to tell a story we thought we knew, the fall of Custer on that hot, 1876 Sunday in Mon-tana. The book is perhaps a masterpiece of form and originality, gallows humor, and eloquence, which is why so many historians hate it. What Connell really decided to do was tell us many of the wacky, tragic, hilari-ous, and sensational things that went into the winning of the West, using Custer as a centerpiece the way Melville had Ahab when that great New Englander decided to write about both America and the whole wide world, setting up his compass with an overture of contradictory defini-tions and references to whales.

While what Connell wrote was a full-length book and not an essay, it made me think about what I believe an essay should do, which is give the impression that one has read a much longer work. It ought to have the poetic power capable of summoning and projecting a larger feeling and a greater sense of information and engagement than the number of pages would suggest. Where Hemingway wrote in *A Moveable Feast* that when he was a kid in Paris he was trying to construct paragraphs that would use the same devices as a novel, I have a theory about the writing of novels that applies equally to the essay of this moment. What good novels actu-ally do is orchestrate onomatopoeia (the poetic device in which the sound imitates the rhythm of the subject). In my aesthetic, the essay should be shaped with such attentiveness to sound, image, and rhythm that it will retain the singular intimate identity expected of writing while simultane-ously asserting the force we expect from other forms in our rapid era, forms such as the television documentary and the feature film, the compact disc and the musical drama, all of which usually assert the compression of power for thematic, narrative, and intellectual effects, with emotion the given that arrives through technical precision.

What about the shorter pieces? Well, they come from my columns in

New York's *Daily News*, where I step into the topical ring and do the very best I can. As a columnist, I have had to learn how to get my ideas into small spaces, the joy of which is moving one's thoughts right out into the street, where the working people give you their attention. I like the pressure of writing the columns and the fact that they make me pay even more attention to the daily doings of life in New York and America than I might otherwise. I also work at using the techniques described earlier in order to make the columns explode into larger areas of contemplation and feeling than we usually expect from such brief turns of mind. They might zero in on events that allow me to look at how certain things are done in our society, or what events such as the fiftieth anniversaries of Victory in Europe and Victory in Japan might mean once we get to the other side of the immature smirks and the self-righteous carpings that are no more than disguises for one kind of sentimentality or another—the maudlin petrified into the hard rock of cynicism. You will be the judge as to whether, in the long or the short forms, I am bringing off what I'm after, but I'm always one who wants to make clear the intent.

There is a small piece here that fits into some category unknown to me, "Trouble in the East," which I wrote and read one version of for a Bosnia benefit sponsored in New York by the Pen American Center in 1994. I didn't actually finish it until January of 1997, when I finally got one line in place that had evaded me. It now has the absolute smack that I wanted, ending with the sound of those boots crunching in the snow.

The collection opens with one speech and closes with another. The first, delivered at the American Enterprise Institute in December of 1996, is entitled "Blues for Tomorrow," an experiment in form and the first part of a two-part overture. This opening lays out much of the terrain the book will traverse, seriously or humorously. It is an intellectual medley comprised of *Daily News* columns organized to exhibit a stretch of our concerns. The second piece, which is about Duke Ellington, provides an alternate, or secondary, overture, laying out a broad set of aesthetic observations. With those two in place, the rest of the book has a more clear feeling. The last piece in Part Seven, a big essay about John Ford entitled "Bull Feeney Plays the Blues," begins the reversal of the form used to open the book, since it is about an artist and is also connected to Ellington. The finale is a summing up, another overview, one way of trying to pull together what I see out here and what I think about it. Where the opening talk is more loosely organized, the last is something so totally orchestrated in its sound and its observations that I am actually proud of it and have enjoyed the challenge of reading it here and there, making those long sentences comprehensible to the ear of the listener. I call what I intend to be a doozy of a conclusion "Blues to Be Redefined."

As one jazz musician friend of mine used to say when kicking off tunes at jam sessions held in his New York loft, "See you at the end."

VICTORY IS ASSURED

PART ONE

To Throw an Arm Around Life and Move with It:

An Overture in Themes

Blues for Tomorrow:

A Gathering of Commentaries

on Our American Condition*

I *am always looking for a form, something new that will allow me to express what I'm thinking about in a way that offers some sort of challenge to the predictable coherence one's own clichés make possible. This time out I intend to make a collage of new material written for this occasion and selections from other works. The other works are, with one exception, columns written for the New York* Daily News. *I am using this form because it allows me to talk about a number of things that have engaged me over the last year, in the worlds of literature, politics, and our popular culture. In a sense, this form allows me to create something akin to a musical set presented by a jazz band, each selection chosen for its role in an overall effect.*

* In a slightly different form minus one piece and featuring briefer introductory interludes between short investigations of national events and themes, this was delivered as a talk at the American Enterprise Institute on December 16, 1996, in Washington, D.C.

As Americans, which is to say a people who have grown up with the Industrial Revolution and with all of the technological developments since,
we almost always find ourselves in a world not quite like any that preceded
it. In order to maintain some sense of our own identity, we reject what we
have been told of the past, or we attempt to reiterate what we think happened, or we invent a past that will work inside the social, political, and
aesthetic conventions we intend to stand on. There is nothing wrong
with this because our century, even as it ends, is something I once called
the "Age of Redefinition." What was meant when I used that name in the
introduction to *Notes of a Hanging Judge* was that we have seen gravity
conquered, the arrival of the automobile, mass entertainment and mass
communications arrive through technology, the redefinition of barbarism
by the Third Reich, the recognition of universal humanity at the United
Nations, the fall of the colonial world, the collapse of Marxism, and, in
our very own country, we have seen minorities and women redefine themselves, sometimes for the better, sometimes for the worst.

Those are just a few examples, some of them central to the meanings
of our time, but they all give you an idea of what I think we need to be
looking at now, which is just how accurately we redefine ourselves in a society that innovated a political structure of unprecedented democratic
clarity. Our system reflects the Western tradition of development through
argument, through contradiction, through reinterpretation. Our American democracy is perfectly prepared to handle the problems of human life
and human consciousness, which tend to break down into folly, corruption, mediocrity, and incompetence. It is because we function from a
tragic base that is also optimistic that we are so well prepared to address
the inevitable blues of human life. This tragic optimism is based in a very
reasonable version of paranoia about power. Our system expresses the
understanding that while human beings might abuse power if given the
chance, we have to have an instrument that will allow us to right whatever policy wrongs arrive through prejudice, corruption, or ignorance.
This makes ours a society which, when it is most like its truest self, moves
always toward integration. We bring together the different and create,
over and over, what the writer William D. Piersen calls "a complex, inter-
continental alloy" in his very important *Black Yankees*.

Off and on for the last thirty years, we have had many troubles un-

derstanding this because we have bought an idea about alienation based
on category that goes in the opposite direction from the blood-spattered
truth of the society. In the last essay in *The All-American Skin Game*,
"Melting Down the Iron Suits of History," I made note of the fact that this
is because alienation has become a commodity and is sold from sea to
shining sea on our university campuses. It is also a staple in our entertainment industry. Negro Americans pretend that they are Africans, women
pretend that they are either the same as men or totally different, and other
ethnic minorities smitten by the trickle-downs from the Black Power pro-
jection of false differences pretend that their essential identities, regardless of how many generations they may have been in this country, are
lodged in cultures at some sort of geographical distance from the United
States. One film after another tells us that all of our problems are the results of corruption in high government places. In fact, the CIA now functions as the *diablo ex machine,* the all-purpose devil in the wings. We also
see in our popular entertainment a tendency to sadism that makes its ap-
pearance when the hero is giving the villain his or her comeuppance.
Such tendencies are rocks in our collective bed.

Our American complexity is such, however, that we also see today a
broader and richer integration of race, sex, religion, and whatever else
than we have ever witnessed in this country. Some of this has to do with
social movements and some of it with the ever-flexible rules of the marketplace. As Michael Jordan and Tiger Woods become icons of excellence, we should recognize that they stand in a New World, which might
not be especially brave but is at least practical. The montage of the Nike
commercial in which individual children of all races and both sexes say,
"I'm Tiger Woods," makes it obvious that Spike Lee's phony baloney ending to his celebration of Malcolm X has moved into a realer world of identification across race. This is based on simple fact, on cold calculation.
Those who work in the business of advertising are not trying to improve
race relations; they are trying to sell products. Only those whom they assume the masses have already identified with, or can easily be identified
with by millions upon millions, will come down front and center in advertisements and get the huge endorsement contracts. Those who conceive these advertisements are only underlining what they know has
already happened in the society. At this time, if a white girl in the suburbs

were to put a poster of Michael Jordan up in her bedroom, the odds are that nothing would happen; there would be none of the shouting and racist remarks she might have encountered as an adolescent sweetie pie if she had put a poster of Willie Mays on her wall in 1960. A black girl in a middle-class and mildly Afrocentric household would probably be the one to catch hell if she had a picture of Brad Pitt on her bedroom wall. So some of us switch positions and refuse to face the music but keep on dancing.

As the rough and refined beast of our society tunes itself up to meet the challenges of the world market, which are arriving at ever faster velocities with digital communication, we will find ourselves functioning on international planes where race and sex will become progressively irrelevant. If one is conducting a deal with someone in Hong Kong or doing some consulting or providing information, the point on the other end will not be one's color or one's erotic plumbing but just how well what one has to say objectively *works* in Hong Kong. Economic thinker Lester Thurow has observed that this new technology will put competition right out in the open and the little person will eventually be able to go toe-to-toe with the Goliaths of industry—if his or her sling shot has the right stuff. Since our America is still out front and will remain so for some time, we need to start thinking about ourselves with the same freedom that will become automatic in the digitalized world economy. We need to see redefinition as it is.

In order to see ourselves as we are and to recognize what we are becoming we need to create a fresh atmosphere of exchange. In that direction, this first selection is entitled "Dizzy Atmosphere."

The recent vote in California to cancel affirmative action, the Texaco scandal in which executives were taped using racial epithets and sneering at minority employees, and the latest charges of rape and sexual harassment in the army make obvious the fact that we are divided on some central contemporary issues. We don't exactly know what to do about the problems of prejudice and we are more than a little upset by the way things have gone.

I, for one, am theoretically opposed to anything being set aside or guaranteed on the basis of race or sex. But then I have heard none of those who are so vehemently opposed to affirmative action come forward with a solution that will handle some of the facts that we now have before us— and the information is irrefutable.

Prior to the Texaco scandal, a commission under the leadership of New York State assemblyman Larry Seabrook got tapes of employment agencies agreeing to send out what have been called "all American types—blond hair, blue eyes, white skin." This evidence led to the attorney general of New York State stepping in.

What are we to do when we have proof of that sort? How many more are out there in America than the ones now caught on the latest tape? Are we to continue whining and howling as though affirmative action has somehow come to equal the sort of racial and sexual prejudice that maintains itself in strong but mysterious proportions? I hope not.

The reason we have so much trouble getting things straight on these issues is that some of us on both sides know just how shamelessly power is abused. There are a good number of middle-aged white people who graduated from good schools and remember quite well what it was like twenty-five years ago when minority students were admitted to top universities on the basis of quotas. A lot money was wasted on minority scholarships because a large proportion of those kids weren't prepared by their grade schools to compete at that academic level. They flunked out or dropped out, embittered or believing themselves inferior. Many millions of dollars gone.

White people who were there on those campuses and saw what they saw are no longer interested in hearing about the historical injustices suffered by minorities, Negroes in particular. Having seen standards ignored and having experienced an atmosphere in which one could be haughtily dismissed as a racist for merely questioning the admissions policy on quotas, they don't believe that any ethnic group is above corruption and are quite sure that those who can will pass favors on to their own. Minorities, they are convinced, are interested only in privileges, not in achieving success on the basis of merit.

From the other side, scandals like the Texaco tapes validate all the feelings of resentment harbored by those black people who complain to one another about the glass ceilings of the corporate world and what they sometimes consider the almost suffocating atmosphere of hostility in the workplace. Where they might previously have wondered if the white people in charge talked about Negroes like dogs when none were around, now they are sure that the white people at the top will do everything in their power to keep black people from moving up. As far as they are concerned, all this talk about meritocracy is bunk.

The latest charges of rape and sexual harassment in the army, if they prove true, are variations on the Texaco tapes. Once again, we have to face the fact that genitalia, like skin color, can attract extra burdens in an already burdensome age. No number of hustlers and whiners who have been exposed for hiding behind race or sex—or both!—will diminish the truth of those problems.

It is also true that those problems *are* diminishing, yet we still have to create an atmosphere in which all complaints from all sides can be discussed free of conservative smugness, liberal-heart hemophilia, and demagogic hysteria. In that kind of atmosphere, we would have the freedom to discuss and debate our problems of prejudice and policy abuse. That is the only way we will get beyond where we are now, exhausted by failed social policies of uplift and enraged by the durable existence of bigotry, even in the highest places.

The tireless rhythm and blues singer James Brown said more than a mouthful in his line that it's a man's world but it wouldn't be anything without a woman or a girl. In that direction, the next selection, formed of three pieces about women in our time, is a little suite that I bring together under the title, "The Prattle of the Sexes."

The Prattle of the Sexes, Part I: Military Ladies

When the Supreme Court recently decided to sexually desegregate military academies, it made more than a good decision. The moment our highest court made it possible for military academies to maintain their traditional single-sex policy of male cadets only if they decline to accept federal funds, we knew what the outcome would be: Ladies, step this way, suit up, and let's get with it!

The reason I think this is a good thing is not because it will blur the distinction between men and women or give the false impression that the sexes are physically equal. The distinctions remain and the edge men have in strength remains. But women who are physically fit enough to try and make it through military academies should have a chance to see what they can do. If they go on to military careers, their preparation will enhance the quality of the armed services. If they choose not to, they will have gotten what are almost always recalled as invaluable leadership lessons in discipline, team work, and learning to assess the measure of others under both limited and sustained pressure.

I say this because our society has to continue to make the best use of all of its talents, no matter the sex, the race, the religion, the nationality, or the sexual preference. All people need to be is civilized and know how to do their jobs. As for women, I come from a family line that included women who were down-home, elegant, aristocratic, and roughhouse when necessary.

My grandmother on my mother's side was the soul of calm, humor, and compassion, but she was just as willing to knock an insulting redneck on his cakes as her husband was. In East Texas, she and her husband were considered "crazy." Consequently, I never thought of women as people who couldn't handle themselves outside of baby showers if they had to.

After all, ours is a pioneer society and we have evolved the idea of the pioneer woman, the type ready to roll up her sleeves and help get the job done—or initiate the job! As Albert Murray pointed out in *The Omni-Americans*, there is no greater example of the courageous, disciplined, and strong pioneer woman than the runaway slave Harriet Tubman, who ventured South many times in order to bring escaped slaves through the swamps and the dangers of the trip to the North.

Even so, Tubman is no greater—perhaps not as great—than Sacagawea, the teenaged Indian girl and scout who was so important to the Lewis and Clark expedition that opened up the American West. But comparative greatness isn't what truly matters because this country has produced so many women who have been important in every field of endeavor, from the arts to the sciences. Arriving from myriad ethnic backgrounds, they have been innovators and they have upheld standards of excellence. As pioneers in the social wilderness of prejudice, they have expanded our conception of what is humanly possible and have pushed the stereotypes about women further and further into the marginal backwoods—where they belong.

Perfect examples in the real world and in the arts are trailblazers such as Ann Richards, the recent woman governor of Texas; Hazel O'Leary, who heads up the Energy Commission; Christie Todd Whitman, governor of New Jersey; Supreme Court Justices Sandra Day O'Connor and Ruth Bader Ginsburg, and the pregnant Minnesota police chief played by Frances McDormand in the film *Fargo*. It doesn't matter whether those women are Democrats or Republicans; liberal or conservative; white, black, brown, red, or yellow; religious or not. They have been involved in helping us realize the values at the center of our social contract.

In *Fargo*, McDormand's character largely sums up where we are right now. She is extremely smart and has the support of her husband and gives him hers. When things are easy, she's charming and down-home. If the going gets rough, she knows how to grill a hostile suspect. When she closes in on a murderer, the police chief, swollen under the overcoat of her winter uniform, pulls her service revolver and stands ready for war in the Midwestern snow. Given our American luck, we can be sure that our military academies will produce some women like that, no matter what careers they choose.

The Prattle of the Sexes, Part II: My Body, My Price

The case of Carol Shaya is an example of where our society is now. Last spring it became public knowledge that this lady who buttered her bread with a badge and a gun would soon bust out with the bimbo moves of showing it all in an August *Playboy* spread. It was another of the remarkable twists we see in our culture, where individual freedom and self-exploitation blend for a paycheck.

Long before Madonna became famous for appropriating every slut direction possible, and equally long before the pop star was celebrated for her willingness to swim through the cultural sewer with her mouth wide open, *Playboy* showed us how easy it was to turn all kinds of women into nude cows mooing for cash.

Forty years ago, *Playboy* began putting a respectable face on stripping and teasing. It also put a sheen on being a peep freak. *Playboy* got in the middle of the argument against sexual repression, supported the Civil Rights Movement, argued for homosexual and lesbian rights, published respected writers, interviewed famous people, did layouts of high-class clothes, yachts, sports cars, fine food, wines, and so on. Those trappings allowed men to pretend that they bought the magazine for everything except the payoff, which was the air-brushed girl next door—naked as a newborn jaybird.

In the process, the *Playboy* "bunny" ripped the seal of sin off of sex. She was expensively photographed and didn't look worn down by servicing the cactus appetites of johns. This young sweet thing had no rap sheet as long as the world's memory of wrongdoing. The buns-bare bunny was just the good-looking American girl ready for the hiss of steamy fun.

As its popularity grew, *Playboy* became inclusive. It recognized the need for diversity and went multicultural. Regardless of color or nation, women were willing to tear it off for a buck. *Playboy* also fought against ageism. It got Vicki LaMotta to pop out her breasts and drop her drawers at fifty.

Eventually, *Playboy* became so serious that it took on the world of the professional woman. A stockbroker was shot writhing on a couch in her office with a photograph of her husband and kids in the background. Even an undertaker went naked next to her coffins.

Now Carol Shaya is suing the New York Police Department for $10 million in order to get her job back. *Playboy*'s $100,000 wasn't enough. She should be free to rip the uniform off of her stuff if she wants to; her job is her job, her free time is her free time. She's an American. She has her rights.

But can 4,600 women cops be wrong? Good riddance is the collective opinion of our Jane Laws. They got harassed on the streets after the spread appeared and were stung to the quick by Shaya's willingness to scrape all dignity from the extremely hard and sometimes brutal job of standing tall in the face of all God's dangers.

Carol Shaya represents how willing some of us are to strut our corruption in public by pandering to any stereotype if the pay is good enough. She is another of those caught in the spiritual whirlwind and the stench of our popular culture at its worst, where bimbo images, endless vulgarity, and coon acts spiced by abundant profanity are sold to the highest bidder.

But Shaya's suit proves that so many of these arrogant and obnoxious people, after all is said and done, aren't quite willing to pay the cost to be the boss. When these little piggies get smacked for putting themselves on the auction block, they cry wee wee wee all the way into court.

The Prattle of the Sexes, Part III: Medea Goes South

The case of Susan Smith, the Medea of South Carolina, says much about horror, empathy, change. The startling velocity of her murder tale fits well within the facts of our celebrated social mobility and makes clear the effects of our emotional identifications through electronic media. That social mobility attunes us to human nuances and commonality. We learn that virtue as well as folly, corruption, mediocrity, and incompetence course from one end of the society to the other. Through our televisions and our radios we are so quickly, so clumsily, and so deeply touched by what happens to others that their sorrows and the dangers that threaten them become part of the vast national soap opera that helps define us.

Give us an inch of opportunity and we'll respond with a mile of emotion. All we need is someone in trouble, especially some young woman and her children, some babies on the verge of starvation, a line of terrified older people caught in a war zone and wondering when the next shelling will start, a number of parents screaming in terror after an earthquake or a flood because they can't find some children they thought were safe. Pull it out, we'll respond.

We'll become sappy and stuffed up, emptying the box of tissues.

We'll get indignant about the slow pace of assistance. We'll tremble with suspense and lose sleep as we stare at the ceiling worrying about someone we never met. We'll swell forward with jubilance when some unmerciful catastrophe is muzzled by a brave team of public servants or the volunteer heroics of passersby.

No matter how often we are manipulated, a strong part of our democratic identity is that willingness to identify with all things human. When someone like Susan Smith tampers with that willingness, we find out how quickly we have moved from what we thought was sudden tragedy to sudden empathy and, now, to sudden shock.

As we face the drowning murders of two children by their mother we also have to face up to what it says about the nature of race relations at this time. Susan Smith is another bumbling murderer who felt that the noose could be slipped by serving up the all-purpose Negro criminal.

Of course, we witnessed this just a few years ago from Charles Stuart in Boston, where red rises in the neck quite easily. Before he committed suicide, Stuart killed his pregnant wife, shot himself, and blamed it all on an invented black killer. As one might imagine, everybody with a civilized sensibility—which is just about everyone—empathized with Stuart, wished him a speedy recovery from his wound and wanted the killer brought to justice with breathless speed.

None of this is particularly surprising. We live intimidated by a degree of crime so unprecedented that it adds a sulfurous edge to the coffee people are always being told to wake up and smell. We also live in a time when the rate of black urban crime is profiled high in the media, the minds, and the experiences of Americans. A killer within the household could easily figure that a trumped-up tale starring some dark-skinned figment ricocheting off of our collective dread would be swallowed whole by the public, no butter necessary.

But we no longer routinely expect a Negro to be railroaded all the way to death row just because a ruthless white person concocts a tale based as much on what is possible as on any simplifying stereotype. Susan Smith thought she could slide by but she didn't count on the ironies connected to the commercial ways in which the national heart is manipulated.

Pursuing high ratings, the media seek real-life perils, flesh-and-blood soap operas for exploitation, which also means that veterans and experts fly in. Professionals and volunteers try to help. The killer is then crushed by so much attentive sympathy that the walls of the whopper start to crack; the cologne of false fear and mourning is sweated away. We then peep through the cracks to see the actual murderer and the bodies and we smell the blood. As Tawana Brawley discovered, the combination of the media's relentless, competitive scrutiny, the serious effort to solve crimes, and the national appetite for melodrama can doom even a damnably plausible lie.

It is equally true that Susan Smith's case, which was cracked by the local police, proves something else we shouldn't forget. In the old, terrorist South, back not so long ago when a white woman's word was considered as pure as a new angel's breath—especially if it was accusing a Negro of wrongdoing—Smith would surely have been believed. Doubtless, hysterical white men—including the police—would have run amok in a familiar pattern, taking what they considered revenge by killing and burning until they got good and tired. No matter how far we still have to go, and how difficult our journey might still be, this South Carolina story lifts a bright, unarguable fact into the gloomy faces of defeatists, making it very, very clear that we have moved a good distance beyond what was once a grim and common kind of injustice.

We all have to grow up enough to embrace a porcupine truth, which is that anything can be corrupted. This corruption is as heavy in the arena of popular entertainment as anywhere. The attention that was given to the violent demise of gangster rapper Tupac Shakur inspired this column: "Flee as a Bird."

When thinking about Tupac Shakur dying in Las Vegas as a target of the thug life he advocated, the facts should be clear. He represented the very worst inclinations in American youth, on or off the stage. Shakur was a charismatic celebrator of scum, whose work helps define our contemporary crisis.

That crisis results from the difficulty of recognizing that there is a difference between this country's many cultural variations on the national norm and the barbaric elements that work against all that is civilized. Some are so confused that when they defend the work of gangster rappers, they assume that those highly critical of its repulsive characteristics are either racist or "too middle class." Too many supposed thinkers, crossing all racial lines, share that confusion.

Whatever their backgrounds, they have no idea what the real issue is.

One does not have to adhere to middle- or upper-class etiquette to live a civilized life. One does not have to speak the English language correctly to live a civilized life. One does not have to be financially well off to impart civilized values to one's children. The ability to live a civilized life is not determined by believing in a specific religion or coming from a particular branch of the human family. To believe otherwise is to be racist or given to religious or class prejudice.

But when one uses guns to resolve even trivial arguments, or resorts to rape and sadism for fun, or becomes part of a shadow world of short-tempered thugs who terrorize lower-class communities—wounding, maiming, and killing innocent bystanders—one is a threat to civilization. When one defines women as bitches and whores, one intensifies all misogynist tendencies, which are surely obstacles to civilization and human understanding.

Those who get their backs up at such statements about gangster rap and its makers usually fall into two categories: fools and opportunists. The fools are the whites and the Amos and Andy academics who are unwilling to call what they see by its name for fear of seeming as though they have no respect for any "culture" other than the ones they come from. There are also the liberal racists who accept any kind of swinish ideas or idiotic behavior from so-called minorities because they don't think we should expect anything more of "them."

Then, of course, there are those youthful black fools who will say, as some of Shakur's fellow knuckleheads have, "Tupac Shakur was the quintessential modern young black man." Such people have bought into an idea about "keeping it real" that always uses the lowest common denominator as the example of the essence. When I see promotional video footage of Tupac Shakur in the updated minstrelsy of thug life, I wonder what such people mean.

It seems to me that we are in a world of deeper trouble than ever if we have to define ourselves in the terms of thugs and sluts. I know of no other ethnic group that has bought such garbage. Have Italians ever defined themselves in terms of the Mafia? Have Jews ever elevated the worst hustlers among them to the position of "quintessential"? Have Asians or Hispanics ever thought of themselves as most "real" when they were depicted as addlepated exotics speaking pidgin English?

I don't think so. This is another Negro "first," confusing one's garbage with one's cuisine. But, after all, isn't the worst aspect of popular culture its celebration of the abrasive and the destructive? That gullibly tragic side of our moment is what truly tells us, no matter our ethnic backgrounds or our class origins, about the troubles that we all share as Americans.

As long as the amoral moguls of pop, both black and white, project antisocial behavior as a form of liberated vitality, we will see energetic but spiritually debilitating confusion in our young, who seek, as usual, to define themselves apart from their parents and adult authority. As long as kids can earn big bucks for chanting omnidirectional rage, misogyny, and celebrations of homicidal violence, all of us are threatened, and thug minstrels, like Tupac Shakur, might pay the ultimate price for trying to be bad as our young are programmed to believe they should want them to be.

This next selection looks at the fairly new face we've seen put on a very old problem: "Liberal Racism."

Though we are more and more accustomed to seeing people from every wing of the human community in positions of authority and expertise, we still have to do battle with racism. But racism is like everything else: It remains the same in some places and changes form in others.

A relatively new kind of prejudice is liberal racism, which is different from Southern redneck racism and from conservative racism. Liberal racism does not intend to protect the group from the dangers of those inferior to it. There is a different conception altogether. Liberal racists think they are holding out for the pigmentationally challenged. The liberal racist wants the best for them and is willing to embrace ideas that would have been unacceptable among the intelligent and educated thirty years ago.

Owing to Manhattan liberal racism, City College buffoon Leonard Jeffries made a bad joke of higher learning as the head of a black studies department for over twenty years. By this I do not mean that there isn't much that first-class college scholars can teach all of us about the complexities of our racial and cultural history in America. As one example, the resounding power of Harold Cruse's *The Crisis of the Negro Intellectual* is proof of racial, political, and cultural discussion at the highest level.

People like Jeffries, separate dorms, separate student unions, and separate eating tables for so-called minority students are accepted because the liberal racist believes that those historically oppressed by injustice have the right to segregate themselves in order to maintain their "identities" and lessen the alienation felt within "white institutions."

Of course, the liberal racist would never allow poor whites from the South to establish student organizations closed to all others than those like themselves. At the suggestion of separate dorms and eating tables for poor whites, the liberal racist would start sputtering and foaming at the mouth.

It wouldn't matter that the poor whites might argue that they felt alienated in Northern situations, felt looked down upon, and knew that everyone thought they were racist trash, children of alcoholics, and had had sex with their brothers and sisters and mothers and fathers and uncles before they were twelve. No deal. Speeches at campus assemblies about tolerance, understanding, and universal brotherhood might be given. That's about it.

Liberal racism doesn't stop on our campuses. It sometimes reeks from the best pages of our press. A perfect example of well-intended liberal racism appeared in the editorial pages of the *New York Times* recently. Entitled "Blood Ties," it was written by Linda Hodges, a white woman who adopted a four-month-old Apache boy with her husband and reared him in the Midwest, where he grew to adulthood. As one who believes that "the pull of ingrained cultural memory is stronger than even the most loving adoptive bonds," she supports legislation that gives Indian tribes priority "when an Indian child is placed for adoption." Opposed to lawmakers who would "remove tribal jurisdiction," she encourages them to "acknowledge the biological and cultural ties that Indian tribes can offer their own children."

Beginning with the title, the piece is liberal racism at its worst. All racist theories are built upon the primitive belief that the blood knows and remembers. "Ingrained cultural memory" is insupportable. What is a "biological" tie—and what is it worth? Doesn't Hodges know that disparities in social rank were traditionally explained away by saying that those at the bottom were incapable of moving up? They just didn't have it in their blood to be more than manual laborers.

Imagine how it would go if a trend started in which well-off minority couples began adopting orphans from Appalachia and hillbilly whites attempted to block them on the basis of the "biological" ties such children had to the "ingrained cultural memory" of poor whiteness. With the rearing of a white child behind her, a black adoptive mother sympathetic to such a vision would be laughed at and considered an idiot for her cultural-genetic theories. The only ones who wouldn't laugh would be those made vulnerable—and dangerous—by their well-intended liberal racism.

As far as Indians go, we can be sure that they are rapidly becoming even more native American than ever. An article published within the last six months pointed out that one Indian tribe in possession of an untaxed casino was caught red-handedly trying to lobby under the table in order to stop another tribe from opening its own gambling hall, which would have created competition. I guess red solidarity stops at the bank line.

We can almost never avoid discussing what talk shows have done to us and to our culture. This next short piece discusses the phenomenon from its very beginning, when the format was innovated. It is, in fact, a critical eulogy entitled "Silver Top Down."

It was recently announced that Phil Donahue is being forced into retirement because of low ratings. Quite obviously, Donahue was mild and fluffy when compared to the hard-core vulgarity that has risen into such prominence on talk television. He even seemed to have an actual feeling for the humanity of his guests. No matter, Donahue could be irritating because he was not subtle.

Early on, Donahue, who improvised the format of the talk show in which the audience participates, was surely provocative. His show went to the other side of what one would expect to see. He would interview, for instance, "women who have suffered the trauma of murdering their husbands." Then the self-made widows would sit there and answer questions.

As his popularity grew and he became the proverbial household name, Donahue developed into the sort of self-important microphone-waver who dominates a genre that has now flooded the stations. It was understandable that the networks would try to replicate Donahue's success. After all, such shows were quite inexpensive to produce.

Through no fault of Donahue's, the genre evolved from the provocative to the crass to the repulsive. As the years passed, all of America discovered that a camera and a studio audience will inspire certain kinds of people to talk about almost anything, no matter how personal, no matter how intimate, no matter how vile. For those of us who needed it, we also learned that rude behavior, crude passions, boundless resentment, violence, cruelty, lunacy, and the impulse to anarchy know no lines of sex or color.

At first, he wore the talk show crown with smug resolution. But after a bit, the silver-topped talk show host was bested by Oprah Winfrey, whose genuine warmth drew her an audience looking for more than Donahue's sanctimonious hand-wringing. What I imagine audiences grew tired of was Donahue flailing his arms and projecting weary outrage in a voice that had the impatient modulations of one speaking to a troubled child.

Donahue so often seemed emotionally out of breath. Or there was the grating condescension that came into his face when he was attacking what he considered some monumental American problem. Donahue embodied the sense of entitlement that has led to so many in this nation feeling as though they have been singled out for injustice when the facts are quite different. Realizing our democratic potential is a big job, made no easier by a lot of talk show deep breathing.

But we should also recognize that the phenomenon of the talk show is another of our insufficient attempts to handle the facelessness that be-devils so many in our society of millions upon millions. We are also in-trigued by the maudlin suffering of others, some so inarticulate that they can barely express the aches that dominate their lives. Then there is our classic American appetite for the vulgar and the forbidden, proof that we are, for all of our flashing of private parts and blabbing of embarrassing sto-ries, as puritanical as ever.

We also have, as one writer observed, an attraction to the bizarre an-tics of the geeks among us, the freaks who no longer work in the circus but now telephone talk shows hoping to get all of the attention for an hour in the near future. Trot them all out here and we will listen; we will show pleasurable shock; we will refuse to turn the dial. We will wallow in the slobber.

To his credit, Phil Donahue chose to go his own way, seriously flawed though it was, and reject the filth. He now leaves the networks a multi-millionaire and a man who fell because he had something akin to in-tegrity. No story is more American.

I was very excited about the Republican Party because of what took place on the first night of the convention in San Diego. My excitement was not the result of any party affiliation because I am more concerned about the nature of Ameri-can discourse than I am Republican or Democrat, liberal or conservative, mod-erate or independent. A fascinated rush lifts up in me whenever what George Steiner calls "the pressure of life" makes itself felt in surprising political places. That happened in San Diego when the Republicans met to nominate a man too disoriented and inarticulate to give Bill Clinton any serious competition. So here is "Down San Diego Way."

The opening night of the Republican convention in San Diego was a his-toric event on a number of levels. While there are those who reach for their machine guns of contempt whenever they hear the word "Republi-can," something is going on over there that will have great impact on that party within the next decade. We are already seeing an effort to liberate the image and the very dialogue within the party itself from conventional criticism. As the selection of speakers and what some of them had to say

proves, there is a small but sturdy revolution taking place inside the cir-
cled wagons of policy and opinion that have given the Republicans a bad
name. These unexpected Republican revolutionaries will not go away;
they will grow in strength and numbers.

That is where the detractors are wrong when they take the position
that the GOP is now and forever a party of rich white men who use
women and minorities as no more than soft icing on a concrete cake.
Those detractors are convinced that the GOP is stuck in a fantasy about
America that avoids the troubles of working people, women, and minorities. The 1996 Republican platform corroborates all of their disdain. It appears to have been written in a xenophobic time capsule by followers of
Ralph Reed and Pat Buchanan.

But the very presence of speakers such as Governor Christine Todd
Whitman, San Diego's Mayor Susan Golding, and Mary Fisher are symbols of unavoidable political facts. The Republicans will have to address
women, back off from pro-life hysteria, and, as Fisher admonished, accept
the human horror of AIDS. Because Fisher has AIDS, her bringing a
young black girl to the podium symbolized something quite obvious—this
problem knows no boundaries of class or race. (The ring in the black girl's
nose also proves that it knows no boundaries of taste.)

Even for all the emotion during the tribute to Ronald Reagan, the
high point Monday night was surely Colin Powell's address, which made
it clear that he might well have won the nomination if he had come into
the ring. Some don't believe that Powell could have gotten over the hur-
dles of being pro-choice and a supporter of affirmative action. I'm not sure
that's writ in stone. Powell may well have been able to come out here with
a convincing and reasoned argument that functioned within the Republican economic philosophy. Statistics could have supported the idea
that affirmative action sparked economic growth in businesses owned by
minorities and women, which were then able to put more jobs on the
market.

Had a nominated Powell chosen a running mate such as Whitman,
Golding, or Kemp, I doubt Clinton could have beaten him. Powell, in the
process, might well have succeeded in running the party's extremists into
the political backwoods where they belong.

Monday night, the general showed his courage when attacking all entitlements, including corporate welfare. And, as one Jewish friend observed, he dreamed of seeing Clinton debate a black man from a strong family who was also a military hero. He joked that at the end of the presidential debates Clinton would have said, "Shucks, I think I'll have to vote for you, too."

What Powell represents—above all else—is the inevitable motion of the Republicans away from one-dimensional politics. Proof of how far we have come is that he was quite warmly received by a convention audience that included North Carolina senator Strom Thurmond, who ran for president on a racist platform in 1948 and became a Republican because the Democrats took on the unconstitutional policies of segregation! Today, any serious political party has to make clear that it has a version of "inclusion" and "diversity," too. That is why the GOP hasn't much of a choice if it doesn't want to become an also-ran party fairly quickly.

Since ours is a country never at loss for surprises, we should welcome these things. As the Republicans expand their vision they will not become Democrats, but they will underscore the fact that this country is a multiethnic mess and masterpiece in which positions change. Eventually, no matter their differences on policy, both parties will include significant numbers representing this nation's variety and its complex of concerns. We will then be much more democratic and better prepared to do protean battle over how to get our opinions pushed into political practice. That's the ongoing story of these United States.

What's good for the goose is supposedly good for the gander, so I should lay down something about the Democratic Convention, which was far less interesting to me. What really made me feel the kind of human moment peculiar to our era was the way Jesse Jackson looked on the final night. I have written about him before and will surely write about him again. Here is a blues for the boss man of the civil rights establishment. It is entitled "Back in Chicago Breakdown."

Under the rubber rain of red, white, and blue balloons and sparkling confetti that fell on the crowded podium at the conclusion of the Democratic Convention, Bill Clinton quickly turned away from Jesse Jackson and went in the opposite direction. It appeared symbolic. Jackson seemed at the end of something. Though bumped from a prime time position, Jackson had given the finest speech of the convention, one filled with gravity, eloquence, and a bruised affirmation suitable to the challenges of American politics and American life.

His no longer being at the center of things may explain why there was a patch of gloom in Jackson's eyes as well-schooled facial muscles hoisted the ends of his mouth to smile at fellow Democrats on the podium. The talk among the toe-to-toe crowd had to be about what a great speech the president had given and how wonderful it was that the party had maintained unity, even while disagreeing over welfare reform. Hope had to be kept alive.

Back in Chicago, which had once been his base of operations, Jackson had come a long way and had done many things. Some of them were as sour as the feeling Jackson must have right now, since he is presently so far from ever being on a serious presidential ticket, top or bottom. In April of 1968, he had addressed the Chicago City Council in dark glasses, a leather coat, and a blood-stained turtleneck sweater.

Half of Martin Luther King's face had been blown off the day before and Jackson, speaking out against the rioting that was going on in Chicago and across the nation, claimed that he had cradled King's head in his arms. No such thing had happened.

As Andrew Young told Marshall Frady for his new biography, *Jesse*, Jackson put his palms flat in the blood and rubbed them down the front of his sweater. What to Young seemed an almost religious attempt to draw into himself the power of the dead was interpreted as an example of how far Jackson was willing to stretch the truth in order to hustle himself into the position of assuming King's mantle as the benevolent godfather of the civil rights establishment.

Jackson had everything he needed for the job. He was tall, quite handsome, and possessed of a charisma that neutralized his speech impediment. He was also young enough to speak across generations, to the Black Power young and the older, nonviolent types. Self-promotion and appropriation were techniques he never shied away from using. He loved the cameras and the microphones and those who used them loved him.

Jackson was clearly the king of the civil rights hill by the beginning of the 1980s, unimpeded by the controversy surrounding the missing funds of his organization known as Operation Push. Unlike King, he had no black nationalists to contend with, no person or movement qualified to steal his thunder. But when he had the bright idea in his 1984 presidential campaign that it would be a racial unity coup to get the members of the Nation of Islam to register to vote, Jackson brought Louis Farrakhan to the mass media and began the process of unintentionally undercutting himself.

For all the excitement and voter registration inspired by his two presidential campaigns, and for all his international accomplishments, Jackson found himself no more than a warm-up speaker for Farrakan at the Million Man March. From the other end of the field, Colin Powell, more popular than Clinton or Dole, has taken on the kind of attractiveness to Americans at large that Jackson dreamed of having. So Jackson, for all that he has done, now finds himself in the shadow of a wacky cult leader and a career soldier who rose to command the greatest military force in history. There is even talk that Jackson's son, Jesse Jr., the congressman, intends to give his dad some tutorials in conciliation.

Jesse Jackson is far from a tragic hero, but when that first wave of blue convention balloons descended from the ceiling, no other color in sight, I thought of him. I was sure he had the blues.

Any discussion of politicians almost invariably leads to a discussion of crime. We all know why. This piece does not look at criminal activity on the parts of various members of both parties or those who help them fill their war chests but, by implication, it makes some suggestions about white-collar crime that could apply to elected officials as well as to those far lower on the rungs of ill-gotten gain. In other words, the proposals here are truly democratic in their application. The title is, after all, "Crime and Punishment."

The continued attention on the crime bill proves that everyone is concerned about crime, from the drug murders in the streets to the high-style, greasy, Wall Street hustles of the suites. Crime crimps our freedom, lowers our feeling of security, creates suspicions that can play themselves out in terms of race and class—if we're talking about the violent crime down below. Up above, we sometimes get the impression that the economy and the work force are no more than toys bent and broken by suavely coated crooks. Our problem is predators, either crude or smooth.

But building new prisons with thick walls and electronic cell blocks isn't the way to go. Such old-time approaches take up too much money, partly because they're neither old-time enough nor sufficiently focused on the demands of our moment. What we actually need to do is reinvent imprisonment while making it spartan and cost-effective. We could save billions.

Military-style prisoner-of-war camps would do it. Barbed-wire fences three rows deep, the middle one electrified. Absolutely no privacy. Barracks under twenty-four-hour surveillance to eliminate rape, violence, and drug use. Cots. Hard labor, not pumping iron. No televisions. No radios. Plenty of high-quality, informative, and witty magazines, newspapers, and books.

An obligatory educational component, meaning that until one can at least read and write, parole is out of the question. In the interest of sentence reduction, educated prisoners would quickly form the bulk of the teaching staff. The reforming wolf above helps the wolf below. This is of absolute importance because releasing an illiterate in a society as increasingly complex as ours is like saying, "We support your going back to crime."

The overall policing of the new prison camps should be handled by the military, which we already pay and have already insured and already offer benefits. Since the military salary is so much less than that of prison guards, we would save an enormous amount of money and could rotate troops to avoid burnout. The military, in a domestic frame, would then extend upon the job of those in law enforcement, which is to protect and serve.

Of course, that sounds harsh to those who feel that prisons should be homes away from home. Some would say, "Cruel and unusual punishment." Actually, those who suffer cruel and unusual punishment are the people who live under the criminal reign of terror that distinguishes this era. Those Americans fear for their own lives and for the lives of their children.

Children have witnessed their mothers killed in cross fires as gang members and drug hustlers banged away at each other. Too many parents have known the crippling wounds inflicted on their children, the deaths of their children, the trauma their children experience after witnessing shootings, stabbings, and murder. They know how difficult it is for their children to concentrate at schools where thugs threaten everyone with anarchic violence.

Even so, since so many criminals are from so-called minority groups, complainers would call these measures "racist." Wrong. They never think about the fact that those criminals represent less than 5 percent of their communities and that allowing them to continue terrorizing honest people actually *is* racist. Black and Hispanic communities shouldn't be denied the protection resulting from new imprisonment policies just because of skin-deep connections to criminals.

Nor should the desperadoes of the suites get sweet judicial treatment just because they don't use guns or knives. In order to mete out justice equally and reduce class resentment, the courts should make sure that white-collar thugs receive much, much more than light sentences and fines. As a friend in the world of high finance says, "That fear of an irrevocably one-sided legal system could be reduced if the public wanted it reduced. People forget that the politicians and the cops work for *us*. They do what we make very clear that we *want* done."

He gave an example with which I completely agree. "Take Michael Milken or the savings-and-loan crisis that we're *all* being taxed billions to pay off. If a guy had all his money confiscated and got twenty-five years to life for that sort of thing, believe me, we would see a drop. That would scare these Wall Street guys to death."

Predators are our problem, and either taming or discouraging them should be our business.

I will conclude this jazz set of arranged commentaries with a short address I gave in October of 1996 at the Century Club in New York City, where R. W. B.

Lewis and Skip Gates brought together a number of writers and friends to recall and celebrate Ralph Ellison, who died in the spring of 1994. I call this concluding piece "The Reach of the Oklahoma Kid."

Discussing the influence of Ralph Ellison is much like describing the impact of strong wind on high grass and natural gardens: the things it touches are bent by its direction while remaining exactly what they are. Ellison had that kind of impact because his ideas weren't the sort that required imitation of his style. One could draw from them and maintain individuality because they were big enough for broad interpretation. His ideas about American democracy, the arts, the far-from-simple meanings of race, class, and culture, and his sense of the hilarious interweaving itself with the tragic, the charismatic with the repulsive, and the courageous engagement that our American moment demands of us all, have— *very, very slowly*—had an informing influence on thinking about this nation and, at least as important in the summoning of the present and the war against time that is art, those ideas have also had an informing influence on the making of things designed to aesthetically capture the strutting, belly-rubbing, signifying, high-signing, profiling, conning, crooning, seducing, aristocratically moaning, tap-dancing, back-paddling, forward-thrusting, Fosberry-flopping, Cassius Marcellus Clay-to-Muhammad Ali butterfly-floating and bee-stinging, and the whole kit and caboodle always-breaking-out epic of collective Americana.

Ellison's impact has come into our national intellectual consciousness very slowly because it had to drill through the rock of pieties and reductions on both the right and the left. He was not easily drafted into movements and his work was resented by those who had decided that the country was finished, down for the count, a done and dirty deal. Ellison wasn't one to be taken in by special interest groups. As patient and as much a tinkerer as the Oklahoma oilmen of his home state, he kept drilling away, recognizing the difference between the liquid black gold that fueled modern life and the dirty salt water of propaganda. Given his understanding of both sides of a question, Ellison would also have been in pursuit of what we now call "clean fuel," the kind that has the lowest level of pollutants. His love and sense of the blues encompassed our battle with the spiritual pollutants that reoccur in our consciousness, moving us rapidly along while destroying our clarity of purpose, our impulse to civilize ourselves and our world. But civilization in an American context has to rise above what is usually meant because it has to incorporate so many things from so many places.

Ellison knew that improvisation is essential to what we make of ourselves as Americans and he recognized that we are constantly integrating the things that we find attractive in others, whether the integration is conscious or unconscious. Ellison knew well that the American wears a top hat with an Indian feather sticking out of it, carries a banjo and a harmonica, knows how to summon the voice of the blues by applying a bathroom plunger to the bell of a trumpet or a trombone, will argue about the best Chinese restaurants, eat sushi with you one on one, turn the corner and explain the differences between the dishes on the menu at an Indian restaurant, drink plenty of Tequila, get down with the martial arts, sip some vodka, recite favorite passages from the Koran, have some scotch on the rocks, show you the yarmulke worn at a friend's wedding, savor some French and Italian wine made from grapes grown in the Napa Valley, charm a snake, roll some ham and cheese up in a heated flour tortilla, tell you what it was like learning to square dance or ballroom or get the pelvic twists of rhythm and blues right, or how it felt in one of those sweltering Latin dance halls when the mambo got as hot as gumbo on a high boil.

Given his perspective, Ellison would well have enjoyed how this last summer's blockbusting thriller, *Twister*, pivoted on the protagonists improvising a way to fix their machine intended to measure the speed and power of cyclones. When they find that the homemade machine is not heavy enough to resist being knocked over by the winds and that the measuring bulbs programmed into their computer aren't automatically pulled up into the storm funnel as they had assumed, the estranged husband and wife—who fall in love again as they make it from one situation in harm's way to another—must face the challenge of the moment with improvisation. This American Mars and Diana who, far more than a century ago, became the pioneer man and woman on our frontier and have now been remade yet again to speak for the rallying point of the sexes in the face of our shifting redefinitions of each other and of the frontier that is now at least partially about how we shall use our technology to better human life. This middle-1990s whirlwind-chasing couple improvises wings for their measuring bulbs, wings made from beer and soda cans, and lash the machine that carries them to a truck for the weight necessary to hold everything in place until the tornado funnel pulls their Christmas tree decoration-looking technology into the air and the big winds reveal their secrets to the computers, lighting the screens with multicolored patterns. The combination of trucks, computers, electronic metal bulbs, beer cans, and mother wit would have gotten to Ellison because he made note of such Americanness in his introduction to the latest publication of John A. Kouwenhoven's, *Beer Can by the Highway,* writing of when his wife, Fanny, brought home a Shasta lemon lime soda can that had been transformed into an object of art by a spieling Negro guy in the street. It was now a goblet with open strips cut into its sides which would have made holding liquid impossible—the image of a banquet chalice appropriated for an aesthetic moment in tin, which Ellison describes sitting on the "glass topped, stainless steel table in our living room."

In the huge cycles of our sorrow and our celebration we now and again find ourselves thinking about Americans like Ralph Ellison, knowing that each of them has in common with all the others the unpredictable magnetism that comes of an illuminated and illuminating individuality. All that Ellison contributed he worked for, seeking out the ways in which he would improvise the wings for the measuring bulbs that he stuck into the funnel of Americana, knowing that there had to be some way of understanding the dimensions of a culture that whirled by so rapidly, sucking up into its center all that it crossed, remaking at the same time that it destroyed, ever realigning and creating new relationships. Unlike the tornado or the cyclone, the huge funnel of Americana can be saddled and ridden by those like Ellison, whose aesthetic and intellectual powers can function like spurs, a bridle, and a saddle, turning the random power of the other into a focused part of the self, fusing one's personality with the force of nature that is the sweep of this society. Perhaps more than anything else, Ralph Ellison was telling us, over and over and over, that our passage on this land need be neither in vain nor narcissistic. If we learn to look closely enough at each other, we will see far beyond the barriers of race, class, religion, and sex. We will recognize the human heart pumping its blood to a syncopated beat, a jazz time in which the double consciousness created by sadness moving at a dance pulsation becomes the occasion to blow the blues away, not forever but just long enough to build up the sober but celebratory strength necessary to face them goddam blues when they make their inevitable return.

PART TWO

A Number One Himself:

Reflections on a Master

Duke Ellington:

Transcontinental Swing

Himself in Overture

Across all idioms and eras we can see that a daunting number of American artists fall apart or fail to realize their gifts completely, owing to dissipation, psychological problems, or career frustrations. In the wake of their youthful peaks others merely cease to be expansively creative, maintaining a style that might deepen but hardly extends its language. Still others, like Miles Davis, become so obsessed with novelty that they make fools of themselves for the last few decades of their lives. If those troubles don't apply, early deaths by self-destruction or because of bad luck do away with the rest.

Duke Ellington was none of those. A star by his early thirties, he sold millions of records; prevailed over the obstacles and setbacks of show business as successive trends rose to dominance then dissolved; and created masterpieces, short or long, in every decade until his death in 1974 at the age of seventy-five.

Yet he is still seen by even those who think they know something about the American arts as no more than a smooth bandleading guy who seemed to be having far too good a time to be taken seriously. (The affected sullenness of the youth culture star affirms that, from pop to the top, we consider the dour European posture a mark of the truly artistic.) The essence of the problem is that Ellington, a perpetually developing artist, was also a master of the bittersweet science of show business. The many ladies who literally and willingly laid themselves open before him, the infinitely bitchy demands of his prickly spirited musicians—including prudes, alcoholics, kleptomaniacs, drug addicts, gourmands, immigrants, intellectuals, and practical jokers—combined with the highly competitive intricacies of an entertainment night world that could write its name in blood as well as bright lights were all unfairly matched against the blue-steel discipline that could shut everything out at will, allowing Ellington to compose somewhere between two and three thousand pieces of music before he joined the immortals.

Considering himself "the world's greatest listener," Ellington maintained such commanding touch with his craft and the culture of the world at large that his fifty years of development constitute what is perhaps the single most comprehensive evolution in all of American art. Much of this has to do with something as American as the bandleading composer himself. Ellington was the greatest manipulator of blues form and blues feeling. He understood it as music and as mood. He knew that those who thought of the blues as merely a vehicle for primitive complaint had their drawers or brassieres on backward. The blues always knows its way around. It can stretch from the backwoods to the space shuttle, from wet blood on the floor of a dive to the neurotic confusion of a beautifully clothed woman in a penthouse overlooking the very best view of Manhattan. The blues, happy or sad or neither, plays no favorites.

In his stark to complicated uses of the blues we can see Ellington quite clearly. He struggles with forms and voices as successfully as Melville; satirizing the skin off of pomposity gives him the same pleasure it did Twain; he measures up to D.W. Griffith in his masterful use of the musical "close-up"—the solo feature within the cross-cutting antiphony and variously lighted tonal support of the big band; the surreal slapstick of certain pieces has the topsy-turvy spirit of Buster Keaton; there are numerous blue and moody parallels to the moments of tragic recognition that Hemingway delivers with a declarative lyricism; the dense intricacy of his tonal colors makes him part Faulkner; one hears a lilting

combination of Bill Robinson and Fred Astaire whenever those percussive ac-
cents in brass flow through suave billows of Ellingtonian harmony; he is a twin
of John Ford in his brilliant development of both his fundamental themes and his
repertory team of players; the worldly melding of satire, gloom, and innovation
is a fine match for his good friend Orson Welles; and, as the master bluesologist
Albert Murray has observed, he is tuned in to Frank Lloyd Wright through his
successful invention of a musical architecture that blends so perfectly with the
shifting inner and outer landscapes of American life.

In Ellington, we hear the story of the Negro, maybe the most American of
Americans. That story precedes the Pilgrims and the Revolutionary War and
has proven epic enough to attract identification across color lines and national
boundaries. For Ellington, that tale, if it goes on long enough, always moves to-
ward some sort of romance. The guy who finds himself fighting dragons, com-
muning with nature, dancing, mourning, celebrating, and stepping through fire
to awaken that sleeping beauty is in for a big, fat surprise. If the initiator is a
woman, a charismatic modern female who will be stopped by nothing, the facts
remain the same. Both will discover that the blues, as Ellington said, is "the ac-
companiment to the world's greatest duet, a man and a woman going steady.
And if neither one of them feels like singing 'em, the blues just vamps 'til ready!"

In order to tell us his epic tale of everything ending up in the arms of the
blues, Ellington had to stay out there for over five decades, writing for every in-
strument in his band, from the clarinet to the baritone saxophone, from the
trumpet to the trombone, for the string bass or the trap drums. He also penned
show tunes for singers, worked on some unsuccessful musicals, did scores for
film as well as for television, and kept himself afloat, no matter how many were
capsized by the ill winds of the trade. Beneath those blue suede gloves were
homemade brass knuckles. Duke Ellington learned early on that his was a world
both sweet and rough and that he had to be able to handle all extremes.

1. In the Magic of the Kitchen

In the same interests of self-preservation that keep ma-
gicians from ever revealing their tricks, Ellington enjoyed presenting himself as some sort of a velvet primitive not quite aware of just what he was

doing, or as the kind of master chef who considered discussions of recipes no more enjoyable than sniffing stink bombs. He had no intention of letting the competition know how it was done. Ellington was well aware of the basic show business problem: an artist who was, in his words, "a number one himself," might someday find that he had been upstaged by an imitator, "a number two somebody else." But it was his systematic approach to sound, his willingness to build bracing or mysterious dissonances into his works, his curiosity about complementary and contrasting textures that gave his art so much depth.

Born April 29, 1899, in Washington, D.C., Edward Kennedy Ellington was, like many Negro jazz innovators, a favored child. He shared with Coleman Hawkins, Charlie Parker, Thelonious Monk, Miles Davis, and others a background in which he was pampered, tucked in, read to, and reared to believe in himself and his own opinions without reservation. Our simple-minded presumptions about color and consciousness frequently dupe us into missing the facts of these matters. The restrictions of race had nothing to do with how such artists saw themselves when accurate expression of their imaginations demanded that they innovate.

He got the nickname "Duke" because he liked fancy pants and was a charmer, ever quick with the kinds of aristocratic lines that pulled in women and even made it easy for him to later fire musicians so gracefully that some described being asked to leave as having the feeling of either a compliment or an assignment of elevated duty. But Ellington didn't go in for social barriers and loved to hang out with anyone whose vitality or skill attracted him. Long after he had become a big success, the Duke might leave his Harlem apartment in silk robe, pajamas, and slippers to sit up all night in a little greasy spoon. While eating or smoking a cigarette and sipping coffee, he gave audience, listening to the stories of the commoner night owls and telling his own.

As were many young musicians of his youth, Ellington was bitten by the night creature of jazz. He was at first thrilled by the Harlem stride piano style he heard on James P. Johnson's 1917 recording of *Carolina Shout*, which he learned by ear and played so well that a local reputation took off among Washington musicians. Since there were no formal ways to study this new music, he absorbed his art in the Washington and uptown New

York streets, during the innumerable jam sessions and the demonstrations where musicians argued technical points or discussed them. He had taken piano lessons as a child but his most important education included observing exchanges between trained musicians and untrained players, each drawing something from the other. This is where Ellington initially sensed that music from both worlds could be fused, something that he worked at throughout his career. During those formative years, when he was still making his New York way in the late 1920s, Ellington would sit with his drummer, Sonny Greer, way, way up in the balconies of concert halls and ponder the problems of emulating European orchestral effects in the language of jazz and for the instruments at his disposal. Alone in his apartment, Ellington also studied the harmony books in Harlem that he forever pretended to have ignored because he was too busy bandleading.

The quality of his recognition was deep. Before long, Ellington figured out what would become the four most enduring elements of his art: 4/4 swing—fast, medium, and slow; the blues; the romantic ballad; and Afro-Hispanic rhythms. That quartet of fundamentals is reinterpreted over and over throughout the history of jazz innovation, from Louis Armstrong all the way to the most fruitful work of Ornette Coleman and John Coltrane. It was Ellington's substantial grasp of the essences of the idiom that allowed him to maintain such superb aesthetic focus at every point in his professional life, no matter the trends and eras he evolved through.

In his 1943 *Black, Brown, and Beige*, a work of more than forty minutes in which all of his innovations had reached a culmination, Ellington built what was then the most adventurous long composition in jazz history. Beginning with a simple motive, as did Beethoven in his Fifth Symphony, he developed it into many different kinds of themes, lyric or propulsive. Ellington used or ignored conventional phrasing lengths, twisted the blues into and out of shape, wrote smooth or dissonant harmonies, and called upon many rhythmic modulations that moved from march beats to swing to jaunty Afro-Hispanic syncopations. It is a perfect example of why Ellington was the truest and most complete kind of innovator; he remade the fundamentals so thoroughly that they took on the freshness of an open sky while maintaining touch with the gutbucket earthiness heard in the best of the very earliest jazz.

Ellington achieved his ends through orchestrated instrumental techniques that were themselves about languages. Those ends were extensions and refinements of the vocal styles of blues and jazz singers. His often saying that he was no more than a primitive minstrel was usually taken as a joke. That was one of the many masks he wore when obliquely throwing historical daggers. In the 1960s he declined Charles Mingus's mischievous idea that they make an "avant-garde" record together by imitating the chaotic squeaking and honking of the day. Ellington said that there was no point in taking music back *that* far. Doubtless, he remembered exactly how it was before jazz became a music of casual virtuosity, back when so many musicians truly *couldn't* play, when they lacked the control of their instruments necessary to execute even the simplest passages. Yet Ellington never forgot the first time he heard just how great the sound of jazz could be, and that experience would inform his music forever.

In Washington, when Ellington was an easy-going and locally popular bandleader, he experienced an indelible epiphany upon hearing the cantankerous, pistol-packing New Orleans genius Sidney Bechet play *I'm Coming Virginia* in 1921. Ellington always referred to Bechet as "the great originator" and employed him for a brief period in New York during the middle 1920s. On Ellington's bandstand at the Kentucky Club, Bechet's soprano saxophone did nightly battle with the growling plunger trumpet of Bubber Miley, whose sound had turned Ellington away from the society music he was performing and convinced him that he "would never play sweet music again."

Bechet was a grand master of both the improvised blues line and a trickbag of vocal effects that he claimed made it possible for him to call his dog—Goola—with his horn. Miley's growl techniques formed a direct line to King Oliver, the New Orleans mentor of Louis Armstrong. What those two brought into Ellington's world never left it. His star alto saxophonist Johnny Hodges had been taught his way around the soprano by Bechet and was to keep the older man's melodic language and inflections within almost every phrase of his own alto style for his entire life, adding to that style a tone so original that it became one of the great instrumental colors of the century. Miley's plunger-muted influence—surely the most

intriguing extension of the African talking drum into American music—
spread through the entire brass section. The growl imitations and allusions
to the Afro-American voice's timbres, inflections, and speech patterns
were stable aspects of Ellington's palette.

The results on all fronts were frequently operatic within the terms of
Ellington's idiom, bringing artistry to what could have easily been just
comic, novelty effects. His brass and reed players delivered arias, performed duets. They wove their elevated, instrumental expansions of the
Afro-American voice through compositions assigning their fellow wind
players the roles of choirs or tuned, jabbing percussion. Under the bandleader's direction, their efforts often disdainfully mocked the sentimental.
One example is *The Mystery Song,* which not only contrasts empty-
headed frivolity with a grotesque mood of fear and gloom, but was recorded in 1931—the same year, as Loren Schoenberg points out, that
James Whale's *Frankenstein* opened in movie houses. As with opera, the
enchanting sensuality of Ellington's many romantic ballads instigated
true-life courtships from coast to coast, several realized within hearing distance of either the radio or the record player.

Yet it was the complex of sorrow and celebration, erotic ambition
and romantic defeat—always fueling the deepest meanings of the blues—
that gave Ellington his sense of tension and release in human terms. That
blues sensibility also inspired him to the sustained development of his
composing techniques, for it could be brought to any tempo. The timbres
discovered in blues singing and blues playing could color any kind of
piece, keeping it in touch with the street, with the heated boudoir beast
of two backs, the sticky red leavings of violence, the pomp and rhythmic
pride of the dance floor, and the plaintive lyricism made spiritual by emotion that has no specific point of reference other than its audible humanity.

One of the things that Ellington perfected as he enriched his expression is what I call "timbral harmony." I refer to Ellington's statement
that when he heard a particular note, he always had to decide *whose* note
it would be. That is to say that the very best jazz musicians in a brass or
reed section have quite individual tones, even when they are playing perfectly in tune, something that was especially true of Ellington's musicians,
whom he called a gathering of "tonal personalities." A given note in

Ellington's three-trombone section could have at least as many different colors as players, and even more when the musicians were called upon to inflect pitches with emphasis on particular aspects of their already distinctive sounds. Such awareness on Ellington's part allowed him to change the sound of a given harmonic voicing by merely moving the players around to different positions in the chord—top, middle, bottom. The shifting might continue as the harmony progressed from chord to chord. A man might be asked to use any of a variety of personal colors—the airy or softer side of his sound, a weightier texture, the lush and sensual aspect, the more stringent dimension.

Further, the emotional and psychological riddles of the blues worked in the contrast between the melancholy or optimistic statement of the melody line and the nature of the surrounding orchestration or the rhythm itself. In the double consciousness of the blues, unhappy revelations might be stated over a jaunty rhythm (a perfect example is the powerhouse pulsation of Ellington's arrangement of *The St. Louis Blues*, recorded at a 1940 dance in Fargo, South Dakota). Ellington also knew that the emotional turns of blues mood made possible the expression of intricate personality, or suggested the kind of expression he expanded upon and refined through the selection and the coaching of his players. Ben Webster could function as a Kansas City Siegfried become a protean tenor saxophonist—innocent, romantic, erotic, combatively heroic—within the course of one performance such as the multitempo 1948 arrangement of *How High the Moon*. Johnny Hodges had a lyric voice capable of much flexibility. It could stretch from the spiritual pinnacle of *Come Sunday* to the glowing sensuality of *Warm Valley*; then, on Billy Strayhorn's *Half the Fun*, render the imperial flirtation of Shakespeare's Cleopatra on her barge or capture Romeo and Juliet's awe and yearning on Strayhorn's *The Star-Crossed Lovers*. As if that weren't enough, Hodges was ever able to croon the blues as majestically or as low down as Ellington wanted at almost any tempo. Ray Nance's trumpet or cornet, given specific timbral access through mutes, plungers, or his remarkably refined control of an open tone, could juggle the puckish, the plaintive, the buffoonish, the high-minded, and the translucently erotic. Consequently, the very selection of improvising soloists, and the order in which they performed a given piece, allowed for the musical, psychological, and emotional aspects of the performance to achieve variational development and operatic counterbalances in idiomatic terms.

Unlike literal singers, the members of the Ellington Orchestra also had the resources to emulate the dark or shining roles of strings, the timbres of wind instruments absent from the ensemble, the blunt syncopations of percussion, the rhythms of ballroom dancers, and various natural or technological phenomena when called upon—all in the service of an epic vision that brought as much detail to the general as to the specific. In the 1934 *Rude Interlude*, for instance, Ellington opens with the trombone quite confidently creating the effect of a French horn! The year before he produced the startling virtuoso display of *Daybreak Express*, one of the most perfect emulations of a train ever written. The 1946 *Happy-Go-Lucky Local* was so good that even the sometimes snooty British critic Max Harrison was inspired to write of it as "the supreme musical train piece, surpassing not only Ellington's earlier *Lightning* and *Daybreak Express* but also the attempts of straight composers such as Villa-Lobos (*Little Train of the Caipira*) or even Honegger (*Pacific 231*)." In much later works, two clarinets shrewdly voiced within the overall sound of the ensemble achieve the weight and color of an oboe; the combination of two clarinets with either baritone saxophone or bass clarinet will create the illusion of a bassoon. In some pieces, a pair of tenor saxophones will play the same note together but their particularly distinctive tones will create a "chord" of timbre that sometimes seems like another—unrecognizable—instrument altogether. As baritone saxophonist Joe Temperley observes, Ellington would also have Harry Carney blow his baritone so strongly for certain effects that the overtones coming up off of the basic notes would add other "imaginary" notes to the orchestration.

Of course, Ellington himself often made mention of the fact that he had thought early on of being a painter. Then, as the story usually went, he would comment on how he had replaced the brush and the palette with brass, reeds, string bass, and percussion. The colors he was able to draw from his ensemble were matched in their remarkable range by the inventive uses he put them to, avoiding pure abstraction at nearly every turn. Almost every sound is connected to something particular in his experience or his mind—even the dimensions of a dream, a fantasy, a myth. There is always the magic of existence, however, which inevitably includes the mystery and the ambivalence. The sense of heartache and of complexity is countered by his affection for the emblematic moxy and charm felt in the rhythmic momentum of jazz swing. Rhythm was definitely part of his business. The endless combinations of piano chords and timbres in combination with plucked or bowed bass notes and the percussion ensemble of differently colored cymbals, bass drum, brushes, sticks, snare, and large and small tom-toms that the jazz drummer has at his disposal were used for beats that anchored or counterpointed or underlined Ellington's featured players. That triangular rhythm section of piano, bass, and drums also sparked, heckled, soothed, and lulled the improvisers it supported.

His orchestration and counterpoint were the result of how much he was taken by the polyphony of the New Orleans jazz bands he heard early in his career, with the cornet carrying the melody as *obbligati* were played above and below it by the clarinet and the trombone. Access to authenticity came directly. By hiring New Orleans men such as Bechet, clarinetist Barney Bigard, and bassist Wellman Braud, Ellington learned, in perfect detail, the specific techniques of the Crescent City style from musicians who had grown up at the source. Works such as Jelly Roll Morton's seminal 1926 *Black Bottom Stomp* taught Ellington tension and release lessons about thematic variety, modulation, changes of rhythm, and pulse that at first inspired progressively profound short pieces with fanfares, interludes, and so on—even though Ellington personally hated the braggadocious New Orleans Morton and was hardly mum about it. Years later and in uncharacteristic anger, he even made the ridiculous claim that he had heard schoolteachers play better piano than the marvelous "Mr. Jelly Lord," who credited himself with having invented jazz and contemptuously accused everyone else of stealing his stuff or not knowing how it was really done, which demoted their playing and their bands to positions below him.

It is highly possibly that Morton, who referred to New York musicians as "cockroaches," might have said something to the young Ellington that was so insulting he never forgot it. Perhaps Morton ribbed Ellington about his unarguable 1927 lifting of King Oliver's 1923 *Canal Street Blues* and calling it *Creole Love Call,* a piece that remained in his repertoire, getting newer and newer arrangements, as did almost every piece that became popular. Still, Ellington, no matter his actual reasons for detesting Jelly Roll, from the diamond fillings of his teeth to the skin on the bottom of his feet, went on to use those Morton lessons for compositional techniques that were individualized and remained central to his sound. As with the unexpected coursings of human events, when Ellington's 1934 *Rude Interlude* appeared, Morton stood out in front of Harlem's legendary Rhythm Club and defended the composition's unusual sound against such detractors as the mighty, hunchbacked drummer Chick Webb, whose ear for innovation was too small to pick up on that particular aspect of it, even from a musician whom he truly admired.

Ellington also took everything he could get from the instruction of bandleader and composer Will Marion Cook, who gave him informal lessons in composition one summer during the middle 1920s as they rode together in open-topped taxis through Central Park. Born in 1869 in Washington, D.C., and a graduate of Oberlin Conservatory who had studied the violin in Europe, Cook was highly regarded. He set down the violin after giving a Carnegie Hall performance in 1895 because of a New York review. The writer referred to him as "the world's greatest Negro violinist," something he considered a demeaning racial slur. Cook soon studied for a short period with Antonín Dvořák, then dedicated himself to inventing a Negro instrumental and vocal music based on the unique elements of the folk styles, religious and secular. It is far from improbable that Dvořák, who was so taken by indigenous American music, may well have helped Cook make his decision to build something from materials native to the feelings and rhythms of the nation.

Success dropped on him early. Paul Laurence Dunbar wrote the lyrics and Cook the music for the 1898 operetta, *Clorindy, or the Origin of the Cakewalk,* a Broadway hit. He traveled to Europe in 1919 with his Southern Syncopated Orchestra, which featured Sidney Bechet, whom Cook had heard in Chicago. So when young Ellington was in the company of Will Marion Cook, he was drawing technical knowledge from one who had been around the block a number of times. He may also have inherited Dvořák's vision as reinterpreted through Cook's belief that a Negro music, something original, was the greatest creative challenge facing an Afro-American musician. Ellington noted that he wasn't able to experiment fully with some of the things discussed with Cook until *Black, Brown, and Beige*, which premiered almost twenty years later.

Ellington also kept his ear on the playing and writing of the stride piano masters of Manhattan—James P. Johnson, Willie "the Lion" Smith, and Fats Waller. He listened closely to the Tin Pan Alley songs that sailed into the culture from behind the footlights of Broadway. The innovations that the writing of Don Redman, Horace Henderson, and Benny Carter brought to the jazz orchestra didn't fall on deaf ears either. Ellington heard everything that was going on around him and made so much of it that he, more than any other jazz musician, perpetually revealed how broad and rich were the possibilities of his art. Alone of the musicians of his generation, he was perfectly comfortable not only performing with the giants who created the fundamental languages of the music for their instruments during the 1920s and the 1930s—instrumentalists such as Armstrong, Bechet, tenor saxophonist Coleman Hawkins, alto saxophonists Benny Carter and Johnny Hodges—but was at ease playing with later innovators from the 1940s, 1950s, and 1960s, such as Charlie Parker, Dizzy Gillespie, Charles Mingus, Max Roach, and John Coltrane. Excepting Bechet, Carter, and Parker, he also made either intriguing or classic recordings with each of them.

In order to do what his creative appetite, his ambition, and his artistic demon asked of him, Ellington had to maintain an orchestra for composing purposes longer than anyone else—almost fifty years. The single precedent in the entire history of Western music was the orchestra Esterházy provided for Haydn, which lasted twenty-nine years. The great difference, however, is that Ellington was artist *and* sponsor, using the royalties from his many hit recordings—and from the multitudinous recordings of his compositions by others—to meet his payroll, making it ever possible to hear new music as soon as he wrote it. That orchestra was, as Albert Murray observed in *The Hero and the Blues*, "booked for recitals in the great concert halls of the world, much the same as if it were a fifteen-piece innovation of the symphony orchestra—which in a sense it [was]."

That hand-picked orchestra was also an Ellingtonian version of the John Ford stock company, which used the images, voices, and cinematic talents of performers such as John Wayne, Henry Fonda, Maureen O'Hara, Victor McLaughlin, Donald Crisp, John Carradine, Ben Johnson, and other, lesser known actors as often as possible. As with those actors, Ellington musicians like Johnny Hodges, Lawrence Brown, Ray Nance, Jimmy Hamilton, Harry Carney, and Paul Gonsalves did their best work in the bandleader's stock company. The contexts he provided for them were far more inventive, varied in mood, and challenging than anything they—or anybody else—could create to suit their talents so perfectly. As composer, arranger, coach, and rhythm section accompanist, Ellington was also the master screenwriter, director, lighting technician, dialect expert, head of wardrobe, set-designer, manipulator of special effects, and makeup man. While his legendary patience with his stars of sound was such that he could ignore a fistfight in a Hamburg hotel lobby between his son, Mercer, and a veteran band member, asking only if his suite was ready, Ellington could also explode, once ragefully slugging a drunkard to the floor because he had been embarrassing on stage one time too many. Yes, beyond extending, elaborating, and refining his themes and the talents of his players, he and John Ford had more than a bit in common.

2. Transcontinental Swing

One of the signal accomplishments of the music of Duke Ellington is its epic expression of American feeling. In evocation after evocation, Ellington proves that he knew in his very cells what William Carlos Williams meant when he observed in his classic *In the American Grain* that by truly exploring the specific an artist will achieve the universal. Ellington's music contains so many characteristics of the nation—its intricate dialogues between individuals and groups, its awesome and heartbreaking difficulties, as well as its skylines and landscapes, city or country. In a work like his three-part 1947 *Tonal Group*, we hear the stone, glass, and steel of industrial achievement summoned through brass, reeds, and rhythm section percussion; urban complexes remade into charm bracelets of sound, a mechanized society in which the technological thrust toward facelessness is met by a sense of transcendence through swing, the democratic pulsation in which responses to song and dance can bring individuality as well as community.

In Ellington's big city of music, one might stand enraptured by romance or share the communal sorrow of the blues; primp for some moment of prominent or private joy; ponder and thrill to the epic humanity ganged up in Harlem and usually happy about it; feel the torrid nostalgia for a period of early courtship; itch inside for recognition of some personal ideal; and experience the mutations of feeling that course through the soul with the swiftness of subway stations flitting at the eye as an express train speeds toward selected stops. Those passions coalesced into the bittersweet joy of modern life, the sense of style and the throbbing vitality that syncopated its way onto the dance floor of the Savoy ballroom. That angle on style made Easter uptown on New York's Seventh Avenue a color-rich display of voluminous elegance. It also ran all the intricate way from pulpits to pitcher's mounds. In fox trot after fox trot, the aesthetic command of those sensibilities individuated the urban momentum of Ellington's music.

If the context was rural or Southern—as in a number of three-minute works, or the 1946 *Deep South Suite*, or his 1970 *New Orleans Suite*—Ellington supplied us with tones that told tales of down-home lore in earthy panoramas, detailing the distances from the sometimes blood-encrusted gutbucket to the ascendant melancholy of the singing in a country church. The music became pictorial, festive, and epic in another key of experience. One could witness the effects of home brew drunk from jars and so strong it was nicknamed "Jack Johnson"; hear the raucously dissonant, metallic percussion of the railroad rhythms that Albert Murray observed had so influenced the ground-beats of the blues; wonder at the hard labor done in the fields, the woods, and at plants; pass the school windows behind which high, high yellow to dark, dark teachers taught with missionary verve; see the old folks sitting and rocking on front porches; witness the visceral dignity of church services; walk in on the culinary splendor of picnics and family celebrations, those events at which you could taste and smell the things experts did with a slaughtered hog, knowing again the succulence of the greens and the sauces, the butter beans, the possum stew, the gumbo in myriad versions; the thin light-brown gravies and the gravies dark as chocolate cake and almost as thick as heavy syrup; those nose-twitching freshly baked apple, blueberry, and peach cobblers; the chicken made golden brown in a frying pan or off-the-bone tender in a pot of dumplings; view the startling richness of the sun-rise and the fields of wild flowers, the trees so weighed down with foliage they were in danger of snapping into pieces; and meet, in ever greater de-tail, the black, brown, beige, and bone people whose suffering, whose cel-ebration, and whose spiritual integrity formed beacons of tragic optimism for our culture. Those who spoke to the murky oracle of the abyss were an-swered with the hard blues, which they mutated into a love song or swung until the cows came home.

While his poetic miniatures were packed with aesthetic action, his suites usually focused on particular aspects of given places or musically de-picted the variousness held together by a common subject. As noted ear-lier, many of the shorter pieces were fashioned by Ellington to capture his beloved Harlem, a bygone cultural jewel possessed of the pulsating light common only to golden ages. That now-mythic Harlem was not the piss-stained slum of those suicidal or smothered jungle bunnies found in the protest writings of James Baldwin. The Ellingtonian Harlem is what Ralph Ellison recalled as "an outpost of American optimism, a gathering place for the avant-garde in music, dance, and democratic interracial re-lationships; and, as the site and symbol of America's freewheeling sense of possibility, it was our homegrown version of Paris." In his own specific paean, *Harlem*, from 1950, Ellington wrote one of his finest longer works beginning with the plunger-muted statement of the title in two notes. There is then a tour through Harlem in montage, cutting from one tempo, mood, rhythm, and texture to another, always maintaining form through, as Wynton Marsalis notes, "its exploration of blues harmony." Near the end there is a marvelous rendition of a funeral that features a fine, fine ex-ample of Ellingtonian counterpoint.

It is quite easy to understand why there is such a rich body of com-position in his canon dedicated to women, for there is no greater show business legend in the world of romance than Duke Ellington, whose ap-preciation and experience of the opposite sex inspired tales of almost mythic proportions. Tall, handsome, formerly an athlete, gifted with a grasp of gab that could mutate into magnetic honey, he quite easily drew women of all races, places, and classes to him. Those intimate experiences are symbolized in his fairy tale jazz history, *A Drum Is a Woman*, which Ellington narrates. There, Madam Zajj—the dark enchantress, muse, and bitch-goddess of his art—says to Ellington: "Come with me to my emerald rock garden, just off the moon, where darkness is only a translucency, and the cellophane trees grow a mile high. Come climb with me to the top of my tree, where the fruit is ripe and the taste is like the sky. Star rubies are budding in my diamond-encrusted hothouse." In short works like *Sophisticated Lady*, *The Gal from Joe's*, and *Lady of the Lavender Mist*, and then in longer ones such as *The Tattooed Bride* and *Princess Blue*, the ardor of Ellington's musical women is complicated by his ability to make them emotionally and psychologically full-figured. The personalities of female Ellingtonia are combinations of grief and vivacity, insecurity and confidence, the childlike and the worldly, the pugnacious and the mystic, the down-home and the regal.

Because Ellington was also a man of the world at large, there was nothing of significant experiential import that he allowed to stop short of his bandstand. If it was human, if he saw it or heard about it, if he went there and felt the air, saw the colors, spoke with the people, ate their food, and got that instant feeling for replication a genius of his sort was prone to, it would end up in music. Ellington had been a local hero to the Washington of his musical youth and made his name working for gangsters in New York's Cotton Club, a segregated room off-limits to all but the most famous Negroes. It was an extended job that sometimes included being called down to the city morgue, where the police asked him to identify the corpse of someone who had been partying in the club the night before. In his memoir, *Music Is My Mistress*, it was made clear that whether or not he recognized the murdered man on the slab, Ellington always answered, "Hell, no," when asked if he knew him. It was impossible for him to be a naif. Moreover, he performed solo piano in a big Harlem benefit for the Scottsboro Boys defense fund, keenly assessed the racial double standards of show business success, saw one of his musicians playing the tuba with the bones in his face periodically slipping out of place because he had been roughed up by gangsters, watched fellow musicians slowly dissolve in the acids of drink and drugs, and recognized the yearning for a fair shot that lay behind the eyes of so many, no matter their class, color, or religion. So his was an art boiled to early recognition in a crucible of glamour, racism, murder, and good, good times. The signal dissonances were perhaps acknowledgments of just how hard and cold the blues could get.

After first crossing the Atlantic in the early 1930s, Ellington and his band eventually toured Europe with the penetration of radio and television broadcasts, went on down to the Middle East and Africa, rode the air all the way to Japan, charmed them Down Under as far as the Outback, and crossed below the equator into South America. Over those forty years, Ellington learned that his versions of rhythm and tune were international languages and that those languages were capable of bringing whatever he knew of the human universe into any room in which he and his musicians were playing. Those foreign lands and societies were brought to the bandstand, sooner or later, their spirits wrestled or coaxed into melody, harmony, tonal colors, and rhythm. As Ellington told the writer Playthell Benjamin, he never composed music about other countries while in them. Only notes were made because he preferred to do his writing after returning to New York, which, for him, ensured the work maintaining an American identity rather than falling into imitation of a particular culture's musical surroundings. None of his efforts, however, stopped the blues from brewing.

3. Ellington and the Misunderstanding

Ellington's sense of artistry over long periods was revealed when he told his nephew Michael James, "It's not about this generation or that. The issue in art is *regeneration*." That was his greatest achievement but it led to the biggest problem he had once his accomplishments sent him to the top of his profession. By 1943, when Ellington premiered *Black, Brown, and Beige* to mixed reviews—some quite hostile—he had already produced far, far more great recorded works than any

other jazz musician or bandleader. A decade earlier he had been celebrated in England as a major artist. But one of the photographs from a
British hall finds the glamorously dressed Ellington bookcased by tall caricatures of the grinning, minstrel figures with banjos that had begun to appear in America a century earlier. The visual irony was that Ellington had
become a hero among Negroes as well as unprejudiced whites for never,
never sinking down into any kind of Tomming.* But as he became ever
more adventurous back home, the minstrel reductions, the simplifications
he gave no quarter to, took on another form in the criticism written by
many who considered themselves supporters.

The misunderstanding that bedeviled Ellington to the end of his life
and that has dominated the criticism written about him for many years is
the idea that his greatest period was from 1940–1942. The ensemble he
led during that period is now called the "Blanton-Webster Band" because
it included the innovative bassist Jimmy Blanton and tenor saxophonist
Ben Webster, both of whom were featured in such classics as *Jack the Bear*,
Sepia Panorama, *Cotton Tail*, and *What Am I Here For?* The conventional
complaint is that Ellington's later work either suffered from his reaching
beyond the limits of his talent in extended works or that his music was less
good because the quality of his ensemble never made it to that 1940–1942
level again. Those critics didn't realize that Ellingtonia is a mountain
range, not a series of hills leading up to one mountain, which is followed
by a descending line of smaller and smaller hills.

The collective way in which Ellington worked, crafting his writing
with his musicians—who might even laugh at poorly written parts and
throw them back at him—made experimentation an ongoing process
that, given the individuals involved, guaranteed development. From the
late 1920s onward, he also left open holes for improvisation or often encouraged a single clarinetist to invent counterlines against the written
parts. In that way, he was much like the film directors who allow actors to
change dialogue or the Hollywood makers of early silent comedies who ar-

*The way Ellington looks at the conventional buffoon Negro characters during his per-
formance in the 1929 short film, *Black and Tan Fantasy*, gives a clear indication of what he
thought about such things. In fact, his low-keyed performance, while no great shakes, is
completely devoid of the exaggerations of silent film and an early example of the subtleties
that developed with sound.

rived on the set with no more than a plot outline or a few situations that were then improvised into form. Yet the determining sensibility was always Ellington's, which is why the music maintained its identity through the many personnel changes, no matter how strong the personalities of his musicians might have been.

In 1939, Ellington had brought the marvelous composing talent of Billy Strayhorn into his organization. Strayhorn wrote *Take the A Train*, which became perhaps the most famous band theme of all time, and he collaborated with Ellington until his death in 1967, cancelling all speculations about how he would do things once the Duke died. Strayhorn came to everyone's attention during the Blanton-Webster years in which the language Ellington had been adding to since the late 1920s reached a golden balance of composition, personnel, and musicianship. The new composer and arranger absorbed Ellington's language and wrote his own invincible works such as *Midriff*, *Passion Flower*, *Raincheck*, *Johnny Come Lately*, and *Chelsea Bridge*.

As his career went on beyond that 1940–1942 peak of creativity and personnel, Ellington composed more and more longer pieces, some alone, some in conjunction with Strayhorn. These works not only expressed his expanding vision but took on the vinyl fact of the long-playing, forty-minute record as a form itself, a space that could be used for the moods responsive to a central subject. While he grew by the decade, Ellington never failed to work on all that he had engaged before. To the very end, as examples such as the 1957 *Where Is the Music?* (over which the shadow of Bechet hovers) and the 1958 *Feetbone* prove, he was always capable of writing the immaculate small and full-band compositions that were once demanded by the 78-rpm era, when discs held little more than three minutes on each side. Classic melodies inspired by women evolved. By the late 1940s a fifteen-minute masterpiece such as *The Tattooed Bride* is an updating—in conception, not material—of *Clarinet Lament*, a miniature concerto for Barney Bigard from 1937. *The Tattooed Bride* opens with a tonally ambiguous overture and introduces its central motive during the piano and bass duet that recalls the ones with Blanton. There is then a snarling, romping fast section, a lovely ballad of pure melody for clarinet, and an up-tempo concluding section that allows Jimmy Hamilton to display his velocity technique against a backdrop of reed writing that both winks at the rhythmic innovations of bebop while extending upon pieces like the 1927 *Hop Head*. Composer, conductor, and transcriber David Berger says of the magisterial *Princess Blue*, from 1958, "It has been really neglected and is one of Ellington's best pieces, incorporating, again, the blues. He's able to change textures and moods very smoothly. It's a seamless piece. It's one of the best examples of counterpoint in Ellington. Then there are the sonorities. It's really a marvelous piece. Genius on the loose. It has a regal feeling, which shows again just how broad the possibilities of the blues were in his hands." The piece is also a catalogue of allusions to earlier Ellington works such as *Creole Love Call*; *Just a-Sittin and a-Rockin*; *Never No Lament*; *Black, Brown, and Beige*; and *Transbluescency*.

Earlier "tonal portraits" of uptown New York—*Echoes of Harlem*, *Harmony in Harlem*, and *Harlem Speaks*—evolved into the aforementioned *Harlem* of 1950, which recalls Bubber Miley as it opens with a plunger-muted trumpet "singing" the title in two notes. The explorations of Afro-Hispanic and exotic rhythms from all over the world heard in Blanton-Webster pieces such as *Conga Brava* and *The Flaming Sword*, however classic, were expanded upon and excelled in the 1960s and 1970s with albums and suites such as *Afro-Bossa*, the *Far East Suite*, the *Latin American Suite*, *Afro-Eurasian Eclipse*, and the *Togo Brava Suite*.

The celebrated arrangements of popular materials such as *Three Little Words* and *Flamingo* weren't put on a lower timeless shelf, but the 1958 reinventions of American standards on *At the Bal Masque*, and the 1962 handling of French street and café songs for *A Midnight in Paris*, move on up to higher places, displaying the distinctions of the past in admixture with the extensions, elaborations, and refinements that experience made possible. Every aspect of arranging—harmony, counterpoint, rhythm, and timbre—is manipulated with the substantially increased authority and depth we should expect of an older master. His joyously sardonic 1934 arrangement of the *Ebony Rhapsody*, based on *Hungarian Rhapsody*, is no preparation whatsoever for the *Nutcracker Suite* and the *Peer Gynt Suites* of 1960. The first selection of each suite—one swinging like mad, the other moving at the stately pace of a cloud—makes it obvious that one of the greatest ensembles in all of Western musical history is at work. The same experience of expanded powers is had when one compares Ellington's quite beautiful score for the 1935 film *Symphony in Black* with his writing for both the 1959 *Anatomy of a Murder* (which works and reworks three themes so well that writer and ex-jazz pianist Tom Piazza calls it "a vernacular American Symphony") and the 1961 *Paris Blues*. In the last, Ellington was able to make use of Louis Armstrong, who was a featured actor in the movie. The results were enduring. In the jam session sequence that produced *Battle Royale*, we hear one of Armstrong's most exciting late performances, his combative horn rising up over the charging band and making Gershwin's *I Got Rhythm* chord changes serve jazz once more. Armstrong's rhythms are still freely innovative, his sound is both darker and brighter, and he maintains a lyric choice of notes no matter how hot the proceedings get.

On *Jazz Party*, Ellington had done the same thing with Dizzy Gillespie early in 1959, coaxing participation from one of Armstrong's greatest sons in two of the album's four masterpieces (the others being the extended *Toot Suite* and *Fillie Trillie*, a jazz version of romantic comedy that boasts Johnny Hodges at his personal Bechet best, a parody of a strip-tease number, and a dialogue between Hodges and the puckish, Clark Terry–crafted, near-bop of the brass). One is a concerto for jazz horn, Gillespie the bop king whispering, bitching, and blasting his way through Strayhorn's *Upper Manhattan Medical Group;* the other a blues summation of things as they then were, *Hello, Little Girl*. The second masterwork also features the silvery, insinuating piano of Jimmy Jones and the Southwestern blues shouting of the magnificent Jimmy Rushing, who had come to national notice more than two decades earlier as part of the Count Basie band that revolutionized jazz swing. After Rushing's bitter, plaintive, and raging tale of romantic turmoil, there is an obvious splice that puts the overall performance into the arena of combined takes in films. We then hear an extraordinary improvisation from Gillespie, himself a revolutionary, clearly displaying his untouchable wares to the Ellington trumpet section with a virtuosity, a harmonic complexity, and a swinging rhythmic intricacy that must have left every one of those trumpeters gasping and trembling. The ending finds Rushing and Gillespie emoting in combination over a splendid saxophone riff, some mightily dissonant brass, and a gutbucket-bottom groove from the rhythm section. Just before Ornette

Coleman and John Coltrane were to open the barn door for the anarchic honkers and squeakers of the sixties, Ellington showed that he was still the master chef capable of bringing together all that was unarguably good.

The uses of singers as far back as the 1927 *Creole Love Call* to imitate musical instruments, or the incorporation of the classical soprano Kay Davis in the 1946 *Transbluesency*, are brought to new levels of exploration and victory in the parts showcasing Margaret Tynes on the 1957 *A Drum Is a Woman* and the writing done for Alice Babs in the *Sacred Concerts* near the end of Ellington's life. While the 1958 version of *Black, Brown, and Beige* is largely a job of editing so incoherent that the form and development of the piece are butchered, it also includes Ellington's supreme liturgical achievement. Because she considered the Duke Ellington Orchestra "a sacred institution," the matchless Mahalia Jackson came to that recording date to sing *Come Sunday* and *The Twenty-Third Psalm*. Then the tragic vocal majesty stretching all the way back to the most powerful spirituals and the twentieth-century achievement of a wholly original language for the idiomatic American dance and concert orchestra reached mutual apotheosis. In the liner notes, it is claimed that Jackson improvised the vocal line of *The Twenty-Third Psalm*. That is more than doubtful, given the distance of the notes from anything the New Orleans high priestess of gospel normally sang. Ellington wrote what is a decidedly modern composition, one so unbeholden in overall sound and effect that it may have created its own category.

One of the reasons that Ellington has been so misunderstood is that we Americans don't always know how to assess ongoing artistry outside of European concert music. We expect the finest concert musicians to ripen and deepen with middle age, but assume that jazz musicians will deteriorate once they leave the bristling province of youth. In fact, Ellington's greatest band was not the one of the 1940s but the one between 1956 and 1968, though he was still able to inspire strong performances from lesser musicians afterward. Beginning in the middle 1950s, what he got from Johnny Hodges, Paul Gonsalves, Harry Carney, Lawrence Brown, Ray Nance, Cootie Williams, Russell Procope, Jimmy Hamilton, and the others could only be achieved by men who had lived beyond forty or fifty. By then, the band members had played every note and register in every key for so long that they had the kinds of intimate and subtle relationships to the identities of their instruments that young players, however gifted, never possess. Their tonal colors could be even thicker or far more transparent, given the assignment. Their life experience brought increasing depths to the emotions they had lived through and had seen played out in the lives of those around them. They had watched children grow into adulthood, handsome men and women lose their looks and shapes, friends and relatives die, innocent girls and boys become whores and ruthless hustlers, misfortune destroy, disfigure, or derange, and wars come and go; they had felt the shock of assassinations; and they had witnessed myriad changes in society and technology. The same was true of Ellington, who invented a piano style so evolvingly creative that the line he improvises on Coltrane's *Big Nick* from his 1962 album with the saxophonist could be transcribed and made into a first-class jazz song. His range of touches and his ear for matching reed, brass, and percussion timbres from the keyboard were equaled by an ability to coax or drive or cushion a soloist that is unsurpassed in the music.

Yet no amount of talent will forever hold out against the limitations of life. Ellington faced his losses as certain great musicians left for good and handled his grief when an irreplaceable man like Hodges died in 1970. Standing up to all responsibilities, he remained in the sway of his muse and continued to create masterpieces. Those who had overstated Strayhorn's unarguable importance and believed that Ellington had become more and more dependent on him for fresh ideas and new material must have been shocked after 1967 when they listened to *The Little Purple Flower* (particularly Part I), the *Goutelas Suite* (the whole of which is built upon the opening fanfare); the *Latin American Suite* (especially *The Sleeping Lady and the Giant Who Watches Over Her*); the finest sections of *Afro-Eurasian Eclipse;* the *Togo Brava Suite;* and the best writing of his *Sacred Concerts*. No matter what happened around him, Duke Ellington kept moving on up what seemed an infinite ladder of personal artistry. His sustained fecundity and the body of his work remain unequaled in American art. As he preferred his musicians to be, Ellington was a number one himself. Fortunately for the world of listeners and musicians, he lived and died in terms of what he had declared in 1959:

I don't want to feel obliged to play something with the same styling that we became identified with at some specific period . . . I don't want anyone to challenge my right to sound completely mad, to screech like a wild man, to create the mauve melody of a simpering idiot, or to write a song that praises God. I only want what any other American artist wants—and that is freedom of expression and of communication with our audience.

PART THREE

Celebrity Nudes:

Bloodshed, Sex, and

Narcissism

Truth Crushed
to Earth

There is something about good versus evil. There is something about truth. Truth crushed to earth will rise again. You can always count on that.

Johnnie Cochran, first evening of final arguments

Race is such a large decoy that it almost always causes us to get very important things wrong. That is why I don't accept the idea that the verdict in the O.J. Simpson double-murder case and the heated counterpoint of celebration and condemnation mean the country is now in greater racial trouble. As Americans, we are all members of an improvising social experiment ever in some sort of trouble. Ours is a country that learns whatever it learns by bruising its ideals in combat with human shortcomings, from the public to the private sector, the mass to the individual. In the long goodbye to those no-good things we are eventually forced to address, context by context, nothing slips by forever. This means that we have serious scars and lumps on our heads from the crashing of idols in every line of high-profile endeavor. "Say it ain't so" is the dark, hot, minor strain of the national anthem.

Yet we always cool off. That's part of our style and part of the heroic drama that defines the evolution of our nation. It happens once the sort of emotion we feel for our individual and group identities wears itself away. We then cease hiding under our beds, where we try to ignore the mature responsibilities demanded by the blues that periodically knocks at the national door, the hard blues dressed up in new duds and full of classic devilment. So what we are presently facing is just another situation in which those looking for something to get happy about and others seeking the opportunity to express their rage about some condition of purported oppression have gotten their moment. Such occasions inevitably work out for the national good because they demand that we face the complexities of our nation and grow up.

A chance to mature is exactly what was put before us in the case that began in a high-rent district with Nicole Brown Simpson's nearly decapitated corpse lying in sticky red death not far from the body of Ronald Goldman, the male model and weight-lifting waiter who came to deliver some eyeglasses and found himself in a losing struggle with the savage blade of murder. We were given fresh access to the kind of human tragedy that is not limited by race or social class or profession or good looks or athletic prowess or intelligence or sex or apparently golden luck. As the media lapped up every drop of blood, fingered every swelling, sniffed out every scent of illicit sex, and listened for every puff and snort of drugs, we came to know brutal and decadent secrets that were bribed or weaseled or forced up from the world of whispers. The swirl of rot reiterated the doubts we Americans lay down right next to our dreams. Something quite adult in us has long made for a suspicion of the anointed that undercuts our adolescent willingness to fall down before almost any person whose fame is a triumph against the anonymity largely guaranteed by the gargantuan world our technology summons. "I told you so" is another heated, minor strain of the national anthem. In our improvising democracy, when a tradition of unfairness is exposed for the low-down thing that it is, we conceive amendments or write new policies, working to keep our politics up on the same level as our human understanding.

In terms of our human understanding, the Simpson verdict crosses a terrain in which something is both amiss and affirmed in our national mythology. Once we cut ourselves loose from Europe, we made the mythology up as we went along. It had to stretch from the backwoods to the cities to the plains, North, South, East, and West. It had to be big enough to handle people from backgrounds as different as those of Jefferson, Lincoln, Douglass, Crazy Horse, Edison, and so on. We needed a cultural myth to explain the flesh and blood illumination arriving from the crude background as well as the smooth. But what we settled for in our weakest moments may well have put far too much emphasis on squeaky-clean human symbols, since we are almost always pulled up short by the tattling of private tales or the public exposure of caked or fresh dung in the drawers of widely admired figures.

Fused to our human symbols were our newspapers which, if they weren't muckraking, did their assumed duty by hiding the dung from us. People in the business figured we couldn't stand the truth and they didn't mind reporting only so much of it as they thought we could take. Censorship functioned in the name of "good taste" (just as bad taste is now promoted as "honesty"). Whenever in doubt, we moved into the recasting of a basic American vision, which is that the common person, the innocent, the mistreated or misunderstood will pick up where others have failed at truly realizing the meanings of our democratic ideals. This person will not be corrupted by the narcissism that comes with large monetary success, excessive power, and inordinate admiration by the mob. This person, one calloused big toe standing on-pointe at the peak of the moral pyramid, will have a messianic effect on our belief in our system.

That is where the Negro comes in and where, at our moments of greatest desperation, we secretly make our most serious bets on something better rising out of something bad. If the Negro can stand the pressure of sustained and unfair opposition, then we all can. If the Negro can get up to the top and hold in place everything this culture has found so charismatic, we have a much greater chance of bringing off this social experiment, especially since the Afro-American's history on this land reaches back beyond the *Mayflower*. The patience, the grace, the rhythm, the humor, the discipline, and the heroic majesty historically found in the best of Negro life have always provided some sort of an antidote to the disorder that Ralph Ellison observed is ever a danger to our society. That is why

identification with Negro aspirations and Negro style has been so important to the development of this country's democracy and its culture. The
Negro has tested our democracy and been central to what we mean by the
spirit of Americana when it sings, when it dances, when it talks to the cosmos, when it gives a certain texture of rhythm to English, or exhibits the
long memory so essential to our recognition of the tragic losses that have
formed the hill of corpses upon which we stand, able to see beyond the
worst of our human limitations while acknowledging their every nuance.

The Simpson case tested all of our contemporary democratic myth-
ologies about good and evil, about race and fairness, about law enforcement, the criminal courts and justice. The Negroes who disturbed so
many by celebrating, by cheering, and by dancing were responding to a
dream of American possibility quite different from what the media assumed. It was all, given the extemporized brilliance of the defense, much,
much deeper than "a brother beating the system." The integrated selection of citizens that magically disappeared and conveniently became an
all-black jury—even in the minds of outraged liberals—delivered a verdict that had nothing to do with racial solidarity or jury nullification.
Those jury members were neither that simple-minded nor that incapable
of understanding what was on display as evidence. The jurors might well
have recognized that they were in the presence of a level of lawyering that
none will probably ever see in the flesh again, day by day, witness by witness, exhibit by exhibit. That, above all else, is what they responded to in
such a swift stroke.

As far as color goes, we all saw just what our country has come down
to, which is not some imbecilic racial divide but interracial teams working both sides of the basic arguments. Just as there are now highly visible
so-called minorities in both major political parties and either heading or
inside the administrations of almost every important city, the prosecution
and the defense in this epic trial were comprised of integrated teams. For
all of the discussion about sinister developments in black and Jewish relations, we saw prosecutor Marcia Clark, a Jewish woman, whose central
partner was Christopher Darden, an unarguably grass-roots Negro, both
backed up by a remarkably diverse group of people appearing as witnesses,
law enforcement, and experts. The same was true of the defense team, first

headed by the extremely smooth Robert Shapiro, whose demotion in favor of Johnnie Cochran may reveal as much about his post-trial sour grapes as anything else. If, say, Shapiro is the kind of guy who is accustomed to being far brighter than most people he encounters, it must have been quite an experience for him to observe in Cochran a level of argument, eloquence, delineated passion, and superbly paced execution that he will never feel nor hear coming out of his own body. He might well have smarted quite deeply as his initial celebrity was gradually but completely overshadowed by Cochran's. That smarting might have reached its supreme intensity near the end, when Shapiro found himself so far down in the public polls that he was loudly booed at a Lakers basketball game and approached in restaurants by social wild cards ranting about his betraying the genocidal horrors of World War II.

In fact, there may have been no issue larger in the overview of it all than betrayal. That sense of betrayal further underlined our double standards. The black jurors were endlessly condescended to for supposedly setting aside the evidence in favor of an irrational sense of duty to group solidarity. Yet nobody in the media seemed bothered by those riled feminist ideologues who freely accused Negro females—on and off the jury—of betraying their battered and butchered blonde sister. The solidarity of victimhood should have transcended the looming presence of a reasonable doubt. Eventually we will be grateful for what the Simpson case forced us to learn about betrayal of the public trust. The dark welts on the souls of athletic heroes and media figures are not new to us, whether we are talking about an O.J. Simpson or a Jessica Savitch. But this time, we had our sensibilities and whatever innocence we could claim pushed right into hard facts about law enforcement, about the risky deals a prosecution team will make with the devil, about the kind of sloppiness in evidence collection and assessment that seems to pass by quite easily in most instances. In the aftermath, we got a chance to see how all of those people who so cynically dismiss "the system" with examples such as Watergate, FBI hanky-panky, the serpentine antics of the CIA, Oliver North, the savings and loan scandal, the Clarence Thomas–Anita Hill hearings, and so on were suddenly and haughtily able to set aside every example of police misconduct and suspicious evidence in the Simpson case.

Those same people—*all of whom should know that juries almost auto-matically acquit when the police are caught lying or red-handed*—turned in the other direction, dropped their pants, and contemptuously mooned the verdict. Turning back around, these people asserted that the forensic evidence should have transcended everything else. They seemed to forget that Americans have a dual attitude toward the kind of technology that lay beneath the DNA evidence. We suspect machinery just as much as we love it, primarily because our society is one at war with the potential anonymity imposed by our technology. So when a good enough lawyer plays into that aversion to the technological, he or she isn't so much summoning up the ignorant impatience of the jury as pulling forth a basic aspect of its American feeling, our fear that our humanity will be compromised by our toys of mathematical definition and measurement. As lovers of the underdog, as people from one group or another who have had the deck stacked against us at some distant or recent time, we don't always take too kindly to statistics and often refuse to be bullied by experts.

Sometimes, like the sort of farm boys whose down-home logic thwarts city slickers, we just want to know why some blood left on a fence for several weeks contains a chemical preservative found in police labs. (Is that a statement on the preserving purity of smoggy Los Angeles weather?) We just want to know why there is no blood trail leading to or away from the infamous bloody glove, which was described by Mark Fuhrman as "moist and sticky" when it was found during his foraging for evidence all by his lonesome—seven and a half hours after it was supposedly dropped by the murderer. We would like to know how even a former super athlete and a seriously mediocre actor could park, leap over a fence, bang into a wall three times, drop a glove, run upstairs, shower, change clothes, and come downstairs deporting himself as just another guy a little late for a limousine ride to the airport. As a deeply disturbed Mario Cuomo observed, there was more than enough to raise "a reasonable doubt," but endless white Americans were distraught because the jury took that doubt's specifically instructed meaning so seriously. The howlers would have preferred that the jurors ignore the law. They felt betrayed.

There are also those who feel betrayed by Simpson's upper-class life to such an extent that a special kind of racism has been put back into play, one that used to slither off of the term "uppity." It now allows William Safire to write in the *New York Times*, "The wealthy celebrity who lived white, spoke white and married white wrapped himself in the rags of social injustice and told his black counsel to move black jurors to vote black." Safire was following the pompous lead of *Time* magazine's head mulatto in charge of darkie correction, Jack E. White, who wrote, "Never one to speak out on civil rights, he seemed to shed his racial identity, crossing over into a sort of colorless minor celebrity as easily as he escaped from tacklers—or from the black wife he traded in for a white teenager."

Twenty-five years ago, no writer, black or white, would have been allowed to impose such a limited vision of "authenticity" on a Negro. Individual freedom was then the issue, not joining a movement, not maintaining a lifestyle that would make certain white people feel more comfortable about the exclusive and fraudulent franchise of their "whiteness," which includes expensive property, privilege upon privilege, the money to do battle with the legal system on equal ground, the proper enunciation of the English language, and freedom of social choice. In this era, when Woody Allen was in the middle of his big mess with Mia Farrow, he wasn't asked to get a cosmetic foreskin replacement because of the women he's chosen over the years. No one asks Allen to suppress his comic urban neurosis in favor of the kind of worldliness Leonard Bernstein possessed. Nor is Susan Sontag told to emulate Fanny Brice if she would truly represent the group. Sylvester Stallone isn't under attack for his lovers or where he lives or whose company he travels in. The only ethnic under that pressure is the Negro, whose unlimited variations on Americanness must now meet not the infinite meanings of our national humanity, but some short-order ethnic recipe of circumscribed taste and possibility.

As we look back on this trial from some point in the future, we will see beyond such recipes and remember certain purely American things that are signal examples of the way our country is going. Ours is no longer a culture dominated by one race taking up all the seats in high places. We will remember Judge Lance Ito—former Eagle Scout and son of parents who did World War II time in American concentration camps—letting both sides have a lot of rope but surely favoring a prosecution that still couldn't serve Simpson's head on a platter. We will remember Johnnie Cochran doing an extremely witty variation on Marc Antony's speech over Caesar's body, pivoting on the phrase "but Christopher Darden loves me." We will remember Marcia Clark coddling Mark Fuhrman through his testimony and F. Lee Bailey getting the rogue cop to say the things under oath that would make him an unarguable perjurer. We will remember Rosa Lopez cringing under Darden's smoldering questions. We will remember Dennis Fung's perfectly modulated voice losing all confidence and starting to quaver as Barry Scheck systematically turned his expertise into confetti. We will remember the way Henry Lee sat there and spun out parables while speaking with such clear, forensic authority that it seemed as though the ghost of Charlie Chan had been brought to life with a deeply human three-dimensionality the Hollywood scriptwriters never achieved. We will remember the enlarging pie pans under Marcia Clark's eyes as the months passed and then the extremely chilling way she ended her summation with the voice of Nicole Brown Simpson calling 911 for help. We will remember the rising and falling of the case, each side apparently losing at one point, winning at another. Then we will remember the final arguments.

By the end, it came down to black and white, Negro and Jew, Christopher Darden and Marcia Clark up against Johnnie Cochran and Barry Scheck. The astonishing one was Cochran. Whatever we must say about this lawyer so foolishly allowing Nation of Islam goons to guard him, or his demagogically attempting to recruit black reporters for the defense point of view, we should also remember that, in the heat of battle, especially during the ninety minutes that followed the dinner break on the first of two days of defense summations, the man was so extraordinary that Brooklyn district attorney Joe Hynes said that in thirty years as a professional he had never witnessed such a tour de force in the arena of advocacy.

Cochran's command of American sound and rhythm was perfectly orchestrated within the context of an argument that tore down the prosecution's case as he ripped apart the state's speculative logic and showed how the testimony of one police officer after another was full of specious contradictions. He convincingly revealed the holes in certain evidence and unmasked the real motives behind the actions of the cops at Simpson's mansion. Part of his compelling virtuosity was the way in which he mixed various straight and street accents, crossing and recrossing the ethnic divide, reaching for an idealistic judicial diction, parodying the "white" voices of the cops, and backing things up with superb pauses and brilliant emphases, then closing out with the repetitions and inflections of the best and more subtle Afro-American pulpit talk. Cochran was so remarkable that, at one point, Ito himself repressed a smile at the quality of the summation he was hearing. The dark-skinned and handsome Cochran, ever immaculately dressed, jumped froggy and brought that Negro American swing to court. One understood right then why Los Angeles lawyer Mike Yamamoto says that to bellow and whine about "the race card" is to deny the fact that this man proved, day by day, that he is the best lawyer in the whole town.

For all that we might find fault with on either side, there is no denying the bottomless humanity we witnessed. There is also no denying that if all we learned as a nation about police misconduct, irresponsible prosecution teams, and sloppy crime laboratories moves us closer to bettering the liberty of the people through the agencies created to protect them, then Nicole Brown Simpson and Ronald Goldman will not actually have died in vain, regardless of who may have killed them. Lying murdered in Brentwood, their bodies brought people and elements into play that let us see how vulnerable we all are to the most brutal treatment and how much we still have to do if we want to move this country closer and closer to justice. Along the way, we will continue to grow up, since the immature can never handle the inevitable blows of the blues. However we get there, as the trial never failed to let us know, we will only achieve our American ideals through multiracial teams of both sexes, calling upon the fullest range of our national humanity.

The Dardenilla
Dilemma:

Selling Hostile Chocolate

and Vanilla Animus

*Now it seemed like Marcia and me against that team of nine
prominent, ruthless lawyers.*

Christopher Darden, *In Contempt*

*The prosecution of O.J. Simpson was the most incompetent
criminal prosecution I have ever seen. By far. There have un-
doubtedly been worse. It's just that I'm not aware of any.*

Vincent Bugliosi, *Outrage*

We know that in the Montana summer of 1876
George Armstrong Custer attacked an encampment of between 5,000 and
10,000 Indians with 300 men. Not a good idea. But, until very recently,
history did not handle him as it might have. For his astonishing blunder,
one of the worst decisions in all of military history, Custer became a national hero, the symbol of the valiant leader standing next to the flag of
the Seventh Cavalry, his flaxen hair blowing in the dusty wind, his mus-
tache and goatee perfectly trimmed, his buckskin jacket hanging as
though tailored, his blue eyes showing no fear as the two six-guns he
possessed alternately blasted away at an endless swarm of bloodthirsty
redskins. In dime novels, on street corners, in office buildings, around
fireplaces, at dinner tables, in pool halls, on front porches, and among
schoolchildren, Custer's story was told over and over. Soon, his proportions took on those of legend; he became emblematic of what the country

had to endure in order to spread the train of its greatness from sea to shining sea. The grit, discipline, spit, and polish of civilization went down before a bunch of whooping savages. It was, however, the last significant victory for the Indians. With the massacre at the Little Bighorn memorially ablaze behind their foreheads, American forces went on to crush the hostiles, tribe by tribe, and the government bureaucracy conceived a way to put them in their place. The various representatives of these United States taught them a thing or two. They'd had their day and it didn't last long.

Now that irrepressible pony soldier, Old Yellow Hair, the Son of the Morning Star himself, has returned to walk among us multiplied. I say this because what the members of the prosecution team in the O.J. Simpson case want to create for themselves is a Custer's Last Stand of jurisprudence, which will allow them a permanent place in the martyr's pantheon of Americana. They want to become heroes for losing, even though their own blunders were substantial enough to make them targets for the kind of scorn athletes are subjected to when they choke up during the championship games that conclude the season. This attempt to define themselves demands plenty of ad hominem in order to take the focus off of those errors, which were watched by who knows how many people both nationally and internationally. If that wasn't enough, hundreds upon hundreds of hours were devoted to analyzing each televised day in court. But there is still a way out. The easiest is to assert that those jurors who decided the outcome were riddled with racial animus or were incapable of assessing complex evidence—or both.

While this willingness to pass the buck seems true of each and every one of them, there is a member of the prosecution team who stands out like a marshmallow in a bowl of chocolate pudding. That one is Christopher A. Darden, the television joy of Geraldo Rivera, Charles Grodin, and Dennis Miller, three examples so different that they make it clear why Darden has become a minor celebrity in the wake of the murder trial. His mask of high moral outrage matches theirs, allowing such people to pat themselves on the back at the same time that they commend him for rising above the irrational temptations of racial loyalty and looking at the facts with unconditional courage.

Darden would agree. When he swaggers on screen for a talk show, barely restraining the smile inspired by the introduction and the applause, the former prosecutor seems intent on becoming Old Yellow Hair himself. This man wants to be canonized as a deep-thinking martyr even though he made perhaps the two most serious on-the-spot mistakes of the trial. Darden is the one who asked Simpson to put the gloves on. Later, his emotions unexplainably running riot, he used sexual allusions and condescendingly badgered the unwilling witness for the defense, screenwriter Laura Hart McKinney, until she angrily blurted out testimony about evidence-planting and cover-ups that Mark Fuhrman had bragged about when she was using him as a consultant for her movie script about cops. This allowed in material that Judge Lance Ito had ruled was beyond the scope of the case. (With typical forthrightness, Darden has failed to address the consequences of the McKinney cross-examination in word or print.) Given such decisions, Darden must have well understood how Custer felt when he was surrounded by the deadly results of his last attack.

Along the way we should not forget that Darden and Marcia Clark exhibited no more shame than the rest who huckstered their relationships to the gore on Bundy Drive. The prosecutors finally responded to the overtures by agents seeking to represent them and, owing to quite successful negotiations, each signed a seven-figure book contract that was sealed with the blood of Nicole Brown Simpson and Ronald Goldman. After all, given the billion dollars or more generated by the case—expenditures and profits for and from electronic coverage, print coverage, press accommodations, transportation, photographs, souvenirs, investigation by the prosecution as well as the defense, expert witnesses, lawyers, long-distance phone calls, and so on and on—why shouldn't a couple of public servants line their pockets? (This makes the case that there ought to be a law against such public servants writing about their work sooner than ten years after the fact.) Those two—pressed by tabloid gossip into uncorroborated copulation—made sure they weren't walking home broke after this one. Having it made in the shade was their intention. They weren't only going to self-righteously morph themselves into victims. This duo would rise rich and famous from the ashes of their defeat, ostentatiously flapping their phoenix wings. Especially Christopher A. Darden.

But Darden's popularity on the talk show circuit and in the rest of the media is understandable, if only because almost anyone, black, white, or any other color, is anxious to hear straight talk about the latest developments in our racial crisis, especially from Negroes. His intellectual clumsiness notwithstanding, Darden is important to many because he is one of the few in the public eye who seems to distinguish himself from those who rant as loudly as possible about white racism but bite their tongues when subjects like Louis Farrakan come up, sometimes asserting that they refuse to pass some white-imposed "test" by attacking other black people. None can improve upon the rationalizations or the passion of the cowardly when it comes to justifying the chicken-hearted nature of their sensibilities. Therefore, Darden is held up by his admirers as just the opposite of those Negroes too squeamish to speak their minds and let the razor-sharp chips of the truth fall where they may. He keeps their hope alive by representing a return to the fresh, unsentimental assessment of our dilemmas, and a rejection of the conventions that embitter racial discourse.

All of this praise for Darden folds into the usually unspoken reservations many white people have about the racial atmosphere that has developed over the last thirty years. When Black Power arrived in 1966, it rejected fundamental democratic reasoning in favor of tribalism, ethnic self-worship, and the idea that a basic standard of conduct was no more than another tool of white supremacy. With Black Power, everything black became good and everything white became, if not bad, at least highly suspect. A twisted cultural relativism reared itself. Rooted in the nineteenth-century European disdain for the bourgeoisie and the lower-class American antipathy toward refinement, Black Power railed against what became dubiously known as "white-middle-class standards." If a Negro adhered to what had formerly been no more than an expression of finesse or the expansion of one's taste, he or she was seen as "trying to be white." Ironically, this interpretation was traditionally expressed by the white racists, who found laughable, pretentious, or dangerously presumptive any Negro aspirations beyond hard labor, cooking, dancing, and singing. One senator even made himself famous during the 1970s by saying all that niggers wanted was some loose shoes, some tight hoonyang, and a warm place to take a dump. So if the Negro's aspirations weren't perfect subjects for jokes, he or she was thought of as "uppity."

None of this, within the context of the Simpson double-murder trial, is separate from the American epic of class hostilities and the tales of ethnic types losing connection to their roots. Simpson's image of success and his change of social context goes right to the center of our country's struggle to understand both our traditional backgrounds and the resistance to our dreams—not to mention our struggle to face the truth that those very dreams might not be substantial. In our history and our arts are the many stories of those pushing their way up from the bottom and those at the top searching down below for a more vibrant relationship to life. But, because we fear being or becoming second-rate, and because we have been so often disappointed by people from every aspect of the social spectrum, we are equally ambivalent toward the supposed vitality of the poor as we do toward the purported sophistication of the rich. We know that although there may be much chaos at the bottom, there may be just as much at the top. We tire neither of satirically cutting through the sanctimonious camouflage of the yahoos at the bottom nor ridiculing the spiritual igloos of the upper class. We hate phony balonies and have made "the real" into our holy grail.

It is this combination of ambivalence and cynicism that makes us potential chumps where race, religion, and sex are concerned. We have trouble picking through to the human reality. At our worst, we might try to resolve our conflicts by accepting some demagogue's definition of a "real" Negro, a "real" Jew, a "real" Christian, a "real" Hispanic, a "real" woman, and so on. What the demagogue wants is a following strapped into simplemindedness by thick belts of hostility and resentment. This allows the demagogue to tell us where our group identity stops and where our expressions of self-hatred, delusion, and gullibility begin. We are admonished to understand that, "Beyond this point you are losing connection to us; you are becoming one of them." (Even Vincent Bugliosi falls for this one in his book about the Simpson trial, *Outrage:* ". . . although Simpson wasn't the classically passive and submissive black memorialized in Harriet Beecher Stowe's novel *Uncle Tom's Cabin*, he easily fell within the more expansive popular definition of the term—a black who has not only forgotten his roots, but virtually turned his back on the black community, striving to become a white man in every possible way.")

In order to understand these issues better we need to look at something Arthur Schlesinger Jr. discussed in *The Disuniting of America*, one of the most clearly thought-out discussions of our "authenticity blues." Schlesinger observes that America has always been a country of miscegenation, even when it was largely only the mixing of different nationalities. He makes it clear that "Those intrepid Europeans who had torn up their roots to brave the wild Atlantic *wanted* to forget a horrid past and to embrace a hopeful future. They *expected* to become Americans. Their goals were escape, deliverance, assimilation. They saw America as a transforming nation, banishing dismal memories and developing a unique national character based on common political ideals and shared experiences. The point of America was not to preserve old cultures, but to forge a new *American* culture." Schlesinger goes on to point out that the twentieth century brought with it many reservations about assimilation. Assimilation was seen as a technique of oppression, a way of victimizing people by tearing them away from their history.

The unrelenting media attention given the Simpson trial brought all of those elements into what most in the profession of law thought should have been, however high profile, a straightforward murder trial, another shocking crime of passion among the rich and famous. On the other hand, Simpson held a special place in our hearts because his was the rags-to-riches tale, and he seemed, in a modest and unpretentious way, to have become the truly American aristocrat capable of traversing our society and drawing out the better human influences, no matter their points of origin. We now know that Simpson, at the time of the murders, was handsome, charming, violent, and illiterate. His years of fame and coddling had infantilized one side of him. He was a middle-aged, muscular brat who narcissistically prowled through his own paradise with the special arrogance of a celebrity accustomed to universal deference. But there are also those outraged by the fact that Simpson didn't make Negro social causes priorities in his life, as though he were required to—which he was not. The man had benefited from the disciplined development of his athletic prowess, not from anything particular to Afro-American culture of the sort that so many musicians, actors, dancers, and writers have built their reputations upon, none of whom, by the way, are obligated to become race crusaders or philanthropists. He had the right to live his life as he chose, marrying whom he wished and socializing according to his own preferences. Yet, there was the rub. As prime suspect, with two grisly murders picked over by the media, O.J. Simpson was still black and he was still vastly loved and he was on trial in Los Angeles, where, in the 1990s, race exploded every few years.

That is where Christopher A. Darden comes in. The man many assumed was brought in to mitigate the negative impression of a very famous black man being prosecuted for murder by an all-white team, Darden is neither simple nor easily dismissed. But he is truly a son of his era. *In Contempt,* his autobiography and his version of the Simpson case, unintentionally reveals that Darden has a rather confused vision of the difference between social determination and individual choice. He is, therefore, both a perfect Californian and a perfect sore loser. In essence, what we get from Darden is another spin on the victim vision. Ours is a time in which we should expect such things and, in some ways, it is perfectly fitting that the conspiracy theory of the defense, which portrayed the wealthy Simpson as a victim of ruthless law enforcement hanky-panky and racism, has now been countered by a theory in which the prosecution, the jury system, and the very law itself have been victimized by some irrational colored people. Darden's excuse is familiar because it is the same one used for so many other kinds of failure—"It wasn't me. Somebody did it to me. I'm sitting here facing accusations because of forces beyond my control. I never got an even break. I got off the bench with two strikes against me. Oh, one more thing. By the way. Take it into consideration. Don't ever forget. Society didn't help me to stack up enough self-esteem in order for me to act the way I should act. I've been had, up, down, and around and around." In Darden's own words, "We were prosecutors, civil servants, and not rich, powerful lawyers." Poor kids.

At the center of this controversy is the question of whether or not one's actions can yet be assessed on individual terms—especially when the stakes are as high as the stakes ever get. Was it possible for O.J. Simpson to be an individual first and a Negro either second or only incidentally? Was it possible for a predominantly black jury to be a gathering of individual experiences and perspectives instead of largely a mass of Pavlovian darkies ready to drool in unison at the opportunity to get back at a legal system demonstrably mottled by racism? This sets up the next question, which is how important one's ethnic group is to what happens in a court of law. Are we so trapped in allegiances to skin color, religion, and culture that justice has a hard time appearing within our system? Do we accept extremely limited ideas about "authenticity" that lead us to certain equally reductive conclusions when we are in the midst of our own experience, not something we have been told about ourselves? Were Simpson and the jurors contemporary examples of how successfully the ignorant, the brutal, the xenophobic, and the provincial have resisted the complex and the sophisticated?

These are questions that completely confuse Darden, who can't for the life of him understand the problems that obsession with "race" and "culture" have wrought in our society. If Darden is the victim of anything at all, it is the body of assumptions he has accepted about what makes him who he is and what makes others who they are. He is far from a racist, but is certainly biased, having bought into insubstantial ideas about "African heritage" long ago. Those ideas are indicative of how shallow is his understanding of this country, however much hard, shocking experience his job has given him. After making the point that "My law school diploma wasn't a black Juris Doctorate," he goes on to write, "I am a lawyer," then comes home with this shiner:

> And I am black. In fact, I love the color of my skin. It is dark and perfect. When you look at me, you don't see the remnants of slavery— light skin, thin lips, pinched nose. You see an African face. I am proud of that.

Darden apparently has no idea how many dark-skinned Negro Americans have both white and Indian ancestors in the mix. He has bought a very simple idea about identity, one based equally in "feel good" propaganda and a rhetorical cliché popularized by Malcolm X during his time with the Nation of Islam. (This reveals Darden's troubled "double consciousness" as a black man who sees himself as standing above the racial divisions in the interest of justice, but one anxious to assert his recognition of "blackness." Though he later attacks Johnnie Cochran for calling some white cops "devils," the Nation of Islam's xenophobic name for all whites, Darden, ever befuddled, talks out of both sides of his own mouth when he defines the very same racist cult as "a strong, proud, and worthy group, but also the very symbol of black separatism.") Darden heard this "historical" genealogy from an admired black studies professor at San Jose State University:

> You are the direct descendants of kings and queens. They didn't load just anyone on those slave ships. They stole only the best and they stole only the brightest. They took the strongest physically and mentally. They took royalty, and that's why you are the sons and daughters of kings and queens. You are the princes and princesses of Africa.

Apparently, this poor man believes that there were enough kingdoms on the West Coast of Africa to be split among the millions who were sold into this hemisphere as chattel slaves! Maybe, back in good old Africa, a man's home is his castle. Perhaps Huey Long was passing for white when he spoke of "every man a king." One never knows. Then there is the "brightness" question. Does Darden think that the Africans who captured members of rival tribes gave them intelligence tests to determine whether or not they would make first-class slaves before they were marched to the coastal beaches and sold to Europeans? Doesn't he know that these people were seen as no more than livestock by the Africans, the Europeans, and the Arabs who made the nasty business truly "multicultural"? (It is interesting to note that Darden's charging the Dream Team with exploiting race was foreshadowed in the mass media when O.J. Simpson played the part of an African in paradise who was killed as the whites began scooping up slaves in the first episode of *Roots*, a miniseries based on a despicably fraudulent work that cashed in on the Black Power appetite for African ancestry, the gold mines of white guilt, and the sob stories of black studies courses, the last far more often about indoctrination than scholarship.)

In addition to his faulty cultural assumptions, Darden is also controlled by a two-tiered system of resentment, one on which racial misgivings are joined by a stew of anger that mixes—in separate but equal parts—class, luxury, privilege, and reputation. Darden unknowingly reveals one of his central concerns when he writes of his classmates from Princeton, Yale, Berkeley, and Stanford when he was a law student,

"These guys with their huge egos and $80,000 educations were always posturing and posing and doing their best not to talk to me." At another point, our genetically untrammeled African complains about how much leeway celebrities are given in Los Angeles. Early in the trail he sulks, "It was funny; I was probably the only lawyer in the room who wasn't famous." But later, when he has become a cap pistol celebrity, our lawyer with the Gold Coast face observes, "Marcia and I were being recognized in more and more places. We were invited to parties where movie stars lined up to meet *us* . . . Movie stars and other celebrities are, as a group, shorter than you'd think. Nicer too." Darden gets so tangled up in celebrity and the courtroom as a place of public performance that he refers to the press coverage as good or bad "reviews." They filled this boy's head with the helium of attention and he just floated away.

In this context, when our prosecutor looks at Simpson's defense— "the whole Dream Team"—and expresses his resentment with such vengeance, we observe a variation on the way Darden felt at law school when he was surrounded by guys with Ivy League pedigrees: "I wondered what the criteria could be for admittance to this team. Among the front-line attorneys, the only thing they seemed to have in common was their penchant for defending spoiled, nasty rich people and their ability to attract and create publicity." He calls them all sorts of names, even refers to F. Lee Bailey as "foul-mouthed" though he frequently quotes Marcia Clark using expletives casually, angrily, affectionately. Darden became furious when Cochran, whom he blames for alienating him from the Afro-American community, attacked him for asking a witness if he heard an unseen man with a "black" voice:

> "I resent that statement," Cochran clipped, leaning on the podium in
> his off-white linen suit, like some angry plantation owner. "You can't
> tell by somebody's voice whether they sound black." His upper lip
> curled underneath his mustache and Cochran came at me again.
> "That's a racist statement!"

Speaking to the reader, Darden justifies his question by reasoning that entertainers "have long fought for the opportunity to reflect genuine black voices—urban, hip, with traces of the South, of the West Indies, of

Africa." The poor prosecutor doesn't understand that region, class, and style, not color, determine whether one sounds "white" or "black." He should tune in to one of the talk shows and turn his back, listening. He will find something out. In today's world, with so many white kids and young adults, from the lower class to the suburbs, taking their leads from rap, black comedians, and so on, what was once heard as "black" might now be no more than another stylistic aspect of Americana, neither a birthright nor a stop sign.

These sorts of confusions on Darden's part only obscure the far more important subject, which is whether or not a murderer slipped through the grip of the legal system. Darden is quite critical of that legal system and believes that the black jurors were sufficiently embittered by how it functions that, when goaded by Cochran over and over, they chose to acquit. This fails to explain how the non-Negro members of the jury—including a very strong-willed older white woman whom many pundits expected to hang the jury—were brought aboard for the ride. It uses the excuse of social determinism to mitigate against a very unpleasant reality. That reality includes a major prosecution witness—a cop—caught lying on the stand. As Darden well knows, such a catastrophe almost automatically leads to acquittal. The reason is simple and obvious, however many mountains of other evidence are on display: juries, no matter their color, distrust any prosecution team that will bring a lying cop to the stand and put him at the center of its case, speak to him sweetly, then attack him as contemptuous vermin when the covers are pulled by the defense. Darden's sociological excuse, however self-serving, is an example of the difficulty we have in seeing the legal and penal systems with the clarity that will allow us to recognize the present criminal crisis while remaining on the lookout for those infringements that allow prejudice to unfairly tip the scales against the innocent.

Here is where the complexity comes in. Even if we accept the idea that the justice system unfairly tilts punishment on lower-class black defendants and that the penal system imprisons a disproportionate number of convicted black men, we have to wonder what we are actually talking about when we balance that idea against the equally disproportionate number of murders, rapes, robberies, and assaults suffered by black people at the hands of other black people who reside within the same communities. The yearly body counts extend far beyond what they were in even the most brutal periods of redneck Southern rule and Northern race riots. The murder and violence have created a racially based national health crisis. The odds that so many young black men will die from violent attacks are not the result of a grim increase in skinheads or Aryan militias bent on race war and genocide. For all the talk of institutional racism—which should be rooted out whenever and wherever its existence can be proven—we haven't developed reasonable emergency policies sufficiently stern to intimidate the bulk of those with thug inclinations into civilized behavior. (As one who believes that we have to face the best we might actually get, I'll settle for good behavior, not psychological rehabilitation or changing a polluted heart into a pure one. They can think or feel whatever they like as long as they keep a collar on the destructive actions that introduced them to law enforcement. Get a job, act civilized, and purge your anarchic fantasies at the movies.)

As a black prosecutor, Christopher Darden earned his living and made whatever reputation he had in that world—before the Simpson case. It is one of the most difficult positions in American society because those sympathetic to the collective sense of racial injustice, black or white, are vulnerable to manipulation by the shrewdest lawyers and criminals among us. This vulnerability was discovered in the late 1960s when the lawyer Charles Gary defended Black Panthers like the murderous Huey Newton. Gary's technique largely ignored the charges and put the society on trial. Since then a trickle-down effect has set in. Now the manipulative lawyer and guilty black criminal can cite slavery, segregation, lynchings, police brutality, prejudiced judges, white juries, and the poverty born of racism and inadequate schooling. Last, but in no way the least, there is the lack of a "level playing field," which guarantees low achievement. So the guilty black criminal, when sufficiently crafty, benefits from the unarguable rap sheet that documents thousands of instances of crimes against democratic fairness. (Critics cite the defense of O.J. Simpson as a variation on this ploy.)

When examined unsentimentally, however, there is a serious flaw in this kind of thinking. Crimes past do not erase crimes present, unless one accepts the idea that society is so much stronger than the individual that what we actually see are not necessarily crimes but could easily be the result of the deformations that come of prejudice and deprivation. The logic of this argument is that those who exist outside of the circles of privilege are driven mad (at least, temporarily) by bitterness, frustration, and the desperate responses to alienation that form an entire code of behavior, one in which values are often turned upside down. In essence, it is a variation on the insanity defense. The individual is not responsible for his or her actions. Anarchic behavior becomes the most harrowing expression of the alienated, they who feel abandoned because of their color and their poverty.

While such arguments might work among the tender-hearted, especially those well educated enough to have had their brains clotted with sociology and psychoanalysis, the people on the receiving end of the actions of predators don't feel much sympathy for them. They are educated in statistics covered by bruises and fresh blood. Their opinions are outside the realms of the academy, where life remains the same whether or not the theorists are right. They who know crime from the point of contact argue that there are many people who aren't doing as well as they would like but that doesn't make it right or acceptable to destroy the feeling of safety and freedom within a community. Those Negro Americans are as bent on law and order as you can get. Where some others might whine about police presence and claim unnecessary harassment, these black people certainly don't support law enforcement excesses but do want *more* police and stronger police action. They want the streets cleared of criminals and, as one woman in a New Jersey housing project said, "I don't care whether they put them *in* the jail, *behind* the jail, or *under* the jail. All I want is for them to be gone out of here."

Darden, who prosecuted violent criminals, from murdering gang members to mad serial killers, came to know the meaning of that attitude. In 1985, he was part of a special unit organized to "hit gangs hard, to coordinate prosecution and specifically target the young men involved in the drug trade, in the random robberies and constant murders of gang life." That year there were 271 gang members; six years later the murdered stacked up beyond 700. Darden saw unarguable examples of what these people had done to their communities:

I drove home at night through neighborhoods in various states of warfare with gangs, some in which the families were held captive behind barred windows because of packs of fifteen-year-olds with semi-automatic weapons; other neighborhoods in which the families just gave up and moved farther away and the houses, the duplexes, and apartments dissolved into bullet-pocked crack houses and shooting galleries.

In 1988, he went on to work in the Special Investigation Division "where public officials, primarily police officers, were investigated for the crimes they might have committed." Darden learned why many people were terrified of the police:

In SID, I quickly found out there was plenty of reason to be afraid. There was a small percentage of cops so dirty, you couldn't imagine a crime they hadn't committed. The files fell onto our desks like dirty snow—rape, embezzlement, fraud, theft, bribery, intimidation, black-mail, assault, even homicide. And that same bunker mentality, that code of silence, allowed them to get away with it more often than other criminals.

So when Darden was brought onto the prosecution team for the Simpson trial, he had seen the casualties wrought by both sides of the sword, those cut down by minority criminals and those done harm by dirty cops. That is why he believes that the system itself is at least partially responsible for the attitudes of black Americans toward law enforcement, both the courts and the cop on the street. While Darden has no trouble recognizing a race strategy in court, he dons the victim's cloak and works so hard to burn Johnnie Cochran at the stake that analysis disappears in the smoke of attempted revenge and self-inflation:

Cochran had decided that everything in this case would be racial strategy and the pundits were playing right along, buying into that hype . . . Everything in this case was sifted through a filter of bigoted expectations, like the pressure Jackie Robinson faced when he broke the color barrier in baseball. "Pretty good hitter for a darkie." It was bad for our case, but it was worse for the country. We were being ratcheted back fifty years because of a lying, murdering ex-jock and his unprincipled legal team. And the media, the pundits, and the starstruck judge played gleefully along.

Though Darden sneers at the idea that O.J. Simpson, "a millionaire who was given every deference by the system," would have the nerve to allow the factual suffering of black people to be used as an abstract shield for his murders, the prosecutor doesn't flinch when comparing himself to Jackie Robinson! He also says, "It was our responsibility to try to appeal to this group of people, no matter how suspicious and bitter they were. And we failed. But I would rather fail than win by perverting and twisting the justice system—as I believe the defense team did." This is whining of the worst sort. It is not possible for a defense team to pervert and twist our system of justice, unless it pays off judges, jurors, and witnesses. Cochran and his crew did nothing of the sort. They raised reasonable doubts that the jury swallowed.

I am also one who doesn't believe we were pushed back to any earlier point in American racial history by the jury verdict in the Simpson case. Those who found it incomprehensible, or thought it proof of Negro stupidity, weren't about to think much of Negroes anyway. Or they would have figured out how to explain why exceptional Negroes outside of athletics weren't at all representative of their group—genetic flukes of no consequence to the fundamental and endless inferiority. It is also true that since the most popular people in today's America are probably Colin Powell, Michael Jordan, and Oprah Winfrey, we don't seem to have lost much ground because of a hypnotic murder trial. Not one of them seems to have lost a single white admirer since the verdict was read.

The real issue, as Vincent Bugliosi points out in his own book, *Outrage*, is that the prosecution completely screwed up its own case by not presenting stronger evidence, not providing sufficient counterarguments to the defense, and not having an overall strategy that would have made use of what Darden says was essential: "Never in our legal system has so much blood and DNA evidence been amassed against one defendant." They were not fallen heroes undone by a justice system that had been unscrupulously devastated by the out-of-order issue of race. Bugliosi takes into consideration the limitations and potential prejudices of the jury but makes the reader believe that Simpson could still have been convicted by the same twelve people who acquitted him. So the greatest disservice to Nicole Brown Simpson and Ronald Goldman was not the Dream Team but the prosecution itself. It was, when all the sentiment from either side is removed, not up to the job.

That makes of this double-murder trial a double tragedy, given our national unwillingness to recognize ineptitude. We allow even the George Armstrong Custers of our day to cover themselves in martyred glory because we would rather kiss the gushing wounds of these public servants than face the fact that they were self-inflicted.

The Dream Was
Not in Place

During these harsh days of dogs sniffing for corpses in the rubble of the federal building in Oklahoma City, the shock, the great sorrow, and the anger are not accompanied by a memory long enough to put our homegrown terrorism in perspective. We fail to remember just when this calculated willingness to kill anybody—man, woman, child—first got national attention in our time.

It was on September 15, 1963, in Birmingham, Alabama, Sunday morning. The Civil Rights Movement was in high gear. Violence had bloodied the movement almost from the beginning. The volunteers had been beaten during sit-ins and freedom-riding buses were firebombed; mobs had fought federal marshals; innocent bystanders, participants, and leaders had been killed; and homes were shot into or bombed.

A second civil war was taking place and the issue was largely the same: white dominion over black in Dixie.

The Southern whites most outraged by the idea of integration and voting rights for Negroes felt they were being invaded by troublemakers and deprived of local rule by the federal government, which meant that their hatred for President John F. Kennedy was as hot as the barrel of a smoking machine gun. It was simple to those Southern whites: no outside force had the right to make the Constitution apply to black people in the South, where segregation was the natural way of a separate America. They just wanted to be left alone with their own rules unchallenged.

Birmingham had been a city of turbulent drama when the Southern Christian Leadership Conference, under the direction of Martin Luther King Jr. and his nonviolent generals, had gone there in the spring of 1963, intent on fighting the segregated order to a halt. There were mass demonstrations and mass arrests. Dogs were loosed on demonstrators and fire hoses were used to knock them down. The motel where King stayed was bombed. There was rioting.

The press covered the conflict day by day. The nation was continually shocked. The feeling of danger was absolute. Finally, there seemed to be victory: the powers of Birmingham agreed to desegregate.

Carole Robertson, Denise McNair, Addie Mae Collins, and Cynthia Wesley were in the basement of the Sixteenth Street Baptist Church on Sunday morning, September 15, almost three weeks after the March on Washington.

At the beginning of the week, President Kennedy had federalized and withdrawn the National Guard troops that Governor George Wallace had used to bar five Negro students from admission to previously all-white Birmingham public schools. Wallace had sent the troops in high defiance of a federal court order and squealed out against the federal government using its power to destroy state's rights.

The following sabbath day, there was a loud explosion in the Sixteenth Street Baptist Church; the murders of the four young girls dressed in white put an emotional whipping on the nation. That bomb brought the meaning of domestic terrorism home to the consciousness of Americans in a new way on that bloody Sunday. We didn't call it terrorism then, but, by now, we should know it was. It was also the twenty-eighth unsolved bombing in Birmingham, each a terrorist act.

Those murdered in Oklahoma City vastly outnumbered the slaughtered in that Birmingham church, but the unrepentant killers of Carole Robertson, Denise McNair, Addie Mae Collins, and Cynthia Wesley were at that federal building in full, raging, spirit. Their madness goes around and comes around. So whatever their politics, those who actually did the bombing in Oklahoma City were different in only one way. They had much bigger plans.

Blues for
Three Widows

In his indispensable *The Omni-Americans*, Albert Murray writes of the extraordinary woman who spirited more than three hundred slaves north from plantation bondage:

> The pioneer spirit of American womanhood is widely eulogized. But at no time in the history of the Republic has such womanhood ever attained a higher level of excellence than in the indomitable heroism of a runaway slave named Harriet Tubman. . . . Tubman was not only an American legend; she also added a necessary, even if still misapprehended, dimension to the national mythology.

It is from that perspective on heroic American womanhood that we should assess what our communications network has made of Coretta Scott King, Myrlie Evers-Williams, and Betty Shabazz. Our media have glued them so tightly together that we are encouraged to think that they comprise our very own Tubman in triplicate—peerlessly heroic (other than in terms of each other); worthy of legendary status; contributors in possession of the mythological dimensions sorely needed in our contemporary world, which shows so little respect to "women of color." There are troubles with those ideas, however, and those troubles home in on what might be considered the "cage of color," that place where human fact takes second place to what we would like to believe.

Whether living or recently dead, King, Evers-Williams, and Shabazz are not suffering from a lack of the kind of respect supposedly reserved for white women. They are celebrated because the three widows bring out an ongoing American sentimentality about the Negro female. From the soothing, ever-faithful, chuckling, and wise mammy to the self-congratulatory slut of Def Comedy Jam, the black woman often inspires responses as superficial as they are intense. The three also share an aspect of identity with Jacqueline Kennedy: their famous, politically engaged husbands were shot down by assassins: Evers in 1963, Malcolm X in 1965, and King in 1968.

Their unavoidable public suffering made them martyr-saints in our pantheon of the abused. While none of them is a Tubman, the three prompt recognition of the struggles with injustice and disorder that have scarred our history. They remind us of our troubles with racism, political murder, paranoid conspiracy theories, self-defeating ethnocentrism, and, specifically in the case of the Shabazz family's problems, the chaos that attends the world of drug abuse, where the out-of-control user—like the alcoholic—puts into motion the sort of horror that can emotionally and physically destroy innocent members of a family.

But when we look back across the history of the nation over the last forty years, the victories in the personal and political areas associated with those widows are rather obvious. The assassins of King, Malcolm X, and Evers have been brought to justice. America is also a very different country from what it was when Martin Luther King came to public attention in 1956 and the Civil Rights Movement demanded that the nation get up off its rusty-dusty and do something about the fact that the Constitution was racially exclusive below the Mason-Dixon line. For all its flaws and its inevitable aspects of corruption, the movement toward a more realized democracy has been quite successful on more than a few fronts, deeply influencing integration across ethnic groups, skin tones, and sexual lines.

Unfortunately, heavy-handed conceptions of race and politics have misled many into conflating the unarguable sufferings of King, Evers-Williams, and Shabazz with the very meanings of their lives. Then, unable to stop themselves, reporters, journalists, and race simplifiers on one kind of stump or another have crazily glued together the platforms of the three slain husbands, sinking down into "all for one and one for all," throwing history out the window in favor of "black unity." To wit, over the last few years we have been given the impression that there was a strong connection between the integrationist goals for which Martin Luther King and Medgar Evers died and the saber-rattling black nationalist ideas of Malcolm X, who is now described—with a straight face, mind you—as a "slain black civil rights leader!"

Given the hagiographic excesses of black studies at their very worst, that should be expected, especially since it long ago became rather chic among easily infected white liberals to say, "They're always talking about Martin Luther King, but they aren't talking about Malcolm X, who may have been much more interesting." In other words, "I respect achievement but when I go to the political ice cream store I like my Negroes served with an outrageous topping." Thusly, the successful organizer as well as the rabble-rouser who heckled the civil rights leadership, rising to public attention as the mouthpiece for the Nation of Islam, were both part of the single fabric of "black struggle." In this martyr-equalizing travesty, it should also be remembered that Malcolm X did not meet his end for his politics. He was doomed by his public statements about both the illegitimate children fathered by Elijah Muhammad and the fraudulence of the racist "liberation" theology that his former mentor had invented along with the Nation of Islam. Malcolm X was the target of a hit by Negro cult members, not those defending white racism.

It is therefore quite ironic that we find ourselves now watching these three women put on one pedestal. It is even more troubling to realize that what they actually tell us, at this point, is how even those strong enough to survive enormous personal tragedy are not necessarily able to ward off the demons of our moment. When it comes to the wages of American life, like any other, there are sometimes no places to run, no places to hide: We are all caught or somehow touched by the general condition.

Coretta Scott King founded the Martin Luther King Center for Non-Violent Social Change, became "the first lady of the Civil Rights Movement," and oversaw the push for the national holiday that honors her husband. With her stern dignity and her coldly resolute intention to continue the work that was so perilous when her husband was alive, King has held her course for almost thirty years. Now she finds herself in the middle of a conspiracy theory about King's murder. The theory has little to substantiate it other than the public statements of her son Dexter, whom scholars like David Garrow feel has been duped by James Earl Ray, the man convicted for pulling the trigger of the rifle that blew half of King's face off. My children, my children.

Evers-Williams has had a successful career as a college administrator, an ad executive, a director of consumer affairs for the Atlantic Richfield Company, a Los Angeles commissioner with a $400 million budget, and director of an embattled NAACP, which she saved from destruction just before Kweisi Mfume became its president. At this point, Evers-Williams, now chairwoman, has said that the NAACP may be on the verge of substantially softening its commitment to integration across all social divisions. If so, this is not clear thinking. It is no more than a defeatist update of the Afrocentric influence on policy, which amounts to accepting a kind of Balkanizing that has never and will never work for Negro Americans or for the society at large.

Shabazz reared six daughters alone, also became a college administrator, but found herself still caught in the vendettas attached to the death of her husband. Her daughter Qubilah was brought up on charges of plotting to have Louis Farrakhan killed, since he had fueled the atmosphere in the Nation of Islam that far more than a few believe inspired the murder of Malcolm X. Shabazz, responding to the "concern" shown by Farrakhan, went through the show time at the Apollo ritual of a public reconciliation with our most highly respected racist and all-purpose lunatic. Then she met her end from third-degree burns, the fatal result of a fire in her home that her grandson by Qubilah, Malcolm Shabazz, pled guilty to setting.

(One story is that the fire was set around her bed, the other that it was started outside her bedroom door, but that, being the selfless grandmother always ready to take the measure of disaster in order to protect her family, Shabazz had spent tragic and dooming time looking for the boy, intent on getting him out of harm's way as the flames burned deeper and deeper into her flesh.)

Qubilah reared the twelve-year-old in a home made so unstable by her alcoholism and drug addiction that the boy was sent to New York to live with his grandmother. Attempting to get back to his home in Texas "by any means necessary," as his grandfather would have put it, the boy now serves the stiffest possible sentence. So neither the death of Malcolm X nor of Betty Shabazz was connected to fighting for mainstream black American causes. They seem, finally, almost the results of a family cursed by violence, whether wrought by racist cults or the reverberations of addiction.

When all is said and done, what we see when we look at Coretta Scott King, Myrlie Evers-Williams, and Betty Shabazz is the fact that our society remains a democratic work in difficult progress, one shining with victory, one as bedeviled by weird theories as by bad, ethnocentric policy, and one sticky with the blood of both rabble-rousers and their well-intentioned widows.

The Huffing and Puffing Military Blues

There are always international and American reasons why I call this century "The Age of Redefinition." One of them is that the democratic evolution of power relationships encourages us to maintain our ideals while maturely realizing that our human shortcomings, like our very best actions, are not necessarily determined by the categories we've agreed to use when identifying each other. In short: We can all be the enemy now. At this moment, hard facts keep rising in the mating game. The recent U.S. Supreme Court decision regarding Paula Jones and President Clinton puts into peculiar or more accurate focus both the battle and the prattle of the sexes as they apply to what has been going on in the armed forces this year.

What we are now looking at is a sweaty torso of information that pulls us into yet another hothouse of casual and caustic scandal, basement to attic. This should obviously be expected, since ours is a time in which we are accustomed to every kind of public vulgarity one can imagine. The media regularly stick their fingers down the throat of our collective libido and geyser up every stinking, greasy clump and string of our sexual urges. We are now supposed to think that almost anything goes.

But we don't really believe that. What we want to do is get on our peep-show knees and look through every available keyhole while simultaneously pretending that power and sex shouldn't stumble into the workplace in the old-fashioned way. A man should no longer assume that his position of authority gives him access to the bodies of women he finds appealing. He can think whatever he thinks but those thoughts and those hands have to be kept to himself. If he gets hopped up and out of order he will have the edifice of his career granulated in public and the feminist troops will take the position that, once again, we have been allowed an opportunity to see just how much women have always been made to suffer while doing their jobs.

This vision is far from inaccurate because one of the prizes that we often assume goes with power is access to—only a fingertip away—far more erotic close encounters than the average person. In the velvet and cactus catbird seat of sex, who's on top hasn't always been about who's on the bottom agreeing to the ups and downs of the proceedings. Our folklore, our fairy tales, our literature, our theater, our film, our music, and our radio are filled with images of women running, jumping, swimming, taking to horseback, flying off in balloons, parachuting from many thousands of feet, hiding in closets, committing suicide, disguising themselves as men and whatever else might work: in order to avoid unwanted advances or the rule of thumb sexual impositions of assumed male entitlement. The story has been long on force and threat but short on empathy.

In the military, we have some very odd problems because we have long accepted the idea that the enemy rapes and pillages while our boys enjoy the spoils of victory. One of those spoils is the female body, so often depicted in our popular entertainment as just willing to avail itself when the irresistible hero thrusts himself into view. No matter how hard she might try, that Indian squaw or that Confederate belle or that Asian or German girl will find herself emitting puddles of sexual goo when she frees herself from conventional allegiance and listens to the unavoidable drum of her very own heart as it sets the rhythm for the torrid march toward two heads on a pillow. Victory is assured the American military hero, no matter the war, no matter the time.

All of that has now changed. The unwritten boudoir rules of the armed forces sticky the public carpet now. We have cases in which boys being boys or the sowing of wild oats while in uniform or the making of the beast with two adulterous backs or the asserting of military rank for sexual pleasures no longer float or travel in the social submarines of unpleasant custom. As with all else in our ever wilder world, we have to face just how omni-directionally human the tendencies to corruption and abuse actually are. Now the definition of innate victim whirls round and round as military Negroes and women find themselves on the receiving ends of charges about sexual impropriety. Uh-oh: the white male can't even maintain his position as high lone demon in the hanky-panky sexual column of the armed services. That old white male devil moons the world solely no longer; he seems to have been born to lose in this era. Leering up from the bottoms, certain so-called minorities and women want a piece of everything, their gash of action, their pound of flesh.

The swiftness of these changes arrives outside the sniper's scope of our conventional protesters. We have had no serious feminist reading of Lieutenant Kelly Flinn's general discharge from the Air Force, where she had become the female Jackie Robinson of B-52 pilots. Those Democratic and Republican politicians, such as Patricia Schroeder and born-again feminist Trent Lott, banged away with the regular rhetoric of double standards, snootily charging that Flinn wouldn't have had to bite the bullet if she were a man committing adultery and disobeying orders to end the relationship. That is bunk, since three hundred servicemen are now in military prison, while others also brought up on sexual charges have either been discharged or relieved of duty, the most recent being Brigadier General Stephen N. Xenakis for supposedly ponying up on a civilian nurse who was treating his critically ill wife.

The conventional complainers also failed to recognize how they would have read Flinn's actions if the sexes had been reversed. Such people would then have said this was yet another example of how men in positions of authority continue abusing those below. But since Gayla Zigo, the wronged wife of the triangle and the female airman with *no* power, hadn't become a feminist heroine by extending military expectations, she was ignored, which parallels the way feminists turned up their noses at the charges against Bill Clinton made by Paula Jones or joked about her "white trash" looks and manner or failed to attack those who judged her merits on class and taste. I guess this means that if one is lower ranked or lower born abuse is not abuse, a kiss is not a kiss. Seems like uncolorized plantation logic to me.

There was no high-profile feminist response to the statements made by those white women at the Aberdeen Training Center who came forward with the NAACP and said that they had been coerced by white male investigators into falsely charging certain of their black superiors with sexual harassment or rape. One would have expected them to analyze this as a contemporary variation on the tradition of white men using white women as pawns in the racist game of keeping black men socially shackled.

That Flinn was guilty of her charges and that black superiors at Aberdeen have been found guilty of rape, harassment, and other erotic improprieties also make one wonder just how frequently historical privilege and resentment play themselves out even in this purportedly new world of sexual relationships. We know that certain of us look forward to the time when we will get a chance to either experience the unfair advantages that traditionally come with the power from which we were previously excluded, or we relish the opportunity to bend the rules the way they have been bent against us or our forebears. In essence, there are women who want it just like the men used to get it, and there are men from so-called minorities who long to conquer or defile the previously untouchable pink-toed females who were made the erotic goddesses of the world by our entertainments and our advertising. Fortunately, such people constitute a small number of those within their groups. But they, like every flesh and blood component that gives shifting complexity to our American blues, prove that trouble can come from every direction, no matter the race, the class, the sex, the religion, the station. Our nation affirms its social greatness whenever it faces those difficult truths of human nature and moves to set our policies straight. At least, until we learn a little more.

The King of
Narcissism

It used to be that if one didn't hurry up and say something about an event, the op-ed scow was gone, leaving the slowpoke commentator at the dock. But now, with the oceanic marketing campaigns calculated to continually flop up sales, one can put two cents in and be right on time for months. It is an unexpected variation on Americans of the nineteenth century mourning Abraham Lincoln for months after his assassination because national communication was then like molasses in January. Now the question is just how much time a product can maintain a position at the top of the huckster's wave, how much media space it can dominate, whether or not it has the strength to rise and disappear, rise and disappear, like a marlin, pulling the ship of public boredom on and on, exciting the crew until—Lord have mercy on us!—it ends up on the deck, not really a real fish but a motorized piece of counterfeit so many have been trained to admire and drool over even so.

*   *   *

Michael Jackson almost seems meant to help us understand the complications of our basic myths and our perennial shortcomings. But because we
Americans often miss the elements of sensibility that connect us, accepting false fire walls of division, we find it hard to see beyond the decoys of
race, class, religion, and genitalia. It is perilous to miss those transcending
essences, be they good or bad. Those essences are at the nub of our perpetually embattled democratic grandeur and our equally persistent child-
ishness. No one, regardless of the point of social origin, is automatically
beyond either the pinnacles or the spiritual sink holes of these United
States—least of all our media figures. That is where the most magnified
entertainer in the world comes in, because Jackson represents both the
hard facts of open opportunity and the swollen visions of self-worth that
have evolved in our narcissistic culture. As a show business product, he
embodies the American dream of rising from nowhere to great wealth and
mass adulation, but Jackson's recent work also reveals how easily the self-
pitying anger that underlies totalitarian paranoia can seep into the content of popular entertainment.

    The King of Pop is a man who would spend a long time in jail if he
were sentenced to counting his riches dollar by dollar. He is an entertainer whom we have watched rise from an itty-bitty cute kid to a man
self-made—or remade—quite remarkably by modern surgical techniques,
all the while maintaining his celebrated submarine position in the pop
music quicksand of adolescent emotion. Jackson extended his stardom by
adding to his concerts and repertoire all the basic trends of his idiom and
the slogans that pass for ideas. Always a mediocre singer given to progressively unimaginative phrasing and overstatement, Jackson will deliver a
shallow version of gospel and some maudlin rhythm and blues, use the
harsh bravado of rock inflection, posture as a love child reciting the
pieties necessary for world peace, stoop to the vulgar gestures that are a
counterfeit shorthand for lower-class rage, and execute a few interesting
dance steps that serve as interludes within a choreographed synthesis of
cheerleading moves, navy signaling without flags, and aerobic exercise.
His work is a summation of the inflated failure that now dominates our
popular arts, where the value of youth is hysterically championed at

the expense of a mature sense of life. This exploits the insecurities of young people by telling them, over and over, that never growing up is the best defense against an oppressive world in which fun isn't given its proper due.

While Jackson's millions allow him to have fantasy kingdoms built, he also usurps the mantle of wealthy nut that Howard Hughes once wore with such unflagging madness. Like Hughes, Jackson also suffers from the distinct kind of paranoia that those who must face legions of jealousy sometimes orchestrate into endless symphonies of plots and subplots, ranging from the press to the government. The alienation that comes with vast success builds upon the familiar theme of the poor little rich kid and becomes the basis for innumerable expressions of complaint focused on the beleaguered tycoon, the adult who sits atop a kingdom of cash angrily trying to duck those who would bloody and destroy him.

This paranoia has not been missed, even in the world of rock criticism, where posterior-licking and the exaggerations of aesthetic value are assiduously taught in the boot camps of preparation for media employment. Though there was some understandable alarm expressed when Jackson's gargantuan poor-mouthing and his lyrics were examined in the new double-album, HIStory, even noting the fascist imagery of the promotional video, what all those rock critics missed was the problem at the center of pop music, which is the function of its incantational rhythms.

Incantation always has two audience possibilities in our culture, one is the collective fused into a throbbing vitality through the repeating groove of a syncopated dance-beat; the other is the transformation of individuals into a mindless mass of putty in the hands of a band or a central figure. The distinction is very important because the vital collective is the highest achievement of dance-oriented rhythm. Essential to that vitality is the expression of adult emotion. While blues might also have simple musical elements similar to those pop has derived from it, blues is fundamentally a music that fights self-pity and even holds it up to ridicule, the singer scorning all self-deceptive attempts at ducking responsibility for at least *part* of the bad state of affairs.

In jazz, for another example, the rhythmic phenomenon of swing is posed as an antidote to the sentimentality of the popular song, with the improvisation allowing for collective inventions that insert emotional irony and complexity into the music. The evolution of pop music is quite different because, far more often than not, the rhythm is used to reinforce the sentimentality of the material. Those pop rhythms now arrive in a form that has largely submitted to the mechanical, often using electronic, programmed "drums" for static pulsations that never interact with the rest of the music, a supreme example of the very alienation it so successfully foments.

It is because of the subordination of everything to the beat that the lyrics so often go by barely noticed. When they are noticed, especially when expressing the choked-up, immature resentment of a demanding adult world in which problems are protean, the words either become anthems of estrangement or bludgeons against some vision of corrupt and hypocritical authority. But, as with fascism, the authority of a mass "conspiracy"—of bankers, lawyers, politicians, educators, law enforcement, and so on—is rejected through obeisance to a figure of gargantuan certitude. That is where the big beat of pop and the big idol of the rock star meet in the fascist garden of dance-oriented totalitarianism. Michael Jackson has been evolving in this direction over the last few years, one video after another showing either the world or his opposition melting into mass chorus lines overwhelmed by his magical leadership. We see this most clearly in the promotional video for *HIStory*, where Jackson marches in front of legions of troops, children scream that they love him, and a huge statue of the King of Pop, one as ugly as any Hitler, Stalin, or Mao would have appreciated, is unveiled. We understand in clear terms the assertion that Hitler was the first rock star because of the way his rallies used technology to create hypnotic rituals of enormously magnified passion.

The Indian poet and philosopher Tagore once observed that the invention of the penknife leaped past the centuries of evolution that resulted in the claw, but that we often find ourselves in a world where those with the penknife mentalities of adolescents command weapons of destruction that they aren't mature enough to handle. When we make those who remain easily embittered little boys into idols by genuflecting before a charisma that has negligible adult application, we shouldn't be surprised at the point of their deciding that they should lead the world into a resurrection of an Eden through which they will walk in the cool of the day, omnipotent as the jealous God of the Old Testament.

PART FOUR

Regarding Books:

Homeric or Not?

Familial, religious, military, and class conflicts drive many works of classic literature, no matter where or when they were written. In our own country, contrary to certain opinions, writing that focuses on race needn't be less good than any other. The challenge staring down at any writer who uses racial conflict in our American context is how close he or she can get to the standards set by writers like Homer and Shakespeare, two champions who were never unwilling to narrate a fight, blow by blow, nuance by nuance.

Two on
the Money

New paperback editions of Richard Wright's autobi-
ography, *Black Boy* (1944), and Ralph Ellison's essays, *Shadow and Act*
(1964), are extremely good and important books to have. Wright and Ellison give two very different visions of American life twirling and twisting
around the issues of race, individual identity, the nation's political
direction, and the way in which our culture speaks to, at, or away from us.

Quite often, the two writers are set against each other. Some see
Wright's unforgiving harshness as a foreshadowing of the 1960s hysteria
that culminated in the Black Panther Party. Others are disturbed by
Wright's almost absolute hatred of the South, black and white, and his refusal to celebrate Negro folk wisdom, religious music, and blues as many
other black writers have. Another group sees him as suffering from self-

hatred, pure and simple. In that direction, his white wives might be thrown into the discussion to "prove" the point.

Wright's actual struggle is usually misunderstood. As *Black Boy* shows, he realized early on that color preceded his essence as a human being. He was a Negro in the skin but intended to become a man of his own making. What he really wanted was to be a writer whose work could stand up next to the best.

Because of decisions at his publishing house, Wright's original title for his autobiography, *American Hunger*, was changed and the second half of it was removed. That vital second half was set in the North and pulled the covers off of the urban Communist movement. Now, in its full form, the book is remarkable.

The reader can feel the sweat, the bruises, and the cold, and understand the dreams as the boy fights the Southern restrictions imposed on him by the Negroes as well as the whites. When Wright comes North, he isn't overly impressed by the black or the white people nor is he taken in too long by the Communists, who have no use for his intellectual probings and his desire for individuality. His insights into the totalitarian techniques of dominating mass thinking are as good as anyone's.

For some, Ellison is an antidote to Wright because of his great affection for Afro-American culture and his richer grasp of the powers of literature. Ellison became rightfully famous for his 1952 novel, *Invisible Man*, which is actually an astonishing variation on the complete *Black Boy*, South to North, but one no less original because of its source.

Shadow and Act, however, is a book about American life and culture that hasn't been exceeded. Ellison, while no racist or self-defensive exaggerator of the importance of Negro life and art, understood the richness black Americans brought to the national mix and had no time for those white "friends of the Negro" who would erect new coon cages. In *Shadow and Act*, his high-class spankings of literary critics Irving Howe and Stanley Edgar Hyman for their limited definitions of Negro life and art are classic moments in the dialogue over racial identity and cultural meaning.

Overall, the complexity, humor, and scholarship of Ellison's ideas are still pretty shocking. They go far, far past the clichés. In fact, since Newt Gingrich speaks so often of "American civilization," it would be very interesting to find out what he thinks of Ellison's essays. The quality Ellison brought to thinking about this nation could greatly enrich our political dialogue.

Black Boy and *Shadow and Act* are two very different books, but, like all real classics, they supply us with a sense of our tragedy, our staying power, and our potential.

Bible Belt
Greco-Roman Blues:
The Shadow of
the Negro*

We completely trust neither the ritual heat of the wilderness nor the humanly calculated flame of civilization. Nature provides us with sustenance, but those provisions are brutally treated because our continued existence is based on consuming things we either kill or harvest. Civilization claims to be here in our interest. It is the world our ancestors invented and the one we maintain, refine, or refute. Civilization assumes that there are fundamental reasons to continue and equally fundamental ways to achieve the action of continuation. From the heat and the flame of the wild and of the humanly organized, the soul, the body, and the consciousness take their third-degree burns. Some of those scars are prints of light, others are the tracks of darkness.

O, ye children of Benjamin, gather yourselves to flee out of the midst of Jerusalem, and blow the trumpet in Tekoa, and set up a sign of fire in Beth-haccerem: for evil appeareth out of the north, and great destruction.

Jeremiah, 6:1

In armies, in navies, cities, or families—in nature herself—nothing more relaxes good order than misery.

Herman Melville, *"Benito Cereno"*

---

*This originally appeared as an introduction to the 1995 Modern Library Edition of *Go Down, Moses.*

1.

As a number of commentators have observed, by the time he got to *Go Down, Moses*, William Faulkner had so extended himself and the humanity of his Negro characters that he and they entered the grand palace of aesthetic revelation together. The development was hard but natural because Faulkner's world is one in which the Melvillian shadow of the Negro either protects white Mississippians from a vicious sun or chills them to a state of spiritual trembling. There is no life untouched by the color, the scent, the hair texture, the affection, the songs, the grace, the lamentations, the instability, the humor, the craft, the mother wit, the intelligence, the ignorance, the food, the religion, the bitterness, the quiet, the dance, the erotic attraction, and the violence of the Negro.

2.

Upon entering this work it is essential to remember at least one thing. William Faulkner was an aesthetic scrapper. He considered it the duty of the serious writer to spit across the line in the dirt and start wrestling with form. This apparent gathering of stories is a case in point. It is not what you might think it is. Faulkner himself told Cleanth Brooks that he considered this book a novel, not a collection. Therefore, we might best understand *Go Down, Moses* as something of an American literary symphony in which each of the seven tales functions as a movement. The novel builds to the looming force of "The Bear," then descends to its conclusion through two quite differently voiced tales, each pivoting on the kind of impatience that leads to an unruffled breaking of the rules.

It has been noted that the material Faulkner brought together had appeared earlier in either shorter or different versions. That he may not have originally conceived the various tales as elements of a novel is no different from the case of the musician who writes a number of themes for separate occasions and then discovers that by adding something here and shifting something there, he has a long piece in which each section is related to the others on the basis of things that were in the front of his mind during a certain period—harmonic ideas, melodic directions, rhythmic approaches, and qualities of texture. In this literary improvisation on form, Faulkner achieves the overall effect of a long work through the interwoven themes, the recurring characters, the place and resonance of the wilderness, the miscegenated bloodlines, and the objects that appear over and over, such as the beds, the guns, the hooch, the razors, the dogs, and the metal cots (iron in the South, steel in the North).

3.

James Joyce and Ernest Hemingway were often on Faulkner's mind and, in this 1942 addition to his already formidable output, the down-home genius wanted to write a book that would stand with *Dubliners* and *In Our Time* (Faulkner was even to blatantly emulate the latter with the 1955 *Big Woods*, which included italicized interludes and material from *Go Down, Moses*). As did Joyce, he intended to tell the moral history of a people. Faulkner's subjects were Mississippians—part European, part African, part Indian—and he knew that their moral history was the history of slavery, segregation, and terrorist practices. In some ways, that history was the day-in and day-out diagram of the horror that twisted inside Mr. Kurtz's dark and damned heart like a small propeller of razor blades. Such blood-encrusted cruelty, rearing up every so often to maintain a regime, was proof of a long, long social war against every democratic idea and amendment in the Constitution. That war demanded endurance and made perceivable another version of what Edmund Wilson called Hemingway's "gauge of morale." Digging into both the rich soil and the gummy, stinking graveyard of Mississippi Americana, Faulkner sought a way of looking at the grace and wit of the people, the inevitable harshness of life, the corruption behind the con jobs of society, and all of the damage wrought by planned and accidental disaster. Like Hemingway, Faulkner was intent on rising above the whining that reduces the power of those tragic facts that provoke the unsentimental crying.

4.

Faulkner decidedly used this volume to further toy with a literary set of themes and images brought forward from the Bible and those Greco-Roman myths of promiscuity that explained how the characters under the thumb of Mount Olympus became all twisted up as half-brothers, half-sisters, and endless sorts of cousins. As earlier work had shown in titles and in the names of characters, Faulkner wasn't one to miss how easily material from the distantly classic past could be brought right into his own world. After all, Southern white men often chose to plant wild oats like the Greek Zeus or the Roman Jupiter, impregnating like it was going out of style, making miscegenation a steamy and heart-breaking part of the tale. It could not have passed Faulkner's recognition that those very same slaveholders might give their chattel Greco-Roman names.

Well-educated, high on etiquette and hospitality, the slave-owning families thought of themselves and their environs as fused extensions of the highest points of Greece and Rome. That is why, in Go Down, Moses, Faulkner mentions centurions, refers to Nero, cites "the fringe of white hair about the head and face of a Roman general," and has Gavin Stevens, in the title tale, use the phrase "by Jupiter" so often. However beautifully they existed in contrast to the tangle of the wilderness, those antebellum kingdoms, owing to human bondage, functioned in relentless opposition to the fundamentals of Christian morality. As with the Roman Empire, the South was destroyed by forces from the North on one hand and forces from within on the other. Where the tribal barbarians came to Rome with fire and steel, the Christians argued against any idea of a chosen people, Hebrew or Roman or otherwise. Though the Roman Empire fell and never rose again, the conquests of Christianity were far more extensive and durable.

All of that stuff supplied plenty for Faulkner to improvise on, just as the biblical tales had given very firm sources of theme and image to the Negroes who invented the spirituals. We understand Faulkner's funda-mental theme because of the book's title, which is that of a Negro spiri-tual, a song in which Moses is commanded to go down into Egypt land

and tell Pharoah to "let my people go." But the novel uses Ike McCaslin's difficulty with the heritage of white-skin privilege to make it clear that all people, no matter their color, need to be liberated from the afflictions rooted in slavery. We see this from a number of perspectives because, just as Nick Adams dominates *In Our Time*, Ike's experiences and reflections at different points in his life dominate this book. The upshot is that the "peculiar institution" and all that followed become metaphors for injustice the world over—past, present, future. As an old man who has lived so long and forgotten so much that he doesn't seem to remember anything he ever knew or felt or even heard about love, Ike, in "Delta Autumn," thinks of these matters as they play themselves out in the Mississippi he has known and the North he has heard about:

> *This Delta.* This land which man has deswamped and denuded and derivered in two generations so that white men can own plantations and commute every night to Memphis and black men own plantations and ride in jim crow cars to Chicago to live in millionaires' mansions on Lakeshore Drive, where white men rent farms and live like niggers and niggers crop on shares and live like animals, where cotton is planted and grown man-tall in the very cracks of the sidewalks, and usury and mortgage and bankruptcy and measureless wealth, Chinese and African and Aryan and Jew, all breed and spawn together until no man has time to say which one is which nor cares . . .

One could even make the case that Faulkner was creating a volume of his own Bible stories, complete with an Eden, with a fall from glory, with the destruction of paradise, with Egyptians, with a people in bondage, with flight and pursuit, with genealogies, all held together by the pyramidal structure of rising to illumination then collapsing under the pressure of temptation or betrayal or hubris that is so basic to the tales of the Old Testament. (Gavin Stevens, by the way, is bent on translating the Old Testament back into classic Greek, which makes us think about the fact that "delta," both a word and a place important to the novel, is also the fourth letter of the Greek alphabet.)

Faulkner does not stop there. He creates an extension into the New Testament with the lynched Rider, whose body hanging from the bell rope of a Negro schoolhouse is a "lesson" that is also a crucifixion. It is a crucifixion because the law, like Pilate, washes its hands of the matter and allows the hysterical to have their way. That, of course, is in keeping with the way blood sacrifice—imposed by hunting or murder or execution—provides initiation or imposes darkness or metes out justice with deadly force.

The novelist was also capable of bringing extraordinary comedy to his Mississippi, using the first two movements—"Was" and "The Fire in the Hearth"—to provoke laughter. Yet those two narrative movements perfectly give us a sense of the range of Faulkner's overview. In the first, as Uncle Buck tries to catch his runaway slave, and Mr Hubert's sister, Miss Sophonsiba, tries to snare Uncle Buck into marriage, laugh is set upon laugh. In the second, because melancholy, rage, the will to murder, and obsession all rise out of the same founts that produce the hilarity, each reader keeps wondering if the course of the tale will lead to comedy or heartache.

That is Faulkner's way. He pulls all of his materials together in complex and subtle passages, repeating words, examining one situation or idea in a number of tones, from the witty to the ruminative to the exciting to the profoundly sad. Much of his vision comes from a deep and original comprehension of Herman Melville. His is the Melvillian understanding of multiple meanings. On one level, the multiple meanings of this literary symphony are improvisations on the significance of limitations. They express the degree to which Faulkner shared Melville's vision of territory—that even the most powerful creature, like the whale, becomes a casualty if he swims too close to land, where he will be trapped in the shallow water and beached. From the runaway slave in the first movement to the last movement's murderer, the comic to serious question of taking too much license comes about over and over. We are encouraged to ponder what going too far means. Is something called to task that ought to be challenged or rejected? Has a terrible mistake been made? Is this action of going too far expressive of greed, arrogance, self-congratulation? Is it sometimes no more than anarchy driven by a bloodlust?

At other places, Faulkner is concerned with the metaphoric meaning of destruction, the moment things change forever. Sometimes, as with the young Ike—who is a son of a Buck—the moment of change is good. He becomes a man when Sam Fathers puts the blood of the forest buck on his face, and that ritual action represents an expansion of his understanding and his having arrived at a firmer place on the complicated terrain. There is also the moment of change that darkens and narrows the world, as when the little boy Roth Edmonds asserts his white-skin privilege and angrily tells Henry, his Negro play-brother, to sleep on the floor, not in the bed with him. The Negroes understand and treat little Roth accordingly. Because he has so insultingly denied his human heritage, the white boy is no longer an honorary member of the Negro family. He is forever after trapped in the category created to honor the surface of color, what Faulkner calls "the old curse of his fathers, the old haughty ancestral pride based not on any value but on an accident of geography, stemmed not from courage and honor but from wrong and shame."

In this matrix, Rider's tale, "Pantaloon in Black," has stumped more than a few, since the characters aren't obviously part of the complicated orchestration that Faulkner weaves on the themes of jumbled-up bloodlines, subjugation, and betrayal of either the codes of nature or those of Christian morality. Though the tale concludes with a monologue so devoid of human empathy that it is surely founded in wrong and shame— sort of a reverse positioning of Delano's superficial observations in *Benito Cereno*—there is yet another kind of brilliant subtlety here. To begin with, "Pantaloon in Black" pivots on love problems and trickery, as do "Was" and "The Fire in the Hearth." Then there are connecting images in two other tales. In "Was" a jovial Tomeys Turl is pursued and jumped upon by the friendly dogs who know him. Rider, laughing while crying, is gradually subdued by the chain gang of Negroes who are initially flung this way and that, foreshadowing the hounds fatally trying to battle Old Ben in "The Bear." Next, we should note that Rider's tale is the first in which a main character or towering animal dies a violent death. Rider's destruction thematically leads to Old Ben and Lion, both forces of nature sucked down a hole of death greased with blood and gore. His end also prefigures that of the last tale's Butch Worsham, who is executed though not by a mob.

Rider's crying-blues narrative is primarily a variation on the theme of love and madness, the second of two consecutive allusions to either the cuckolding or the torment of Leopold Bloom, who so deeply mourns his lost son. In "The Fire and the Hearth," the movement preceding "Pantaloon in Black," Lucas Beauchamp is the central character. Lucas, usually so aloof and wily, loses his mind to greed, which is somehow crookedly passed down to his grandson Butch, whose dooming occupation is, "Getting rich too fast." But Lucas himself is not doomed; he is pulled back from the madness of endlessly searching for gold by the threat of losing his wife, Molly. Rider, such a Hercules on the surface, is broken inside by the loss of his wife, Mannie. His consciousness swiftly crumbles into a condition of mad grief. As Leon Forrest points out, that extraordinary grief is another contrasting variation: In "The Fire in the Hearth," Zack Edmonds, the white man who loses his wife, makes little of her death.

The two tales are also connected by extreme defiance of the social order, the refusal to accept the unwritten laws of unfairness. That order wasn't so simply divided into white on top, black below. With his clear delineation, Faulkner kicked the simple Northern sense of the South in the shins. At the very bottom of the Southern social register were not Negroes, but "white trash," the rednecks whose social respect was limited to thimbles of juice squeezed from the puniest fruits of racism. Those sips of white privilege led to an obnoxious drunkenness and access to them was maintained by an hysterical bullying that could extend all the way to murder. Negroes who looked up to no one and had their own sense of the world understood all of that quite well. Lucas Beauchamp was that kind. The novelist writes, ". . . to the sheriff Lucas was just another nigger and both the sheriff and Lucas knew it, although only one of them knew that to Lucas the sheriff was a redneck without any reason for pride in his forebears nor hope for it in his descendants." When push comes to serious shove, Lucas will not bend to get through the ritual eye of the Southern needle. Somebody will have to die first.

Lucas goes into Zack's home ready to kill because, after long and steady brooding, he refuses to accept the unnatural order of racial cuckolding, the idea that a pale suitor can disrupt his household at will. Like Rider, the whites of his eyes gradually disappear as a countrified Greek rage rises in his blood. A Mississippi Odysseus come to settle a score, Lucas stands over the sleeping white man with a razor. Rider, while playing a rigged dice game in which he and numerous other sawmill Negroes always lose money, does something far out of the ordinary. He catches the redneck Birdsong palming a second pair of bones. In what is suicidal self-defense, Rider pulls his razor and cuts the white man's throat before the cheat can reach his pistol. Like Melville's Babo, he will pay "for barbering white men without using no lather first." (As for further barbering, Butch has his head shaved before he is electrocuted.)

In jail, as Rider wrenches the metal cot out of the wall, he grabs a connective symbol of repose and demise: The ancient Ike, not long for the world, lies on one in "Delta Autumn" and another supplies a brief resting place on death row for the cop killer Butch, who, when he seems to smile through a bleeding mouth in a flashback, also appears obliquely related to Babo. (If we were to forget that this criminal's grandmother, Mollie, calls him "my Benjamin," we would miss the symbolic significance of Butch and the irony that the heavenly Chicago Southern Negroes dream of can as easily be a destructive, Northern hell.) Rising as he does above others, his strength more a metaphor for natural force than for that of a man, the grief-hounded Rider is surely a human relative of Old Ben, the "taintless and incorruptible" bear who lords over the forest that men like the Herculean Negro whittle down for the sawmill.

Much has rightfully been made of the wilderness and the elements that Ike is introduced to by Sam Fathers, the descendant of three bloodlines—part Indian, part white, part Negro. All of the novel's themes reach their peak and pitch in "The Bear." The success is due to the interplay within an animal and human universe that Faulkner makes so simultaneously real and mythological. There is the huge hunting dog, Lion, also a mixed breed—part mastiff—a mongrel given a name that connects him to Africa. Like the Africans transformed into breathing instruments of labor, Lion is domesticated by Sam Fathers, turned into an instrument of the hunt, his baleful and savage authority, for all its beauty, no more than a serving tool in a blood sport. There is the part-Indian Boon, who climbs up on the mountainous bear and slays him with a knife, reaching back to the frontier Americana of Daniel Boone, whose bear-killing claims are carved into Southern trees. There is Old Ben himself, the white whale remade, rising out of and disappearing into the ocean of the forest, remaining the focus of all hunting obsessions. In the terms of our time, Faulkner quite obviously had an ecological set of concerns but he also felt that since destruction was basic to living—killing something to eat, destroying something in order to build—the prevailing question is how well the destroyed are honored by the conduct of their destroyers. After all of the suspense and the wondrous excitement of the tracking and panting and shooting, the issue is whether or not the lessons of sportsmanship might serve our civilization by encouraging us to recognize why we should struggle to hold at bay the excesses of pride and the dark gloom of resentment.

The famous debate in the fourth section of "The Bear" is about the brutal and decadent nightmare of Southern history. Ike is attempting to wake up from that nightmare, and in the snarl of twisting time, genealogies, and the nose-thumbing of willfully unnatural dialogue, we are given a metaphor for Ike's struggle. It symbolizes, in an onomatopoeic manner, the confusion and difficulty of truly addressing a set of situations so tragically dominated by the decoy of race. As Ralph Ellison observed, "Here . . . Faulkner comes most passionately to grips with the moral implications of slavery, the American land, progress and materialism, tradition and moral identity—all major themes of the American novel . . . And it is in the fourth section . . . that Faulkner makes his most extended effort to define the specific form of the American Negro's humanity and to get at the human values which were lost by both the North and the South during the Civil War." In essence, Ike does not feel that the moral history of the South is even slightly justified by the biblical assertion that Negroes are eternally cursed because they descend from Ham. Faulkner has Ike respond to that quite clearly: "There are some things He said in the Book, and some things reported of Him that He did not say." In other words, all biblical passages that clearly set up pecking orders founded in injustice are the words of men, not the words of God. There is an Old Testament of Western history and it has its marvelous eloquence and its brilliantly argued prejudices, but in the New Testament of American life, all prejudices must be set aside if the empathetic meaning of democratic freedom is to realize itself.

But there is no hiding place down here. We don't always carry our ideals with us. None of his brave and various insights as a young man help the ancient Ike of "Delta Autumn" when he discovers that the denied miscegenation, the casual incest, and the heartbreak seem never to end. Startled and angered by the same kind of payoff that disgusted him when he did some homemade detective work and deduced the miscegenated truth about his family line, Ike, now in his seventies, screeches the very same words at the young mother who is not exactly white that a frustrated Boon bellowed at him many years before in the last lines of "The Bear"— "Get out of here!"

5.

There is superb writing in so many places that quoting *Go Down, Moses* for any further accuracy would even *further* outdistance the allotted space. But a little more must be said in conclusion. William Faulkner profoundly understood that thorough investigation of the particular achieves the universal. His people are not the pulp chattel of simple-minded politics, his animals are more than sticky lollipops of the forest luridly licked away by a wicked civilization, his Mississippi is all Mississippi but not just Mississippi. His world, as Faulkner often pointed out, is the world of the human heart in conflict with itself, and that world is made no less grand because it is spoken of in an accent rising up from the miscegenated grace, hospitality, verve, tragedy, and slapstick of our America below the Mason-Dixon line.

The Blues Is
the Accompaniment*

The actual American story is always colder, hotter, and more mysterious than we would like it to be. But the reason why we are always attracted to the serious tale of American life and place is endlessly at hand. Any impressive fiction with a United States pedigree subtly or muleheadedly opens discussion of the known and the unknown, reminding us of the heartbreak, the inspiration, and the moxie at the center of the way we in this country have shaped a life so completely modern it has made the rest of the world into a variety of mirrors. Even so, one part of our American blues is that we so often refuse to create the emotional technology necessary to fashion our own spiritual mirrors. Our pref-

*This originally appeared in 1996, as the introduction to *Blues and Trouble*.

erence is the distortion, usually the distorted sense we have of ourselves. We are on the run. We believe happiness is a matter of geography, or a matter of class, or of color, or that happiness hides its wiles inside a pile of money. Motion to *somewhere* is what we wish for. All along the run, the blues disturbs and reminds us, hiding like a pebble inside our favorite jogging shoes or sitting just under our skin, a long splinter of emotional recognition denied. The blues never refuses to tell us whenever we are fugitives from the mirror.

These are some of the things Tom Piazza is clarifying in *Blues and Trouble*. In his stories we read and hear a voice that has no fear of the dissonance between appearances and essences, the discordant harmony that results from so many out-of-tune lives. But these are neither self-righteous morality tales nor sneering attitudes disguised as stories; they are tales of our time and of our dilemmas. They have the empathy that gives them human momentum and pulls us into the deeps, where we, too, must hold our breath and feel the pressure of the water. In various ways, the collection talks out of school about the fantasies underlying the poor workmanship that goes into the making of our contemporary American gods, who are usually human, past their prime, and so misunderstood we too frequently fail to realize that they were shoddy even at full power.

If those targets of worship are not human, they form some version of heaven on earth. That heaven on earth is the other side of the fence, the other side of town, in another state, or even a place left not too long ago. It is some slice of the world ungooed by the difficulties of where we are, some place where loneliness has no dominion, where love has the snugness of a bug in a rug. Or the preferred fantasy is some immature idea of freedom, a kind of life never caught in the bear trap of decay, dissolution, and death; a kind of life in which we might strive to enslave someone else in a ritual of performance based on repeating forever or as often as possible the shadow plays of a golden time, when all was green and every dream seemed nearly palpable.

Huge splinters like that pass through the flesh of these stories, which are so American that they don't accept the contemporary rules of the game. These stories take place in the North and the South, the East and the West. The characters are black or white or both; are Mexican or

Anglo; are Jewish or Christian. They are Americans, not solely the members of a single group the writer has been assigned to by virtue of an imposed and closed-off ethnic identity, a category at odds with both the challenges of democratic imagination in narrative and the precision necessary to achieve epic command of the varieties of the national voice. Tom Piazza's people don't belong to any particular class but they are trying to make do within the heavily starched rituals and customs of the places where they find themselves. If not, they might snap the running legs of their spirits in the gopher holes of desperate nostalgia, in the demon cups of booze, in the Never-Never Land clouds of marijuana, in the snorted up lines of white powder laid out on a mirror that reveals no more to the whizzing onlooker than disembodiment. Whatever they are and whatever they do, the blues knows them well and is never shy about saying so.

That Tom Piazza is able to bring such different kinds of people and problems to the page while holding together the form of his book with the themes and nuances of that deathless twelve-bar form on which so many variations have been played is something of a signal achievement in this period. Because Piazza knows the blues—the facts of having rambling on the brain, the facts of loss and longing, the resolutions of romance and the harsh, deceptive antidotes of anger—he is able to weave those conditions through his characters and give an overall structure to this volume that is willfully musical in its sense of variation. Try, for instance, "Responsibility" and "Burn Me Up," back to back, if you would understand my meaning. In that respect, Piazza is throwing his hat in the ring where *In Our Time* did its timeless tricks, or where *Go Down, Moses* went for broke, each of those books a monument to the shaping of American tales for the gathered force of a novel. I am not trying to put the burden of competition with Hemingway and Faulkner on this writer; I am just laying out a way for this work to be understood as a whole. In their quick summoning, their mix of the concrete and the lyrical, all given orchestral balance by pitch-perfect dialogue, the first eleven tales achieve the literary success of a blues suite. The last, "Charley Patton," is an evocation of the blues singer and the world that inspired his sound, the world that remakes that sound into flesh, blood, bone, machinery, cuisine, and shelter—the community that always sits on the edge of nature and carries the human part inside, where the percolating and the bursting of the bubbles within the heart detail the mysterious arrivals and collisions of passion. It is a worthy coda of twelve paragraphs that concludes a fine, fine mess of blues.

Some Words about Albert Murray:

Universal Counterpoint from the Bass Clef*

Who knows but that, on the lower frequencies, I speak for you?
Ralph Ellison, *Invisible Man*

1. Bassically Speaking: Bottoms Up

*I*n jazz, the bass is protean in its identity and function. *That jazz bass is percussive, harmonic, and lyric. It is the Southern end of the music, the bottom, the lower frequency. Known as the bull fiddle, its player is sometimes a matador whose imagination is a syncopating cape turning the snorting power of that wood and those four thick strings this way and that. Blues on the hoof. Said bass functions in the musical position where the individual beat is given multiple dimensions as the propelling nuances of swing are sought. That*

*Though written as a paper delivered at Claremont-McKenna College in the fall of 1995, a fuller version was published in 1997.

beat is usually a four-in-one event—a single note, a specific degree of the chord, a particular part of the meter, and an unaccented or emphatic aspect of the rhythm.

Everything sits on top of the bass—the singer, if there is one; the trumpets, the saxophones, the trombones, the piano, and the drums. The bass is down there below all. It helps to define and interpret the form and keep the tempo in place; that voice of the lower frequencies responds to ensemble inventions and makes inventions of its own; that Southern end of the music helps accent and extend rhythms.

The bass is the Atlas of the music, the bull fiddle shouldering and turning the globe of the sound. It has a perfect place in the triangular rhythm section that includes the piano and the drums. Part piano because of its pitch and part drums because of its percussive pizzicato, the bass is not only a violin with a deep voice, it is also something of a satyr, possessing the intelligence of a man and the power of a horse. In essence, subtlety and force are its specialties.

2. Blues at the Crossroads: Getting Down

Somewhere down there where we tend to think that it is darker than in any other part of the country; down there where we seem to feel the stickiness of murder tinting the air and where we recollect through our senses the smell of magnolias without even knowing their scent; somewhere down there in that place where the moon shines bright and we conjure up those who once drank white lightning and committed the startling and hot deeds of thunderbolts; all over that part of the land where we so often believe that the jungle of the human soul rules by growl and claw or by the extensions of the claw that are the knife and the bullet; down and out of this upper industrial range and so low on the rural map of this continent that its meanings ring out the bass tones so heavy that only the elephant aspects of our hearing can recognize the melody with absolute clarity is the American South.

That South is always something of a myth and a mystery. It is our national symbol of the dissonance that rattles the American soul with the conflict between hospitality and the ruthless willingness to use the very harshest means in order to maintain subjugation. The South also holds such unimpeachable significance in our national mythology because so much of what our country has become began down there. The history of the lower region is thick with so many tales and so many different kinds of adventure. Pirates used to sail through Southern waters and unfurl their black flags. Men as different as Ponce de Leon and Daniel Boone made their names down there, one looking for the elixir of perpetual youth, the other for a place beyond the reach of neighbors and civilized noise.

The South is where the Indians knew those various terrains, the forests and the swamps, the birds and the bears, the deer and the merciless swellings of the Mississippi. All kinds of fighting took place down there, backdropped by the frieze of the wilderness. Along the Natchez Trace in the 1790s, just a few years after thirteen British colonies had become the United States, monsters like the older Micajah and the younger Wiley, notorious as Big and Little Harpe, killed men, women, and children with the sustained brutality we now attribute to serial killers. Down South in 1812, the British at the Battle of New Orleans got their cans kicked and dented for good by Andrew Jackson and Jean Lafitte. In that same Louisiana, trivial displeasures led to so much ritualized killing—pistols drawn, knives at close quarters, swords, and whatever else might be considered suitable—that dueling had to be outlawed.

The relationship of pride to bloodlust was transmuted into the vision of mad gallantry that took John Brown to Harper's Ferry and made possible those reckless attacks by Confederate troops that resulted in the green fields turned red by the gore of defeat, defeat at the hands of Yankees, Midwestern farm boys and Northern kids scooped up out of the cities, all backed up by the indispensable help of the Negro, whose freedom was the issue of that war in the first place. The South is where most of the Civil War battles were fought and where Washington, D.C., is located. So we too frequently see the South as a place of dislocation and barbarism, imbecility and decadence. We, presumptively perched in the alto and soprano reaches of the nation, look upon Southerners, the residents of the bass clef, with a mix of pity and contempt.

That is where Albert Murray comes in. His bull fiddle has a different bass line and that line—those melodically interpreted harmonies and the rhythms he uses to give them extra thrust—takes us around a very different set of corners in the massive counterpoint of our national mythology. Murray's South is neither William Faulkner's nor Richard Wright's nor Robert Penn Warren's nor Flannery O'Connor's, though his command of place and idiom, his understanding of the historical and genetic curlicues, is second to that of no one who has ever written about the bass clef of American life. Almost all of Murray's work is informed in some very specific ways by the land where the blues began and where jazz was invented, the very same geographical space in which the writer began fusing his idiomatic sense of his nation's identity with the ever present and universal themes that stretch across the entire sweep of Western civilization.

Murray's South, because it is shaped and orchestrated by a writer of grand ambition, has a range of intellectual probings and realizations we rarely associate with the humanity so often masked by the vaunted eloquence of Southern rhetoric, particularly when that humanity is Negro. Murray is at war with conventional thinking and conventional condescension, but his basic intention is to avoid the kind of social protest that we associate with Southern Negroes who feel it absolutely necessary to make sure that the shadows of hanging trees forever darken their pages, obscuring any recognition of family, religious ritual, adolescent whimsy, romance, the passing on of transcendent wisdom, and so on. Murray is, to make a Joycean allusion heel, concerned with the burning brightness within a blackness, a brownness, a beigeness, and a boneness as varied in humanity as in skin tones, a brightness unpredictably softened and intensified by the broad and mythic range of Americana—the sweep of spirit and grit that was given such charismatic reiteration in those poetic snake hip patterns of rhythm that rose from the gutbucket of the blues and evolved into jazz. Murray's theorizing, his reporting, his technically splendid insertions of memoir into his musings, and his fictional efforts shape a considerably detailed strategy in which he makes the case that Negro Americans have far more to offer the nation than is historically or commonly understood. Those things have not only already made themselves evident in music and in the best of Negro culture. Importantly, Murray believes, they might lead to more creative political thinking and ways of combining ritual, philosophy, and engagement that could positively influence how Americans handle the inevitable and unpredictable demons of life.

As a literary man, Murray's instrument is that most extraordinary extension of painting, the written word, itself the largest step after the pictograph. Murray uses that instrument to achieve great variety. Like the cars of freight trains that are made differently in order to carry specific cargoes, all connected by couplers and rolling in the same direction, Murray's work sometimes seems to invent its own structures as it goes along, taking epic advantage of the imagination's transcontinental rails, traveling in so many directions by association—passing through, visiting, connecting the far and the near. This makes reading him almost always one version or another of an adventure, whether or not the individual work succeeds. In an excellent article about Murray that appeared in the August 1, 1993, issue of the *Boston Globe* magazine, Mark Feeney gets to the grit of the matter when he writes that "Murray is as close to a classic 19th-century man of letters as one might find in this country today." Feeney's observation is backed up by Murray's prolificacy. Though born in 1916, he didn't begin producing books until he was fifty-four years old. As of 1997, he has had nine works published, each differently conceived and executed.

Beyond his interest in stylistic flexibility, however, Murray is a writer whose output, if far better known and heeded, could mightily enrich the quality of our discussion of this country, its ethnicity, and the many powers that fill the universe of Western aesthetics. Whatever his shortcomings, Murray essentially has the goods and has put them to use in creating a perspective formed of interconnecting materials, ideas, and techniques. Hindsight allows us to see his output as an autobiography of consciousness and vision, established first in nonfiction, then fictional nonfiction, then aesthetic theory, then fiction, then as-told-to autobiography, and, most recently, back to fiction and aesthetic theory. From the very beginning, as we shall soon see, the late start seems to have caused Murray to have been in a hurry to establish himself as one of the major voices on the American scene.

His first two books arrived one year apart. *The Omni-Americans* (1970) is a collection of social essays and reviews which is still outstanding by dint of its distance from the racial and cultural misconceptions that continue to tangle us up. *South to a Very Old Place* (1971) is a shrewdly ordered succession of autobiographical travel meditations and conversations given shape and direction by the subjects, which are Murray himself and his quite personal take on the lives below the Mason-Dixon line, white to black, black to white. The immediate function of the book, however, was to allow Murray an opportunity to prove himself a top rank intellectual and writer whom you may not have known but whose virtuoso execution and unexpected thoughts would make it clear that he was far from a somebody come lately in the areas of serious cultural engagement and personal refinement. Essentially, it was a boldly confident advertisement for his own importance, one in which Murray poses himself as the worldly kind of hero upon whom he would soon base his fictional counterpart in a series of novels devoted to creating a Negro American *hombre de época*. *The Hero and the Blues* (1973) is a collection of three related lectures that comprise a fine and unique literary theory intended to illuminate the challenges facing the writer who would make something of the convolutions that propel and confuse American life. It also proposes fresh ideas about what constitutes the avant-garde while beginning to clarify how the blues sensibility can function in the world of literature. In the process, Murray opposes farce to tragedy as a better way of handling the mysteries and absurdities of life. *Stomping the Blues* (1976) is the first and only poetics of jazz, twelve chapters that rise far above the too typical sociological clichés and academic foggings of perception that have made it so difficult for the aesthetic triumphs of jazz music to achieve understanding. The journey from apprentice to past master that defined the life of Count Basie is the autobiographical tale Murray co-wrote with the Kansas City bandleader, *Good Morning Blues* (1985), spending a diligent but largely wasted decade on the effort. *Train Whistle Guitar* (1974), *The Spyglass Tree* (1991), and *The Seven League Boots* (1996) are three parts of an ongoing vision of the epic hero that I call, after the name of the protagonist, "The Scooter Novels." Though an unbending personal ideology seriously mars the second and third novels, each of the three, as the underground Negro intellectual Michael James says, "succeed in getting the sound of 4/4 jazz swing on the page, that rhythm." Another book of theories on art is *The Blue Devils of Nada* (1996), subtitled *A Contemporary American Approach to Aesthetic Statement*. The subtitle is a typical stance beyond the decoy of race.

A true radical, Murray has neither sold out to defeatism nor raised a flag of pirated ideas declaring alienation and animosity as the fundamentals of American race relations. His unwillingness to compromise a grandly sophisticated vision in favor of political and academic trends seems to have cost him the kind of recognition his substantive canon should have automatically guaranteed. All of his books are now available but the fact that major works of his such as *The Omni-Americans*, *South to a Very Old Place*, and *Stomping the Blues* were out of print for long periods is a major indictment of black studies departments on college campuses. Those departments are so numerous that they guarantee consistent sales of the books chosen by their instructors and professors for course study, written analysis, and discussion. Get on those lists and your books stay around. Obviously Murray's writing is too complex, or too contrary, to be absorbed into the polemical crucible out of which the coin of ethnic curriculum is frequently poured. Then there is the world beyond the jugheaded American campus. The writer, while well reviewed in almost every case, has conceptions quite far removed from the fashionable evolutions of literary form and content that have emerged over the last twenty-five years. Recent induction into the American Academy of the Arts notwithstanding, American literary types basically never heard of the guy. So Murray has labored beyond the spotlight, creating a stack of books designed to maintain dialogue with the literary achievements of the titans. His is the stuff of metaphoric connections summoned to the job of transcending race and place while reveling in the specifics of our multi-layered culture. No small job, no small heart.

3. A Lighthouse on a Dark Sea

Thus does the American species of negritude bring itself by a commodius vicus of recirculation back to protest fiction and Marxist environs. Whereupon enter the old effeterati, now become the politerati, doing an ofay version of the one-butt shuffle

> *to the fading but still audible strains of the old nineteen thirties*
> *dialectical boogie woogie.*
>
> Albert Murray, *The Omni-Americans*

      Albert Murray's vision was already quite cohesive when *The Omni-Americans*, his first book, appeared in 1970. It was not the work of a young man and there is no patience to be found in the book for any separatist ideas about American life. Its purpose was to reassess what had become central themes in racial discussion and propose that there were more answers in the world of art than in the simplistic rhetoric of black nationalists and the questionable disciplines of one-sided social surveys. In that sense, Murray was in the line of Goethe who, as Alain Finkielkraut observes in *The Defeat of the Mind*, rejected the nationalism of Herder in favor of recognizing that while one might have been initially shaped by the culture of his homeland, the truest recognition and understanding of life would come from intellectual, emotional, and technical interplay with the learning that came from the world at large, where human themes were essentially the same but were interpreted through a variety of particular attitudes that could enrich the individual in ways that nothing provincial ever could.

      But by the time that first book was published, what Murray calls "Afro-Carib Zionism" had successfully hijacked the dominant political vision of the Negro movement. So *The Omni-Americans* came on the scene as Negroes were being encouraged to think of themselves as if they were West Indians or Africans struggling with a distant "mother country." Nationalism of the sort that Stokely Carmichael espoused in 1966 when he made famous the thinking compressed into the term "Black Power" was concocted of alienation, paranoia, and the politics of colonial liberation from an external power. As its theoretical base extended into ancestor worship, African identity became a refuge from all the troubles of American life, a recognition of paradise lost, a way of stepping free of supposed self-hatred and the intimidations imposed by life in Western society.

      The globe was then color-coded. The West was white and the rest of the world was dark. Europe represented coldness, exploitation, and rot; the dark world warmth, collective cooperation, and vitality. Polemical generalization took precedence over subtlety, but the head-snapper is that the black nationalist alternatives were no more than poorly ingested forms of oppositional Western ideas that were German in origin, both politically and culturally. The Afro-Carib Zionist was singing a segregated version of the Communist theme "Workers of the world unite!" and assessing ethnic reality in the terms of a cultural "authenticity" that the Germans most bitterly intimidated by the French had been preaching for two hundred years. The latter were the very ideas that Goethe had turned away from by 1827, envisioning both the arrival of a world culture to draw from in pursuit of one's individuality and a world economy based on international trade.

The Omni-Americans is a thorough attempt to redress the confusions that have since distorted our sense of American identity. Murray submits that recognition of the deep commonality underlying our many cultural variations is a necessary intellectual foundation if the problems of color are to be addressed appropriately. The Negro has no need to look backward to Africa for ethnic or cultural validation. True Americana will do.

Murray understood exactly what Ellison had made clear before him in *Invisible Man* and *Shadow and Act:* Polemical reductions, if believed and acted upon, were capable of draining away all of the human complexities and the cultural facts of American life, which were far different from the patterns and policies of prejudice. In the argot of today's sidewalks, Murray was "dropping science," another way of saying that he was cutting through the bull. The writing already dismissed the unscientific idea of "race" in favor of ethnicity, foreshadowing what were to become prominent elements of discussion twenty years into the future:

> As for U.S. Negroes being non-white, nothing could be further from scientific accuracy. Indeed, no classification was ever less accurate. By any definition of race, even the most makeshift legal one, most native-born U.S. Negroes, far from being non-white, are in fact part-white. They are also by any meaningful definition of culture, part-Anglo-Saxon, and they are overwhelmingly Protestant.

The "non-white" classification that irks Murray is a basic aspect of the society at large and one that preserves fraudulent suppositions about unchanging wedges. He knows that those wedges cannot be shown for what they are unless Americans develop a much more real understanding of their own culture and its human ingredients. That is why a signal argument of Murray's is clearly rooted in the work of Constance Rourke and her cultural observation that by the nineteenth century the American had become an amalgam of four elements—the Yankee, the backwoodsman, the Indian, and the Negro. Ours, then, is a country of people emphasizing or deemphasizing their gumbo ingredients, either unconsciously or at will. Speaking to that point, Murray writes:

> Identity is best defined in terms of culture, and the culture of the nation over which the white Anglo-Saxon power elite exercises such exclusive political, economic, and social control is not all-white by any measurement ever devised. *American culture, even in its most rigidly segregated precincts, is patently and irrevocably composite. It is, regardless of all the hysterical protestations of those who would have it otherwise, incontestably mulatto.* Indeed, for all their traditional antagonisms and obvious differences, the so-called black and so-called white people of the United States resemble nobody else in the world so much as they resemble each other. And what is more, even their most extreme and violent polarities represent nothing so much as the natural history of pluralism in an open society.

Another theme that will run throughout his work is also introduced. Murray quite confidently asserts that Negro American life in this nation is not one unrelenting humiliation after another, not the perpetual feeling of inferiority in face of the white people, not a condition of anger ever threatening to make someone a bloody mess. This is why the writer rejects theories in which Negroes are described as no more than victims of "cultural deprivation," misshapen by prejudice, and existing as nearly human in an abominable situation. To the contrary, Negroes, like everyone else, pick and choose from the national influences, sometimes reinterpreting, sometimes inventing what they want when it is unavailable. At one place Murray doubles up on Ellison and observes that Negroes are at least as ambivalent about so-called white culture as they are attracted to it, ever wary of all the difficulties, pitfalls, and frustrations that have been reported to them from the friends and relatives employed in white homes, at hotels, in social clubs, and so on:

> Most Negroes, far from believing that white Americans have only the lowest opinion of black Americans, are forever revealing the fact that they are firmly convinced that even those white people of wealth and power spend a highly significant amount of time emulating Negroes while pretending not to. No conviction is more indicative of Negro self-esteem, the appreciation of other Negroes, or the ambivalence of which their response to white Americans is seldom free.

Murray also makes a couple of points about black Americans that are basic to his aesthetic concerns, since they arrive not through the blood but through a specific and shifting set of interpretations of the national culture:

> As for behavior or life style, no other people in the land have as yet evolved a characteristic idiom that reflects a more open, robust, and affirmative disposition toward diversity and change. Nor is any other idiom more smoothly geared to open-minded improvisation. Moreover, never has improvisation been more conditioned by esthetic values . . . When such improvisation as typifies Negro music, dance, language, religion, sports, fashions, general bearing and deportment, and even food preparation is considered from a Negro point of view, there is seldom, if ever, any serious doubt about how Negroes feel about themselves or about what they accept and reject of white people. They regard themselves not as the substandard, abnormal non-white people of American social science surveys and the news media, but rather as if they were, so to speak, fundamental extensions of contemporary possibilities.

Bending for his own purposes the distinction Kenneth Burke makes between the ritual of "the poetic" and the methodology of "the scientific" in *The Philosophy of Literary Form* (which he will do again in *The Hero and the Blues*), Murray renounces the spin-offs of utopian ideas that burden us in one way or another, falling on our heads from the windows of Marxism, sociology, psychiatry, and all of what he terms "social science fiction," which amount to statistically justified theories of why the darkies should be both pitied and kept in their place. Outraged by the constant citing and discussion of what became known as the Moynihan Report, a study in which the single-parent Negro family is underlined as an explanation of black social problems, Murray writes:

> At a time when Negroes are demanding freedom as a *constitutional right*, the Moynihan Report is saying, in effect, that those who have been exploiting Negroes for years should now, upon being shown his statistics, become benevolent enough to set up a nationwide welfare program for them. *Not once does he cite any Negro assets that white people might find more attractive than black subservience.* Good intentions notwithstanding, Moynihan's arbitrary interpretations make a far stronger case for the Negro equivalent of Indian reservations than for Desegregation Now.

The point that Murray puts in italics is an example of his belief that Negroes have not only survived but that they have done much that, if taken up by the society at large, could comprehensively better the quality of American life and add, from the sensibility of the blues and the rituals that surround it, another philosophical perspective, one geared to an "affirmative disposition toward diversity and change." Elsewhere the writer, who has argued that Negroes are not only American but more deeply rooted in the culture than the immigrants who have long gotten preferential treatment, looks at another aspect of the social science fiction problem:

> The major emphasis in the large surveys is never placed on the failure of white Americans to measure up to the standards of the Constitution. The primary attention repeatedly is focused on Negroes as victims. Again and again the assumption of the surveys is that slavery and oppression have made Negroes *inferior* to other Americans and hence less American.

The melody that rises from Murray's intellectual bass line also says that access is more important than the lesser meanings of assimilation, and that the problems of our society are traceable to whether or not some-one has a chance to make it or break it in open competition, no matter what overall group the person supposedly represents. He goes after those who confuse "the politics of philanthropy with the real politik of munici-pal, state, and national government. The exaggeration of black suffer-ing . . . may be a time-hallowed means of obtaining benevolent handouts, but it is hardly the best method of developing rugged political power. In fact, many of the white politicians who back stop-gap poverty appropria-tions bills do so because they assume that this is the surest and smoothest way of delaying active and equitable participation in the power mecha-nisms." Those exaggerations keep Negroes at a distance, giving them an exotic identity outside of the mainstream and outside of the struggle that was based on the rights of American-born citizens.

Self-imposed alienation was no more than a way of aiding and com-forting the enemy, which was a composite of racism and racist policy. The slap-dash conflations of minority experience even led to Negroes such as James Baldwin and Kenneth Clark describing black life in terms that, by implication, made it secondary to the European experience of immigrant Jews, which added another galling layer of condescension: "It is not at all unusual for second generation Jewish writers to refer to native-born multi-generation U.S. Negroes . . . as a non-white, unassimilable minority. Unassimilable with whom? Is Norman Podhoretz more assimilated than Count Basie?" Murray discusses at length the unacknowledged but rich qualities of Negro community life, paddling Baldwin, Clark, and the others who chose to impose the inappropriate description of "ghetto" on black communities, segregated or not:

> But what useful purpose is really served by confusing segregated housing in the U.S. with the way Jewish life was separated from the gentile world in the days of the old ghettos? After all, in addition to physical segregation, the real ghettos also represented profound dif-ferences in the religion, language, and food customs, and were even geared to a different calendar. It is grossly misleading to suggest that

segregated housing anywhere in the United States represents a cultural distance that is in any way at all comparable to the one that separated a Jewish ghetto from the life styles of various European countries. . . .

Not even the most degenerate rituals of the South are more infuriating to multigenerational U.S. Negroes than the pompous impertinence of those European refugees who were admitted to the U.S. on preferential quotas, who benefit by preferential treatment because of the color system, and who then presume to make condescending insinuations about the lack of initiative, self-help, and self-pride among Negroes.

Further dispensing with what had then become the periodic barking of the Negro militant and the race hustler but has since evolved into respectable status on our university campuses, Murray uses the writings of prominent black and white historians as well as cultural theorists to demolish hostile soapbox propaganda, its sources usually some intellectually bilious crossbreeding of ideas from Massa Karl Marx and overwrought paeans to Mother of Civilization Mama Africa. One of the prominently crushed propaganda ideas that made its way into pop political and historical analysis is Malcolm X's absolutely inaccurate juxtaposition of "house" and "field" slaves. In this bit of political rock and roll, the "house nigger" was described as a mansion chattel totally in love with the master and protective of him, while his counterpart did the hard labor of the fields but was so full of an unsubmissive, revolutionary hate for the master that he became ecstatic whenever there were problems on the plantation or valuable things were destroyed. In 1970, those images had taken on class variations that amounted to "good" middle-class Negroes being defined as subservient "oreo" extensions of the house slaves and "bad," unlettered street types given the mantle of "authentic" representatives of the feelings of the people.

Murray knew the distortions of historical reality left out all sorts of Negro cooperation across backgrounds and income levels in education and politics, since the majority of important black leaders on local and national levels were from the so-called middle class, not the bottom.

What Murray was not able to do was warn Negroes away from buying "into," as he wrote, "what amounts to the promotion of a black intramural class struggle." Had he been listened to, or at least had his ideas well promoted through the national machinery of high school and college education, the catastrophic difficulties that black students now have seeing themselves as both studious and "authentic" might have been avoided.

A retired military man, Murray was similarly disturbed by the static of black saber-rattling that might well have supplied excuses for the kinds of whites who became violently hysterical at even the slightest Negro threat, real or imagined. The writer backs up his sense of strategy by pointing to the history of lynch mobs and the tradition of Northern police officers overreacting with deadly force. Trampling simplistic conceptions of "good" and "bad" Negroes, Murray gets all the way down into the center of the issue, lifts up his down-home, low-voiced Stradivarius, and thumps out these bass notes:

> In all of this nonsense about black good guys and bad guys—in their varying shades of militancy and class and coloring and status—what is most often forgotten is the nature of the problem. *So far as white people are concerned, the most revolutionary, radical, and devastating action any U.S. Negro can engage in is to compete with other Americans for status, employment, total social activity, and basic political power.*

4. Reminiscing in Tempo

Hey you who you how come you got to be the one running your mouth so much and so proper-talking like don't nobody else know nothing just because you passed a test in a book or something. Hey you who you let me tell you one goddam thing mister little-old-know-so-much smart-ass goddam nigger you don't know no goddam more about it than no goddam body else because don't no goddam body give a goddam shit about none of it no goddam how. You can read all them old white folks books you want and you still ain't going to be nothing but another goddam nigger just like every goddam body else. So don't come getting so goddam bright-ass

smart-ass about me goddam it like somebody supposed to think
you so much because you over there running up behind Mister
goddam-ass Baker and them old hancty-butt goddam Mobile
Country Training School goddam teachers.

South to a Very Old Place

In *South to a Very Old Place*, which is invaluable to an appreciation of his formal creativity, the writer takes off from André Malraux's *Anti-Memoirs*, which is itself an exceedingly brilliant series of autobiographical meditations, conversations, and monologues on the politics, the wars, and the artistic discoveries of the twentieth century. Murray's reharmonization for his own purposes, while no match for Malraux's extraordinary international context of world-shakers, is still quite something. The writer creates one of his most original books because its form allows him to address his fascination with the various ways in which the present moment arrives from the womb of the past. Murray looks at the history of our South through a Proustian structure of association that, to use a well-deserved jazz metaphor, reaches a high point near the end as a down-home jam session of orchestrated voices playing with the themes of American life in a Southern frame. Overall, however, *South to a Very Old Place* is largely a series of solo improvisations that interweave the grand past, the past of the writer himself, and the present, almost always contesting the cultural disfigurements of social and political clichés.

Not only does Murray take on whites, he does battle with the condescension Northern Negroes have long shown those from the South, especially those of Murray's generation, who were told things such as "I would rather be a lamp post in Harlem than the mayor of Mobile, Alabama" (meaning, "I know those crackers had a good time giving you all hell day by day. I couldn't even *breathe* in the middle of all that mess"). In *The Omni-Americans*, he responded to that statement and predicted this part of his war plan when he wrote, "as any black Mobilian old enough to remember will readily confirm, educators down-home would have regarded such empty-headed arrogance with contempt at least as far back as thirty or forty years ago." For one and all, whatever the color, whatever the geography, he meant to prove that Southern white racism hadn't merely handcuffed Negro experience just before it was locked in a trunk that was then wound round by chains before being dropped to the bottom of the ocean. Southern athletic heroes who went on to the big time, local educators known only to their students, and musicians abound, images and memories of them arriving every which way. Through an infallible ear, Murray puts to literary use his deep, deep appreciation of John A. Kouwenhoven's conception of American culture and art as an ongoing dialogue in which the vernacular enhances higher forms as it is appropriated.

The book began as an assignment for *Harper's* magazine, Willie Morris commissioning Murray to, as the original jacket copy says, "travel around the South, interviewing leading white Southern intellectuals and writers." It turns out to be something else altogether. Right under the close reader's eyes, the writing becomes a wild and subtle embodiment of the "non-fiction novel," a term Truman Capote gave us so that we might recognize the novelist's sensibility arriving in the world of uninvented incidents.* The result is that Murray perceives and, in his very own way, extends upon what William Faulkner had been revealing for many years—at the most intense moments of segregation, Negroes were functioning in the households of whites, setting examples of excellence, standards of behavior, spinning tales, entertaining, and passing on exactly the way all wisdom finally does. This is made explicit from Murray's position on the field when the subjects of mammies, Southern belles, and courtly gentlemen are examined. In one of the italicized monologues that so often lift the narrative out of the present or place the vernacular speaking rhythms in sort of an omniscient time range, more or less an Olympian statement, Murray drops a double bass blues chord voicing on us in which we hear just how the black and white notes are truly together:

> *A frisky tale gal is a frisky tale gal, don't care how much they pay for her perfume. You see them white gals sashaying around actin all stuck up and making out like they just stepped out of a doll house or somewhere, well I'm here to tell you they ain't no china dolls, don't care how much powder and*

---

*The recent—and withering—attacks on *Anti-Memoirs* for its factual inaccuracies, its self-promotion, and its invented dialogues make it rather obvious that the work is far more like Murray's than the writer could have been aware of at the time.

rouge they got on. Who you reckon keeping the dollhouse clean, such as it is? On top of washing and ironing them clothes and tying them ribbons and bows. Who you reckon they mamas learned to from, and they mama's mamas? Who you reckon the last one of all them always come to show themselves to just before they go flouncing off somewhere to make a fool out of another one of them little old mannish white boys all growed up putting on airs and calling hisself a gentleman? And don't bit more know what they doing than the man in the moon? Who you reckon the one made him learn them fancy manners he showing off?

Murray takes the point even further when he jars against the conventional ideas about the overwhelming influence of white over black, which is always supposed to be the coating of spiritual genocide, as is any kind of import from outside one's own group in our day of alienated "authenticity." "You can only wonder," he writes, "what happens to all that fancy Teachers College-plus-Bruno Bettleheim jive about the first few years of childhood being the most crucial, when the topic is the black mammy's relationship to the white child?"

That is not at all a one-way phenomenon because Murray is nostalgic about how a film star of the old days looked to him as a child:

As far as you were concerned just about the only white man who really knew how to strut his stuff walking back in those days was not anybody anywhere in and round or even near Mobile, Alabama. It was a western cowboy. It was the one and only Tom Mix walking neither pasty-faced nor red-necked but bowlegged; and then standing not like a flatassed cracker deputy but hip-cocked and pointy-toed, with his thumbs hooked into his low-riding two-gun cartridge belt, his silk neckerchief knotted to one side, the angle of his ten-gallon western cowboy hat as sporty as a flashy-fingered piano player's gambling hall fedora.

This is an example of Murray at his most personal, for he brings together what might be termed a "mulatto association." That is, beginning with Tom Mix, who was a Saturday afternoon hero to all young American boys of the 1920s, Murray brings together the grace of the Westerner with the

Negro piano players like Jelly Roll Morton. It is another of many examples in which the subtle reader observes the writer's absolute willingness
to make something his own from whatever touches him inspirationally or
entertainingly, regardless of where it comes from.

At that time, Murray became the first Negro writer since Ellison to
so unflinchingly embrace an American identity that transcended race
while working so well within the specifics of his own cultural background's variations on the elements that define and delineate the national
feeling of and for life. Murray achieves this by bringing to bear his own
memories as they apply to his travels and through the themes that arise
either from contact with his subjects or in the work they have written
themselves. Murray's layered vision of the South gives human texture to
the ideas about the vitality of Negro American experience that were observed in the theoretical format of the combative social essays that heat
up *The Omni-Americans*.

Here Murray makes his own keen observations and recollections the
autobiographical validations of the ideas that do such battle with "social
science fiction," his perpetual nemesis. Again moving outward from the
themes of his first book, he is intent on exploring the things that Negroes
would not *want* to give up just to get fair treatment. Murray is also setting
up his own riff on an observation from Ellison's *Shadow and Act*, which included a previously unpublished 1944 review of Gunnar Myrdal's *An
American Dilemma*. Ellison wrote that Negro culture contained "much of
great value, of richness, which, because it has been secreted by living and
has made their lives more meaningful, Negroes will not willingly disregard." But some have been irritated by the approach used in *South to a
Very Old Place* because Murray didn't give C. Vann Woodward, Robert
Penn Warren, Walker Percy, Jonathan Daniels, and others much of a
chance to do more than a little talking. It is charged that they are made to
sit still for Murray's summations of their individual importance in American culture, then allowed to drop a few vamping chords that send the
writer off on his own tangents. When the writer briefly comes to rest,
these established figures set up interludes or transitional figures for his
next extended rumination.

The complainers are right. Murray puts those white Southern writers in the rhythm section, keeping time while he swings, flits, croons, and

celebrates himself and his background with a self-referential arrogance quite surprising from one who was then an all but unknown writer. In other words, instead of making *South to a Very Old Place* his book about *them*, he chose to make it his book about *himself*. That is why the respectful introductions almost always fall away as Murray pulls rank, making it clear that he doesn't care what anybody else has said, he knows the South, its beauties and its dangers, as well as any other writer and, in certain ways, far, far, better than any who have ever approached the subject of black and white down there in the bass clef. So Murray "vouches for" or dismisses the ideas of men who had already produced considerable bodies of published work and were recognized major figures in American letters across the disciplines of art, criticism, history, and journalism. Murray is merely applying to the universe of the written word what he observed about jazz musicians in *The Omni-Americans*—artists who improvise their own lines by ear "not because they cannot read the score but rather because in the very process of mastering it they have found it inadequate for their purposes."

What we get is almost a reverse version of the traditional Southern tale of the stage, the screen, and the page, in which the white people live romantic, exciting, and refined lives while the Negroes shuffle in to make short statements that are, by turns, funny, wise, ridiculous—bits of comic relief, peasant expressions of illiterate wisdom, examples of how innately ludicrous the colored people are destined to remain. But we are not visiting the slave compound to wonder at how much fun the darkies have in face of all their dramatic plantation troubles; we are taken into a training ground for aristocracy, a vast source of literary possibilities. Murray is filling in the spaces that even Faulkner couldn't fill and that were not sufficiently filled by anyone else.

Through Murray's appropriation and swinging, rhythmic reorganization of Malraux, Joyce, Hemingway, and Faulkner, we are essentially given what also appears to be a symphonic, jazz-soaked expansion of chapter sixteen in *The Life and Times of Frederick Douglass*, "Time Makes All Things Even," where that titan of nineteenth-century America writes of returning to the South after his major role in the Abolition Movement, after the Confederate loss of the Civil War, and in the wake of his world travels. Douglass was then no longer a runaway slave but a hero respectfully treated by his dying former master as well as by other whites. His very presence brings joy to local Negroes, who share a complicated past with him, not all of which is even close to sorrowful. The great man wrote of his formerly cruel master and himself, then, at one point, of the nostalgic memories of his childhood that are sparked by places that transcend his former social condition:

> Our courses had been determined for us, not by us. We had both been flung, by powers that did not ask our consent, upon a mighty current of life, which we could neither resist nor control. By this current he was a master, and I a slave, but now our lives were verging towards a point where differences disappear, where even the constancy of hate breaks down and where the clouds of pride, passion, and self-ishness vanish before the brightness of infinite light. . . .
>
> This carriage house was of much interest to me, because Col. Lloyd sometimes allowed his servants the use of it for festal occasions, and in it there was at such times music and dancing . . . there was the shoemaker's shop, where Uncle Abe made and mended shoes, and the blacksmith's shop, where Uncle Tony hammered iron, and the weekly closing of which taught me to distinguish Sundays from other days. The old barn, too, was there—time worn, to be sure, but still in good condition—a place of wonderful interest to me in my child-hood, for there I often repaired to listen to the chatter and watch the flight of swallows among its lofty beams, and under its ample roof, Time had wrought some changes in the trees and foliage. The Lom-bardy poplars, in the branches of which the red-winged blackbirds used to congregate and sing, and whose music awakened in my young heart sensations and aspirations deep and undefinable, were gone; but the oaks and elms, where young [white] Daniel . . . used to divide with me his cakes and biscuits, were there as umbrageous and beau-tiful as ever.

In the "New Haven" chapter of his own book, Murray toys with his own oblique relationship to Douglass's life—and the great man's *own* bass line—when he recalls what the older people said about the obstacle course of local racism, then moves through musical association from North to South and on to a recognition of down-home commonality within the broad context of human concerns:

> [It was] the same situation on which some of the old heads by the fire-side were musing when they used to come to the end of some story about somebody being in trouble, and mutter: "You got to know how to handle them; you got to outthink them, you got to stay one jump ahead of them"; but which so far as any number of others, old and young, yourself included, were concerned was a very good rea-son to un-ass the area. Not simply in flight, escape and hence abdi-cation, however, but also in exploration, quest, and even conquest.
>
> One snatch of either whingding or rooty-toot and even as you sit looking at the midtown Manhattan skyline from 132nd Street, looking south as you once did from the northward outskirts of Mo-bile, you are also back in the old spyglass place seeing all of them that once more. But in better perspective, in proper complexity and with proper awareness of the ambiguity and ultimate obscurity of not just black and white motives down home but of all human motivation everywhere. Because after all that instantaneous, popeyed, no-matter-how-fleeting-expression of drawing-room outrage you register at the impropriety of all that old narrow-nosed, shaggyheaded blue-eyed talk when you hear it outside the South is perhaps as much an ex-pression of kinship as aginship whether you can admit it or not.

His overall literary ambitions are well served in passages such as those wherein Murray mulls rhapsodic over his early education as well as his college years at Booker T. Washington's Tuskegee Institute, on which campus he first meets fellow intellectuals. Then we see some of Murray's goal come into aesthetic completion as the points are made: The South produced Negroes such as himself, almost none of whom, in all their so-cial rituals and intellectual aspirations, ever made it to the pages of our lit-erature. These descendents of Douglass's world often rose from blue-collar backgrounds that denied them none of the wonders of childhood dreams and encouraged them to go beyond everything by which they were surrounded. Such backgrounds also prepared the children—in spirit and mother wit—to study hard in schools that might have been the result of segregated policy but, contrary to cliché, contained teachers and students obsessed with and thrilled by the broad world of universal concerns, the full and complicated menu of human meaning and human achievement, from the sciences to the arts, from the making of war to the making of love. Murray gives us this untapped universe, chapter and verse, in a brilliantly constructed section called "Tuskegee," a tour de force of lyricism, humor, and nostalgia. The chapter brings us right into the circle of young Negroes who live the college life of stylishness, popular entertainment, courtship, and athletics while intellectually stretching themselves into new dimensions. Effortlessly counterstating the now and again dismissive picture of Tuskegee that Ralph Ellison gave us in *Invisible Man*, this chapter is a high point in post–World War II American writing.

Through memories of his teachers, Murray fashions the human extensions of a man Douglass described during his return to the South, "Dr. Copper, an old slave [who] used, with a hickory stick in hand, to teach us the Lord's Prayer." Those extensions and their context have become quite complex. Of Tuskegee's Morteza Sprague, an intellectual mentor to Ralph Ellison, Murray, and Murray's roommate, Jug Hamilton, of the good feeling to be had hanging out with "the fellas" prior to a dance, and of the Negro humor toward the whole matter of doing one's racial duty through high-level student performance, the writer recalls:

> Morteza Drexel Sprague expected you to proceed in terms of the highest standards of formal scholarship among other things not because he wanted you to become a carbon copy of any white man who ever lived, not excepting Shakespeare or even Leonard da Vinci. But because to him you were the very special vehicle through which contemporary man, and not just contemporary black man either, would inherit the experience and insights of all recorded or decipherable time. Because to him (as to everyone else on that all-black faculty) your political commitment to specific social causes of your own people went without saying. What after all were the immediate political implications of *Beowulf* and of all epic heroism? Nor was true com-

mitment ever a matter either of chauvinism or of xenophobia. To him as to the bards, the scops and gleemen in Fall Quarter Literature (201)—as to Mister Baker at Mobile County Training School—commitment involved such epical exploits as penetrating frontiers and thereby expanding your people's horizons of aspirations. . . .

All of that too was part of what being there was like in those days. And who, having known it will ever forget the tuskegeeness of The Block back then when the best fountain Cokes and milkshakes and freezes in the world were made by Alonzo White and the second best by one of the faculty-jiving students named Happy White? Nowhere could you go and find a more steady flow of out-of-town sharpies, athletes and big-league musicians to jive, wolf, and signify with than in and around the Drag, the Drugstore, and Bill Washington's clothing store, which was then known as Harris and Washington in those days. Not even the main stem of Sage Hall (which after all was only undergraduate stuff as much fun as it never ceased to be) was as much of a charmed circle as The Block—*especially in the Yardley's English Lavender euphoria of that postgame predance twilight time when happiness was simply being there standing not tall as ofay drugstore squares in their rolled-sleeved open-collared white shirts did, but stashed fly in the gladness of your most righteous threads, whether tweed or hard finished, hanging loose like a blue goose with, say, Lunceford's "Dream of You" on the jukebox for your background, until White Hall clock chimed the hour when you would pick up the trillies for the stroll to Logan Hall.* . . .

Nevertheless the here-and-now tuskegeeness of those days . . . was also such that back on the upperclassmen's main stem of Sage Hall the noble inscription (chiseled in the stone pedestal of The Monument) which read: HE LIFTED THE VEIL OF IGNORANCE FROM HIS PEOPLE AND POINTED THE WAY TO PROGRESS THROUGH EDUCATION AND INDUSTRY had become: *"Hey lift the goddam veil, man. Hey, man, lift the goddam veil." Had become: "Hey, horse, you know what the man said; Unka Buka say lift that shit, man, goddam." On occasion it could also become: "Hey looka here pardner, damn man; here I been drinking muddy goddam water and sleeping in a hollow goddam log hitchhiking my mufkin way all the goddam way from chittlin goddam switch to get here and now I ain't going to get to help y'all lift that chickenshit goddam veil because you gone hen-ass-house and ain't going to help me work out this mess for old Red goddam Davis.*" Or from somebody like the one and only Mister Big-Goddam-Double-Jointed-Door-Rolling and Door Roller: "*Hey, damn man. Unka Buka say let down your somiching bucket right where you dog-ass goddam at, cousin. Say, that's all right about all that other shit. Say, you take care of this shit, and, man, if I don't have this shit for Jenkins I am going to go back home and tote that barge. Ha! ain't them up-north crackers a bitch? Tote that barge! What kind of bullshit talk is that? And old potgutted Paul Robeson up there singing it like it's a goddam spiritual or something. Hey but come on man, let's tote that goddam veil outa my goddam face for Jenkin's goddam English. Hell, man, we can't be letting old Unka Buka Tee down.*"

The vitality of Negro speech so takes Murray that he doesn't replicate the voice-limiting technique of his "chats" with the white and famous throughout. In *The Life and Times* Douglass wrote, "Leaving the great house, my presence became known to the colored people, some of whom were children of those I had known when a boy. They all seemed delighted to see me." That kind of delight is a parallel joy to Murray's ears. If just about any down-home Negroes are praising the writer for leaving the South and making something of himself (something made clear by neither the down-home flatterers nor the writer), he largely drops into silence, only popping in his comments every now and then. Through them we learn that Murray was a legendary student, a pitcher who could have become a professional, a ladies' man, and a traveler. This is also true when they share his opinions. Mostly nameless black people in Mobile, Alabama, are *allowed* to talk with almost no interruption for more than thirty pages of the Modern Library edition. They express themselves about social changes, black nationalism, and Lyndon Johnson in a virtuoso jazz fugue that captures many different kinds of Southern black speech.

Yet there is something oddly evasive about the book for all its masterfully layered and lathered narcissism. We learn a great deal about how

Murray felt as a child, as an adolescent, as a college student, but little about his experience in the Air Force during World War II. While we are told at least four times that he is on an expense account—gee whiz!—and though he brilliantly telescopes his Douglass-updated memories of periodically returning to Mobile and talking with Morteza Sprague or writing to him in order to give readers references to and quick pictures of the writer's experiences in Key West, or a vacation from Casablanca to the Swiss Alps, or his trips and the time spent in Venice, in Paris, in California, London, Rome, Athens, and Istanbul, in "the Andover Shop on Holyoke Street off Harvard Square," and at a New York literary party with Norman Mailer among others, we finally learn next to nothing about his professional life at Tuskegee, where he taught in the forties and the fifties.

Had Murray chosen to remember such things, he would have had to let us know the details of how fellow Tuskegee Airmen lived, thought, and felt. What a contrast that could have provided to the scenes of campus dances, events, and discussions. We know that Murray was well aware of the difference between the mood set by college life and the preparation for roles in the big war. Murray had to personally know those military Negroes who received segregated training and fought for the United States but, when captured, "preferred," as he wrote in *The Omni-Americans*, "the treatment they received from the Nazis to that which they had endured at the hands of their fellow countrymen in Alabama, whose solicitude of German internees was beyond reproach!"

What exactly was that endurance in response to? How were they received by Tuskegee Negroes and whites when on leave and in their spit-and-polish uniforms? What did they think when the atomic bomb arrived and forever changed warfare? We might also have learned what it meant when Truman desegregated the armed services. Were Negroes jubilant or indifferent or a bit of both? How did it feel to be an officer, the major that Murray became, who exercised power over white men that was largely unprecedented in civilian America? There Murray could have run some fresh bass line changes upon the book's ideas about how white boys in the South have benefitted from the wisdom of the endless Uncle Remuses who helped prepare them for adulthood. As an officer commanding men black and white, and a superior as intellectually engaged as he surely was,

Murray must have been some kind of an impressive force and source. And who knows how the Murray sense of humor would have handled an observation made by a retired Negro officer of the writer's generation: "Man, those guys from the South had trouble when we started getting some rank. That really put their cracker asses in a sling. Those country boys would be on the lookout for a Negro with some stripes. That was hell walking on two legs. When they saw you coming, they would drop everything and scoot off as fast as they could because they would rather kiss you than stand there in public and salute you. You could have a lot of fun with that." Given the deft conglomerations of perspective, history, ritual, and feeling that the writer almost always brings to the places and people he visits in order to avoid the limitations of the familiar and the academic, it is extremely unfortunate that Murray didn't include those military aspects of his past, since he moves as far away from the South as Europe or Los Angeles when his memories of his past are called upon to add color to the narrative or deepen some point.

Had Murray written of teaching in the South during the years that he did, we might have been informed of what it meant to become the college teacher after having been the gifted student. We might also have come to know the way it really was among Negroes in the academy as the Civil Rights Movement began to take off—the thoughts and emotions among that fringe of black refinement as the nonviolent troops began experiencing the terrorist actions of rednecked dragons. I am not talking about the "pissing and moaning" Murray is so contemptuous of, ever mindful of how strain and heartbreak are so easily shredded into political pulp and protest writing. I mean something else altogether: the elaborate cross references and angles of impassioned perspective revealed in the fugue of Mobile's Negro voices are probably but an indication of what could have been done with the black intellectuals and the local elite that the writer must have come to know. Such material as remarkably rendered as other subjects are in its very best passages could have meant that *South to a Very Old Place* would not have had miles and miles to go in order to reach the region of the masterpiece. It would either have gotten the book there or taken it close enough for another measure of glory.

5. Blues to Become Better at Beating the Devil

In order to have a story, you have contention. You have a desire, a wish, but something's in the way. So you have agon—struggle. The one that carries the values we identify with, we call the protagonist. The one that threatens those values is the antagonist. One is indispensable to the other. No dragon, no hero.

Albert Murray, interviewed in *American Heritage*, September 1996

The Hero and the Blues, Stomping the Blues, and *Good Morning Blues* form a trio in which an aesthetic theory about blues and literature is extended into a poetics of jazz, then followed by an as-told-to autobiography of Count Basie in which Murray has a figure whose career exemplifies what he calls "the velocity of celebration." These all fit perfectly in his canon because the writer knows that there are occasions in the development of art when the personal declaration of an aesthetic is necessary. This makes possible a proper assessment of the work one intends, or at least an assessment in terms of its purpose and its creator's actual sense of order.

From *The Omni-Americans* forward, Murray, building again upon Kenneth Burke, had been working on redefining the blues and the blues musician, then removing the house party, the juke joint, and the dance hall from the purported world of escape and putting them in the world of ritual. He successfully brought the full cultural discussion of jazz and blues beyond the mess of narrow sociology, polemics, gee whizzery, and academic dullness that missed the substance of the two arts. Murray sees the jazz ritual in very basic terms. He names those terms "the dynamics of confrontation," which he knows that too many mistake "for the mechanics of withdrawal, escape, and relief!"

In Murray's overview, "The sense of well-being that always goes with swinging the blues is generated, as anyone familiar with Negro dance halls knows, not by obscuring or denying the existence of the ugly dimensions of human nature, circumstances, and conduct, but rather through the full, sharp, and inescapable awareness of them." Extending that assessment with those who did large deeds in the flesh, Murray presents men such as Louis Armstrong and Duke Ellington as epic American heroes whose art has not only given us a superb image of ourselves in rhythm and tune but has added another twentieth-century way of handling the inevitable shortcomings of life to our human strategies. He makes it clear that at the same time that the slow blues might complain about the low-down dirty thing that love is, the sensuous feeling of the tempo acts as an aphrodisiac and, we might add, also provides an onomatopoeic form of instruction to the young male who aspires to be a smooth and easy lover, not a bumbling brute in the boudoir. Murray is victorious from page to page of his theoretical books on aesthetics and music, convincing the reader that elements such as vamps, riffs, breaks, and fills allow jazz musicians to develop their variations in ways that are decidedly American. He makes us think quite seriously about the implications of the whole idea of stomping the blues, which is, we might realize on our own, somewhat akin to the Mexican "Day of the Dead," when that inevitable winner is toyed with, made into candy skulls, and parodied. Writing of the feeling that shifts everything around as a jazz band takes off into its swing, Murray says what he thinks it all comes down to, which is establishing the combative human magic of jubilation:

> The atmosphere changes so instantaneously that it is as if a Master of the Revels had suddenly interrupted the proceedings to command: *"Say now, hey now, that's all right about all that other carrying on and stuff, I say let the good times roll!"*

Murray's ultimate ambition was to create a stage on which he could present his own version of the epic hero by the time he got to *The Seven League Boots* and made his Scooter a bass player armed with fairy-tale magic, a young man capable of trekking through mud in a white suit but never getting it dirty. The preparation made it most of the way. *The Hero and the Blues* and *Stomping the Blues* are two exceptional books, but *Good Morning Blues*, the autobiography with Basie, while containing some stretches of information and wit delivered in the voice of the Kansas City bandleader from Red Bank, New Jersey, is quite often flat, lacking in much human observation, and has long, long dull passages in which we get little more than the band's itinerary. The autobiography is so disappointing, in fact, that Murray felt obligated to write an essay in *The Blue Devils of Nada* to try and explain away its many shortcomings. On aesthetics, however, *Blue Devils* contains not only fine writing about Ellington, Armstrong, and Romare Bearden but a piece as insightful as it is excessively generous to Hemingway, whom Murray tries to make into "an honorary Negro," never seeming to have taken into account what Gene Seymour raised in a review for *The Nation* as he alluded to Roy Campanella, Jr.'s essay in the collection *Cult Baseball Players*: "He calls Hemingway a 'man of active goodwill'—the same Hemingway who, back in the late forties when the Brooklyn Dodgers were in Cuba, barred Jackie Robinson and Roy Campanella from his home while inviting their white teammates inside." To make everything absolutely clear, the great catcher's son wrote, "An oversight? Papa Hemingway specifically requested that the Dodgers bring no black ballplayers." That would only make Hemingway, on that occasion at least, another of those American geniuses who melted down from full height and slipped, as redneck clay in dragon shapes, through holes in their socks when confronted with the Negro. One wonders how skillfully Murray could have handled that question while rightfully praising the Michigan master for his invincible contributions to twentieth-century writing. Would he have remained an "honorary Negro" or would he have become a dishonorable honorary?

Further, if what we see in Negro American popular culture at the moment is as unfortunately vulgar and willfully ignorant as it quite obviously is, Murray's aesthetic ideas are not, as one reviewer pointed out, contemporary at all. As Wynton Marsalis observed in the summer of 1997, when the master trumpeter Clark Terry, who was having problems with his black, uptown audience in a free outdoor performance at Grant's Tomb for the Jazzmobile in New York, went into the great *Jeep's Blues*, assuming to communicate through the time-honored form Murray has celebrated and described as so basic to Negro American culture and what it has to offer the world, "It was amazing." Marsalis added, "Those Negroes had no idea what he was playing. They had no feeling for the form and no emotional rapport at all. He could have been playing to the wind." This suggests nothing other than a crisis in Negro culture, a clear example of serious decay, a formidable loss of taste of the sort that black academics would do well to combat through teaching the work of Murray in an attempt to spark the kind of vital renaissance this country needs, an antidote to the decadence that knows no limits of skin tone or class or anything else.

6. And One, and Two, and Three, and Four Is to Begin at the End

Goethe quickly drew up a plan of action. Since literature had the ability to conquer or transcend differences attributed to time, race, or culture, it had the obligation to do so. The possibility of achieving such a goal became his ideal. Reaching this utopia, this nowhere beyond time and place, became his true vocation, leading him to value only those works in which the questions of "where and when?" could not be resolved with certainty.

Alain Finkielkraut, *The Defeat of the Mind*

While Albert Murray's greatest contribution has been in the arena of thinking about the character and texture of American life at large, his ambition, at least partially, is to write fiction that will parallel the idiomatic power of Duke Ellington, our national composer with the broadest and richest canon. In fact, he often says that all of his other work, whatever anyone thinks of it, is an overture to the fiction he writes. Above all, Murray wants to create a character whose tale proves out his vision of "the dynamics of heroic action." In *The Omni-Americans* he spelled it out like this: "Perhaps every serious writer proceeds on the assumption that a sufficiently vernacular and revolutionary image can be created to initiate a millennium during his generation."

Whether or not the octogenarian Murray will reach that particular goal remains to be seen, especially since all three of his novels zero in on the first-person experiences of an essentially untested hero named Scooter. The eternal schoolboy, Scooter is quite charming and effortlessly brilliant but fails to face, after most has been said and most has been done, the very dragons that the writer himself defines as basic to earning the wings necessary for a position in the heroic pantheon. As Murray writes in *The Hero and the Blues*:

> Promising young men in stories, as in life, do not become heroes by simply keeping their police records clean and their grade point averages high enough to qualify them for status jobs and good addresses inside the castle walls. Nice young men are the salt of society, the soul of respectability, the backbone of the nation, and their faces appear at court functions and their names are recorded on official documents. But those young men who become heroes, whose deeds merit statues, red-letter days, and epics do so by confronting and slaying dragons.

Given *those* criteria, the great hero of Murray's canon is, as he was quite willing to far more than imply in *South to a Very Old Place*, the writer himself. *His* are the deeds that most truly define those "dynamics of heroic action." Though the novels do slash down certain imposed visions of automatic Negro deprivation, the vast majority of the dragons Murray has slain, their hills of bones rising upward and upward, are not in his fiction. In the novels, as Tom Piazza pointed out in an essay on his work published in the *Boston Phoenix*, Murray has assigned the devil beast an offstage position. The dragon never stands at full height in Scooter's path, his claws sharp, his leathery wings expanded, vast sheets of fire roaring up from his belly. Scooter hears some tall tales of all God's dangers but they never actually blight his life. Other than some frightening moments in his childhood, a few powerful initiations into the hard facts of murder—one on water, one on land—Murray's hero never knows terror nor doubt nor confusion nor disillusionment nor heartbreak nor deep loss, the moods and conditions of emotional affliction that the traditional hero must control and transcend in order to triumph over the opposition. Murray is not unaware of those traditions by any means. He just seems to have ignored another of his own dictums from *The Hero and the Blues*: "Indeed, since in the final analysis the greatness of the hero can be measured only in scale with the mischief, malaise, or menace he can dispatch, the degree of cooperation is always equal to the amount of antagonism."

Scooter is also decidedly at the other end from those Negro characters ground into hamburger by racism and wrapped in the butcher-paper prose of propaganda. The writer is going at an about face in an unsuccessful attempt to redefine heroism just as Joyce did when he made his Odysseus an Irish Jew named Leopold Bloom, whose existence was at a tremendous remove from the violent and bloody universe of the wily Greek who wandered so far and so long just trying to get home from Troy to Ithaca.

The goal is a Negro American realization of what is, finally, the aristocratic novel in which the development of sense and sensibility is the central achievement. Therefore, these Scooter novels are about the making of a civilized person whose concerns, while informed by race, are far from limited by it.

Whether set in the South or moving across the length and breadth of the nation, the narrative is tinted by the blues and its propulsion is sometimes informed to the individual syllable by the momentum of swing and the lyricism of the ballroom romantic song, either of courtship or nostalgic reflection. The vision of life that Scooter embraces and puts into more and more of his personal decisions as he grows from childhood into early manhood is infinitely beyond the provincial. It allows and drives him to pick and choose from the world at large and put whatever he likes into the cultural gumbo that is his own personality. In that respect, while only one of the books is completely successful, the Scooter novels are unique in our fiction and stand apart from just about everything else written about Negro life in these United States.

Train Whistle Guitar is an especially good evocation of a Negro childhood in the South of the 1920s. *The Spyglass Tree*, moving the recollections of *South to a Very Old Place* deeper into fiction, supplies us, in its best parts, with another invaluable clarification of how all of those stunning Afro-Americans who came through Negro colleges in the 1930s looked at themselves and at the world, what they learned, and how it made the best of them into the exemplary types whose exploits are only now being recognized within that broad context of triumph, which is just as emblematic of our society as any of its shortcomings. The first two novels are under two hundred pages, but *The Seven League Boots* is almost twice that length and moves through a mythical time frame of such elasticity that the narrative stretches from the middle 1930s to the early 1960s, while never getting stuck in either period and maintaining the kind of continuity only a superior craftsman could bring off. This is even more impressive since only about three years actually pass in the life of the hero!

The Seven League Boots was intended to be the culmination of what Murray has been working toward in his other books, especially the nonfiction, which has introduced most of the ideas that Murray puts in the mouths of his characters, taking a well-formulated analysis of American culture, history, and the universal meanings of aesthetic style into the narrative world of a hero who squeaks his perpetual cleanness through a language inflected and orchestrated by an ear tuned to an impressive stretch of Afro-American rhythms (a "multiplicity of voices from the same land," as Finkielkraut would label it). On the other side, whether white or black, the characters who exist primarily to spout Murray's aesthetic ideas and his unfortunate attempts at epic reverberations, sound like just so much essay palaver:

> That's what the marquis has in mind when he talks about the ideal person that should be the natural product of the American experience, that our schools should be geared to turning out, given the ready accessibility to modern innovations in ever more precise and efficient communication and transportation facilities we enjoy.

Yes, it is often that far from real human talk.

Murray's Scooter is a bass player by the time he arrives in this novel. As such, he is symbolic in his musical register of all bottoms, all lower frequencies, all depths, all of the Southern parts of the Western world, from America to Southern Europe and back. That down-home bottom is the swing porch of Scooter's Alabama childhood; or it is the preparation for swinging in a jazz band that he draws from the communal wisdom of the many different kinds of adults who give him much more than the time of day. Central to that wisdom from the bottom is a sense of inventive interplay, reinterpretation, and adjustment that Scooter comes to comprehend even better through high-flying, witty, and unfortunately pretentious exchanges with his dorm mate, the Snake, as they attend a Negro college quite reminiscent of Tuskegee, Murray's alma mater. The intention is to match the intellectual potency of the conversations in Joyce, Mann, and Malraux, which is admirably ambitious, but the troubles are the same ones that arrive when Scooter talks with white Americans and Europeans: Murray ineffectively attempts to inflate the mythic significance of his narrator until he becomes part Odysseus, part Telemachus, part Jason, part Joseph, part St. George, part Douglass, Armstrong, and Ellington.

Scooter's pride in his roots centers this traveling man's rhythmic trilogy. Murray's point is that his hero, from baby talk to college chatter, gets everything necessary to assess the world and adapt to its demands through the folk and formal instruction of his own background. That background is one in which white people play no significant part in the flesh, where all of the teachers are Negroes of one sort or another, from illiterate talespinners to lovers and discussers of books. This arena of instruction is as rich as just about any other and Scooter draws his various lessons from an increasingly demanding context of fun and games. The *Homo ludens*–derived world of play, the point at which the species achieves the freedom that comes of invention—evolves into the novel's ultimate context. That vision of Man-the-Player expands from intellectual jam sessions in college to the professional bandstand playing of a jazz orchestra and, finally, becomes Scooter's personal willingness to quite seriously horse around with the mysteries of art and artistic style wherever and however they appear. Along the way, all of the significant playmates, manual laborers, barbers, main squeezes, war veterans, barrel house denizens, prostitutes, musicians, and professional illuminators of the classroom make Scooter feel that the very best accomplishments of mankind are both worthy of his pursuit and demanded by the dreams the youngster's people have for him, those projected but democratically imprecise aspirations that Murray dubs "the ancestral imperative." In other words, lofty achievement in the field of choice.

Beyond that, *The Seven League Boots* is a very ingenious realization of the bass metaphor in literary form, an orchestration that is nostalgic, didactic, romantic, humorous, and whimsical. At some points, one is reminded of the way Ellington assigned the innovative bassist Jimmy Blanton to improvise interludes between the composed statements of the full band. Those bass improvisations, known as "breaks," ended up with the lower strings seeming to say, "This is what those orchestrated full band melody lines make me remember and spark me to invent." At other places, one recalls how Ellington gave the full poetic assignment of the featured melody line to the bass in *Sonnet in Search of a Moor,* from his Shakespearean suite, *Such Sweet Thunder.* In specific literary technique, it goes like this: Everything, no matter the race or the class or the place, is underlined by a contrapuntal set of flashbacks in italics that take the reader into some aspect of Scooter's Southern preparation. Those italicized passages constitute the experiential bass notes of the hero's earlier life, the human resolutions to the fundamentals of the outer world's chords, the deep, deep triads that sing up from the bottomless well of the past. (Among its many purposes, the design of *The Seven League Boots* may also constitute a rejoinder to the metaphoric order of *The System of Dante's Hell* by LeRoi Jones, an autobiographical novel from 1965 that is uncommonly influenzed by jazz in its rhythmic flights, equally as filled with literary allusion as anything of Murray's but far more esoteric at the same time that it is shockingly confessional. In Jones's novel, Negroes in Newark, New Jersey, twist and turn and destroy each other in various circles of torture. But, using the geography of the nation's map for his own spirited variation on Dante, Jones makes the South the very lowest point in Hell: Bigoted violence rules, Negroes receive short sentences for killing each other, and the Devil resides not in a block of ice but hidden beneath a house at night, a white man on his knees stage-whispering lewd sexual propositions to young Negro men as they pass in the darkness.) And since Murray chooses to have his Scooter toy with the wandering associations of Odysseus, another Southern boy, we are apt to notice by the end of the novel that the bull fiddle player—his spyglass tree of symbolic omniscience transformed into a jet plane—returns home, just as his creator did in *South to a Very Old Place.* The lyric line along which the third novel progresses resolves as Scooter, his fingers crossed, anticipates reunion with a thinly drawn Negro Penelope. The homing pigeon structure was probably inspired by this passage in John A. Kouwenhoven's *The Beer Can by the Highway:*

> Our history is in the process of motion into and out of cities; of westerning and the counter-process of return; of motion up and down the social ladder—a long, complex, and sometimes terrifyingly rapid se-

quence of consecutive change. And it is this sequence, and the attitudes and habits and forms which it has bred, to which the term
"America" really refers.

Surely inspired by the short list that Stephen Dedalus made in *Portrait of the Artist,* moving him from town to country to continent to planet
to universe, Murray's Negro American frame of refined experience is designed to be inclusive of (and in vital dialogue with) the arts, popular
entertainment, sports, cuisine, society, education, politics, and so on.
In brief, a world. *Train Whistle Guitar* is the first novel and it develops
around the information gathered through two senses, the ear and the eye.
Scooter learns almost everything either from hearing a tale told or from
seeing something happen. When he begins reading children's stories, the
eye takes on a different function. In that first novel, we can easily see that
Murray went in the opposite direction from what Diderot called, in visual
art, "moral painting." Diderot meant raising ordinary human events to the
state of human tragedy. But when Murray takes the ordinary Southern
Negro situation, which is often no more than some Negroes sitting around
talking, he transforms it to the condition of human affirmation. Here arrives Murray's ongoing polemical point, from novel to novel: being a good
little boy and listening to the wisdom of the elders is the way one absorbs
the fundamentals of an oral tradition as well as all the determination necessary to extend those fundamentals into a richer intellectual world but
one that is no more human, finally, than where one began. Doing one's
work and playing by the rules when they're right and planning to change
them when they are wrong is the best way to go forward in this life.
    Train Whistle Guitar is full of rhythm and syncopation, memories and
many voices, each element used to realize the kind of jazz influence American novelists and short story writers have been periodically struggling to
bring to the art of fiction since the 1920s. Superbly evocative and a poetic
epic, the novel shows its hero discovering through the story of his forebears that he is obligated to make the high end of its aspirations come true
through his own accomplishments. In ways that bring together the arche-
type and the plausible character, Murray invents figures who represent
certain backgrounds and are composites of Negro American history in the

flesh—ex-slaves, folk blues players and sophisticated jazzmen, World War I veterans, schoolteachers, and so on. This allows the boy to look history in the face and listen to what it has to say through the people who know what they know. So Scooter hears tell of many things, the broad lore of the omni-directional bloodline, and comes upon one man murdered in some bootlegging mixup, another stabbed to death by his girlfriend, and is told of yet another who has been done in by the down-home legend of barrelhouse piano, Stagolee DuPas. The latter scene might be a variation on a violent moment in Faulkner's "Pantaloon in Black." Stagolee has to put a concluding exclamation point to the deputy's life because the redneck kicks the keys off the piano, which is the symbol, in this context, of the harmonizing blues powers that men like DuPas have become famous for.

(This fight to the death that Scooter doesn't actually see arrives again in *The Spyglass Tree* as an act of racist violence, and once more near the end of *The Seven League Boots*, appearing there as a professional boxing match. Scooter, now a veteran of bandstands and expensive boudoirs, is caught off guard and misses the moment when his friend begins to lose the bout. In a work of negligible dramatic impact, this third variation seems an attempt to bring off what Burke observed about a favorite Murray novel in *The Philosophy of Literary Form:* "Horrors strike deeper when they strike out of a sweet and gentle context, as the highly contradictory genius of Thomas Mann's *The Magic Mountain* testifies. When they do strike, note how they strike: for one has been responding to the humanity of humans; one has been warmed; one presumably is aglow—and then of a sudden one sees the human concentration-points of courage and tenderness blasted into hell.")

In *The Spyglass Tree*, Jug Hamilton of *South to a Very Old Place* has become the fictional young man from the North, Snake or Snake Doctor, replacing the partner that Scooter had in *Train Whistle*, Little Buddy Marshall, who was kind of a boyhood Falstaff, a person who traveled with the developing prince into the lower reaches of the gutbucket. (Little Buddy's final meeting with Scooter before he hops a train and leaves town has a cutting melancholy and is the culmination of the twelfth chapter that, in its entirety and its focus on loss, is some of Murray's most well executed and moving writing. The exit from his life of such a great friend is perhaps the moment when the narrator's childhood most truly ends: he is now on the verge of entering arenas too big for Buddy, whose own universe is now too small for Scooter.) As was noted before, when Murray was reminiscing in tempo about Hamilton in the earlier book, we got an insight into the intellectual development, pride, and raucous humor of young Negroes during the Depression years. This same theme dominates the second novel, which is not as exciting as *Train Whistle* though it, too, has very good portraiture. Murray pulls the feel and smell of the seasons to the page and the details of coming into early manhood within the environment of a college world made storybook rich by the scholastic introduction to new worlds and ideas, all of which are undergirded and counterpointed by the cultural bass line lessons Scooter picks up from the sturdy Negro men and women whom he becomes attached to in situations beyond the campus, where he expands himself, again, by listening, watching, and obeying.

There is a lot of learning and there are a good number of flashbacks and flash-forwards; the game of controlling time—the nub of the novel at large—is played so that every moment or situation is part of time past, time present, and time future: Murray's orchestration of what Eliot meant by "the present moment of the past." When telling the tale of Will Spradley, a Negro beaten and terrified by a redneck he's sure will kill him, the writer also uses a version of the high-handed technique Melville pulled out in *Moby Dick* when he freed up the narrative line so that Ishmael could move, at will, from the first to the third person and into the mind of another character. Murray is not as bold as Melville, however, for he finds it necessary to explain the shift in narrative by having Scooter tell the reader that Spradley "had told me about his trouble with Dudley Philpot so many times over and in such personal detail that forever thereafter I was to feel that I had not only been an eyewitness but had also been a party to it step by step, breath by breath." Still insecure almost a hundred pages later, Murray writes, "He recounted everything, not only word for word but sometimes also thought for thought and almost breath for breath for breath. So much so that it was not only as if you were an eye and ear witness but also the actual participant himself."

Spradley's offense leads to a wonderfully tense and nearly violent confrontation between Dudley Philpot and Giles Cunningham, a sophisticated Negro businessman who is the second Ellington variation to find himself locking horns with a Southern racist, the first being Stagolee Dupas, who stood up to a bigot with a badge in *Train Whistle Guitar*. The fear felt by Spradley allows Murray to make variations on the "prayer" at the end of "A Clean, Well-Lighted Place" by playing on the idea that even accidental infringements of white privilege can lead to death: *"Ain't none of it nothing and here I is, all messed up in the middle of it. All tangled and mangled up in it like this and it ain't nothing and ain't about nothing. . . . All of this now. All of this and it ain't nothing, plain flat-out nothing . . . I ain't done nothing. I ain't said nothing and ain't done nothing. I ain't done nothing to nobody."* The memories of childhood, always the best parts of Murray's fiction, are masterful in their sound and in the feeling of discovery. One of Scooter's memories is of an adolescent romance with a white girl that sets up a motif which interweaves with Snake's further development of the kind of coupling Ellington referred to, in his *Deep South Suite*, by the name *When Nobody Was Looking*. The segment also allows Murray the opportunity to describe how the looks of certain models associated with Manhattan or East Coast aristocracy were actually no more than what the world saw when white Southern beauties made it into the big time up North. (In *The Seven League Boots*, interracial romance is taken up again in two instances, but neither adult female character is anywhere as real as the girl in *The Spyglass Tree*. One is an upper-class tramp whose name, Fay Morgan, plays at least four ways with literature, region, and slang, alluding to Morgan le Fay, the sorceress and sister of King Arthur; to "ofays" or "fays," the pig latin black slang for whites; and to the Morgan horse developed in Vermont, which, by the way, slyly connects to the Negro description of big, pretty women as "stallions." The other white woman is a movie star whose name is Jewel Templeton. Temple jewel—get it? Of course, "family jewels" is a seasoned slang term for testicles. Mix 'em up and roll 'em, Pete—I mean Scooter.)

In artistic terms, *The Spyglass Tree* is deeply flawed by the fact that just about everybody loves Scooter so much that he has little resistance to his dreams. The college boy isn't ever truly tested. He never really feels tempted to do anything other than stay on the straight and narrow. The desire to run away with Little Buddy was thwarted for good in the first novel. But here is where we see the didactic and personal ideology that is a cyclical, propaganda theme begin to take an ever larger position in the novels, creating another form of determinism, one imposed by the writer himself. Warren Carson wrote of this problem in an essay about Murray that was published in the *African American Review*: "Essentially, Scooter behaves as we expect him to behave, achieves what we expect him to achieve, and thanks and celebrates whom and what we know he will, based on the course he set upon in *Train Whistle Guitar*." In the first novel when the blues-plucking, twelve-string-guitar player known as Luzana Cholly stops Scooter and Little Buddy from hopping a train out of town, their very own folk hero in the flesh starts mashing the writer's point of view—"the ancestral imperative"—on the two boys: "He said the young generation was supposed to take what they were already born with and learn how to put it with everything the civil engineers and inventors and doctors and lawyers and bookkeepers had found out about the world and be the one to bring about the day the old folks had always been prophesying and praying for." Did I hear somebody say Messiah?

One of the things that *The Spyglass Tree* does quite well is show how the nature of racial confrontation changed according to the place. Southern racial convention, what the narrator calls "that very old and very grim down-home game," wasn't hard and fast. There were Negro laborers who didn't take anything off of white people, Negroes who gathered and were so ready to do war with the Ku Klux Klan that when the boys in the sheets found out what was in wait for them they satisfied their urges with a march and the burning of "a chickenshit cross." In the college town when a problem arises between Philpot and Giles Cunningham, things come close to sparking some serious racial atrocities, but are settled by interracial cooperation between the highly positioned in the white and Negro communities, preparing the way for what happens to Scooter when he moves through the fairy tale world of *The Seven League Boots*, simply gliding along and astonishing one person after another, no matter how accomplished, no matter how great, no matter how understandably legendary. Yet the bass line fails because what only slightly mottled *South to a Very Old Place* devastates the third novel: The legions of the Scooter-awed must sink down into passages such as the almost unbelievably embarrassing farewell speech from the movie star who couldn't be allowed to

stop once she had called him *El hombre de época* a hundred pages earlier:
Jewel Templeton must continue and continue and continue to tell us how
wonderful the guy is and how thankful she and all her friends are that
Scooter was ever born. The two are in France, sitting in her Jaguar, and
have met her friend the Marquis de Chaumienne, who is a jazz fan and another person for the narrator to test his intellectual mettle on:

> When I turned to kiss her and go because it was time to move to the
> boarding line, there was her voice vibrating that close again and her
> saying, I really must thank you once more for being so wonderful
> with the marquis, who thinks you're just fantastic. Oh, it was as if I
> had used my magic movie star wand to conjure up a golden brown
> storybook prince who was by way of becoming the very embodiment
> of what the music you play is all about.
>
> Oh, I very much doubt that anybody from *Burke's Peerage* or
> the *Almanac de Gotha* could match your impact on him. As for my-
> self there you were once more as you were the night I accosted you
> as you stood at the curb outside The Keynote with your arm around
> the neck and shoulders of that rich toned earth brown earth mother
> of a bass fiddle looking for all the world as if you had just alighted
> from a foam flecked steed. Oh, I must say, she said.

No character as hip as Murray would like us to think that Scooter is
ready to cite such overwrought, tin-eared praise. Would that the writer
had done something with the insecure narcissism and coat-of-paint-thin
humility his character exudes, obviously troubled by his illegitimate pa-
ternity but constantly covering it over with an international cast of flatterers. That in itself is enough of an internal dragon to have given him
something to struggle against.

Then there is the stuff about music. In *The Seven League Boots*,
Scooter's partner becomes Joe States, the drummer with the jazz orchestra
of The Bossman Himself, Murray's version of Duke Ellington. The Bossman is always thanking Scooter for setting aside his studies and doing him
the large favor of coming out with the band, while the jazz band itself is
unlike any ever read about or known. Everyone likes and respects every-

one else. There are no internal rivalries, no enmities, not even a shouting match. It is jazz heaven on wheels, a gathering of brown angels so false only a devoted maker of fairy tales like Murray would have the nerve to put on paper. The temptations—and trademarks—of alcohol, whoring, reefers, gambling, and heroin never appear. Nor are there any gifted musicians who are exasperating and get a wide berth because—no matter their problems with addiction, their prickly personalities, their arrogance, their selfishness, their gloom, their narcissism, their jealousy of the leader—they sound so good that it would either be irrational or impossible to replace them. Murray again ignores his own aesthetic positions, such as this one from *The Omni-Americans:* "There is first of all the serious novelist's complex awareness of the burdensome but sobering fact that there is some goodness in bad people however bad they are, and some badness or at least some flaw or weakness in good people however dear."

Every last one of the musicians, by the way, is in awe of Scooter, who has now become Schoolboy, the golden child of the road band world— "You hear that deep stuff Schoolboy is saying?" But this Schoolboy never really convinces us that he is a musician, especially through the senses. This is odd for one so given to Hemingway's dictums of weight, balance, smell, texture, sight, temperature. We never get any physical sense of even carrying the fragile thing that is a bass, much less working one's way through the pain of calluses, battling to stay in tune, learning how to hear one's place in a rhythm section, developing different strategies of accompaniment, exchanging and transforming phrases in the high-speed combination of catch, hot potato, tennis, and teamwork that is the essence of rhythm section playing. Finally, the unexplainable difficulties of consistently sounding good don't face this band, which never has an off night, one on which the players either can't catch or can't hold a groove. Everything is always in musical place so that Scooter can say: "That was the way things got going that first night, and the next night just picked up where we left off and kept going, and the same thing happened the night after that and night after that and after that."

This latest of the Scooter novels, even so, offers a whole batch of extremely good writing and a mythical time frame that allows Murray to realize what the down-home singer Hortense Hightower said to his hero in

The Spyglass Tree when she, pushed forward by an obvious pun, gave him the bass that had been in her basement, "I already know how you whistle and hum along and how you don't just *keep* time but also have to play around with it." Yes, the time frame is quite impressive, not only in its spanning about three years and about thirty years at the same time, but in its sidestepping World War II, the Cold War, the Civil Rights Movement, and the Balkanizing arrival of black nationalism. There we have the dual identity of the book. The upside of Murray's structure allows for exceptional plasticity of scene and place that is perhaps innovative, with Scooter realizing his personal nickname of "Jack the Rabbit" by fluidly moving through the briar patch of eras that modulate like musical meters and keys; the downside finds the writer picking and choosing only the pleasant aspects of experience in that masterfully executed three-decade sweep. This means that the character's conquest of time present, time past, and time future is never jarring, but it does become a device that frustrates the possibility of dramatic intensity. If something unpleasantly real might take place, the narrative either stops short of the inevitable or shifts to a later period when such a problem had been conquered. That is why when the band members travel to the segregated South, they don't get off the bus, which would reveal the undifferentiated contempt that forced celebrated Negroes into piss-poor accommodations or the private homes of local black people. Instead, Murray's musicians trade observations about the Civil War and Southern military statues. This eluding device also allows the writer to have The Bossman and his musicians stay in first-class Hollywood hotels and motels that they could not have in the 1930s or the 1940s, when Negro musicians lived in the Dunbar Hotel on Central Avenue, the black mainstem of what is now known as South Central Los Angeles. It reminds one of the complaint that Hemingway made about how protective James Joyce was of Stephan Dedalus. The result is that Murray's strategy, however impressive, still removes his Scooter from the heroic world of endeavor central to the writer's own aesthetic.

Then there is the question of feeling. Unlike the wonder-and-warts of *The Spyglass Tree* in which there was a visceral realization of blood and thunder whirling *around* Scooter in a much more compelling universe of inspiration, wisdom, humor, eroticism, risk, danger, and human pain, this novel is spiritually and emotionally air-brushed clean of all deep hurt and heavy trouble. It makes no attempt to show us, from the top to the bottom, the varieties of human experience found in that second novel, varieties that clearly add much of substance to American fiction, whatever the novel's overall drawbacks as a work of art. Truly serious human problems of the sort that usually make for superior fiction wouldn't have fit in the contrived emotional narrows of Scooter's world, and might have demanded something more of him than close listening and coolly intelligent responses. He might have gotten heated up about something, or felt the weight of the age with some actual depth, or known the gloom that followed the arrival of the atomic bomb or the shocking Nuremberg blues that became international with the detailed atrocities of the Nazi war criminals, or he might even have been tempted to take some kind of actual risk, or felt some doubt. At the very least, the bass-playing supposed hero might have had to set someone straight who wasn't overly impressed by his vision of life or his experiences (which he did in a rather contrived and, par for the course, *near-scrape* with some winos in the second novel). The dragon might then have stood tall and "the dynamics of confrontation" would have had to become literal, not just another subject for the exceptional to slick musings of Scooter and his fellow intellectuals, black and white, North and South, here and in Europe. In this much broader human context, Murray's hero might have then come to grips with what his creator said in *The Omni-Americans*, "The unpredictable is the very stuff of storytelling. It is the very stuff of dramatic power, suspense, thrills, escapades, resolutions; the very stuff of fears, hopes, quests, achievements. It is the very stuff of the human condition."

Either attempting to fictionally realize his total war with the conventional renditions of Negro life as one set of overwhelming troubles and brutalizations after another, or perhaps now incapable of coming to terms with the literary demands of unsentimentally rendered disillusionment and human suffering, Murray has gone too far in the opposite direction. Of course, no true American writer should offer us the clichés of racial antipathy that amount to a hand-me-down stack of extinguished matches, all literary illumination charred out; the job, as Pound would have it, is making a match that strikes—burning and lighting anew. Scooter does not prevail over any bracing confrontations so inventively remade that we experience something we think we know with the freshness that artistic conquest—as with some of the racial troubles in *The Spyglass Tree*—makes possible. In this virtuoso fairy tale, there are no dues and no blues.

That may be why the central character lacks any spiritual fire or mystery. This problem also arrived in *The Spyglass Tree* when Scooter was drafted to ride shotgun toward a potentially violent situation that might have ended all of his dreams for good or sent him fleeing town for participating in a shoot-out or brutally landed him in jail. None of this crosses Scooter's mind, though he displays omni-directional contemplation whenever anything else of import takes place. Much like an automaton, the young man (as usual) listens to his elders, follows orders, and goes along, sometimes wishing he were back on campus but never feeling any deep dread, any cold fear, any resentful misgivings—none of the underlying emotions that would have made his involvement a decision expressive of courage, something Murray's man Hemingway was surely well aware of and used quite skillfully to make his own creations actual heroes, not main characters who were constantly referred to as such but did nothing—internally or externally—to earn the appellation.

On the other hand, when such a superior talent is at work, you have to avoid assuming how everything will go. There is one marvelous exception of twenty-five exquisite pages. Scooter, who is now living in Los Angeles with the white movie star, visits a Negro woman whom he met earlier in the novel, shortly after he had joined The Bossman's band. The woman, a Calypso remade to blues contours, is enamored of musicians and emotionally full-figured. She is quite ready to tease him, express envy and bitterness toward the white woman, tell him wild erotic tales, explain her own willingness to be kept by white men, and show Scooter the sort of delicate to contradictory human feeling wistfully unmatched by any of the other characters he encounters. Were the rest of the cast as fully drawn as she is, this might be some sort of a masterpiece, since we meet so many faces in so many places, almost every one of them no more than eloquent but servile talking heads. If they aren't assigned to reiterate the ideology of "the ancestral imperative" in didactic cadences, the writer inducts them into an argument so repetitious and one-sided that the case for jazz as a major twentieth-century art is, I'm sure, unintentionally turned into a mantra of special pleading.

But Albert Murray is much more than your normal fox. He is not finished with Scooter, and the way in which he is given to playing so boldly and brilliantly with time, place, and situation, we have no idea what he's putting together right now. The grit and improvisational verve of *South to a Very Old Place* surely prove that, illustrating so skillfully how the weights of racism didn't diminish the vitality of a people or reduce their ability to identify with the problems of man's fate—decay, dissolution, disillusionment, and death. Whatever that future book might be, it will surely maintain the vision of one of our most original writers and thinkers, a presence in our culture we should be grateful for and honor while we can.

Somebody Knew

1.

      Few American memoirs have opened up the intellectual essences and the human quirks of a major urban community as well as Anatole Broyard's *Kafka Was the Rage*. Broyard achieved national fame as a book reviewer for the *New York Times,* and his recollections of living in Greenwich Village just after World War II, while brief, are so well executed that the little book seems to me an essential part of what New Yorkers and those interested in the nation's intellectual history ought to give a close reading. The focus is predominantly on the literary community of the time but the observations are so shrewd that they bring forward many of the issues that gum up our moment. At exactly the same time that we understand much better how different America was then, we also recognize in some measure why our nation has had such a terrible time resolving the oppositions of privilege and resentment, love and sex, adventure and masochism, freedom and repression. Though surprisingly wacky, his was still a much more innocent America than ours.

2.

Broyard's name was recently recycled through the circles of gab after a long and elegant *New Yorker* gossip piece revealed that the writer lived out his professional life "passing for white." Uh oh. Written by the ubiquitous Skip Gates, the piece called upon the memories of many who had known Broyard, personally or professionally or both. One friend remembered Broyard being black in Brooklyn but turning white by the time he got off the subway stop at West Fourth Street and Sixth Avenue in Greenwich Village. The piece kicked up so much dust because Broyard, who died in 1990, had made a reputation for himself as a number of things—a Village intellectual, an owner of a used-book store, a ladies' man, and a respected book reviewer—none of them under the flag of Negro.

Born in 1920, he was from New Orleans and had moved to Brooklyn with his family as a child, the reluctant brother sandwiched between an older and a younger sister, the former light-skinned, the latter too dark to get over the racial fence. The younger sister was a secret Broyard kept from his two children by an "officially" white woman whom he met in 1961. Broyard climbed the fence and never looked back. This was a guy not particularly interested in the narrows of Negro culture as it was defined at the time. Constantly discussing the few black writers worthy of analysis had no place among his deepest concerns. Jazz wasn't an aesthetic and spiritual emblem for him. In opposition to Negro writers, superb, good, mediocre, and bad, he considered jazz a bracing folk art encumbered by hopeless complaint and an aggressive sentimentality mistaken for wisdom. He didn't approve of building an identity on the stance of the outsider. Broyard wanted to get all the way into America, no limitations imposed. This is made very explicit in the memoir as he recalls sitting down with Delmore Schwartz, Dwight MacDonald, and Clement Greenberg. Schwartz had accepted an article of Broyard's for *Partisan Review*, "Portrait of the Hipster:"

> They were talking about the primitive: Picasso, D.H. Lawrence, and Hemingway; bullfighting and boxing. I was a bit uneasy, because my piece was about jazz and the attitudes surrounding it, and I didn't want to be typecast as an aficionado of the primitive. I wanted to be a literary man, like them. I felt too primitive to be comfortable talking about the primitive.

There it is. And there it isn't. Had we realized what we have yet to get straight, that there is a Negro culture but no Negro race, Broyard would have just been another writer in flight from his personal or ethnic background, like so many Jews, Catholics, Italians, Southerners, Irish, and so on. While there are those who will hold that against him, assuming that he had repudiated his racial duty as a sentry or a point rider, no such vision of duty matters when one goes through his memoir. Oh, the blood-line facts that are left out may glare very brightly every great once in a while but those omissions are made largely insignificant by a caustic wit delivered with such controlled, worldly insight that it never abandons grace in the interest of cruelty. The memoir's title is made more than appropriate by the very deep melancholy, the needling anxiety, and the oppressive feeling of inadequacy, of having done something so hickishly wrong that no one feels required to explain what it is. "You'll never be a man," one of his lovers says, intent on knocking him off balance, "until you can live without explanations." Its complexity and frustration makes this an intelligent book for adults.

3.

When Anatole Broyard was discharged from the army fifty years go, America wasn't yet steeped in the violence, hostility, and trash that it is now. The pornography issues hadn't been fought to the point that *Hustler* can be bought on most newsstands across America;

there had been no sexual revolution; ethnic, racial, and genital narcissism hadn't pushed our Humpty-Dumpty optimism off the wall; the battle between high and low wasn't resolved by the high raffishly imitating the low, if they weren't mirroring the very bottom desperately or self-consciously; even Lenny Bruce had yet to open the way for *Def Comedy Jam*. Then was another time. While we know all of that in so many ways, what makes *Kafka Was the Rage* so good is how distinctly it clarifies the ancestral line of so much willfully offensive contemporary material. The experiences rendered take place during the writer's middle twenties but it is still a coming-of-age tale in which this greenhorn goes along, questions, assesses, and pulls away from the herd. Broyard eventually realizes that shock, no matter how contrived, was what some people in the Village assumed was good enough to stand in for originality. Rebellion against middle-range standards resulted in contrived behavior, dirty apartments, dress that could cross the line into costumes, weirdly fashioned ways of talking, and oddly gullible responses to the untested ideas of the period: the pioneer spirit screwed up and put on a boomerang double-whammy. Broyard outlines the overall mood in his italicized introduction:

> *The tragedy—and the comedy—of my story was that I took American life to heart and with the kind of strenuous and ardent sincerity that young men usually bring to love affairs. While some of my contemporaries made a great show of political commitment, it seems to me that their politicizing of experience abstracted them from the ordinary, from the texture of things. They saw only a Platonic idea of American life. To use one of their favorite words, they were alienated. I was not. In fact, one of my problems was that I was alienated from alienation, an insider among outsiders. The young intellectuals I knew had virtually read and criticized themselves out of any feeling of nationality.*

This is an example of what I meant earlier. Since we now know that Broyard was something of a Jay Gatsby, his own actual alienation would have made this passage even richer but what he detected still has an importance. It foreshadows the animosity toward America that has taken so many forms over the last half-century, on and off campuses. The flight from "any feeling of nationality" not overwhelmed by guilt or bitterness began to get a Manhattan head of steam in the middle 1940s, when the hatred of America became a staple of the New School for Social Research:

> Known as the "University in Exile," the New School had taken in a lot of professors—Jewish and non-Jewish—who had fled from Hitler on the same boats as the psychoanalysts. Because they were displaced themselves, or angry with us for failing to understand history, the professors did their best to make us feel like exiles in our own country. While the psychoanalysts listened in their private offices— with all the detachment of those who had really known anxiety— to Americans retailing their dreams, the professors analyzed those same dreams wholesale in the packed classrooms of the New School.
>
> All the courses I took were about *what's wrong:* what's wrong with the government, with the family, with interpersonal relationships and interpersonal relations—what's wrong with our dreams, our loves, our jobs, our perceptions and conceptions, our esthetics, the human condition itself.

The following passage makes the verbal floggings that the students received seem very obvious foreshadowings of the highly influential racial and "revolutionary" harangues Malcolm X popularized:

> They were furious, the professors, at the ugly turn the world had taken and they stalked the halls of the New School as if it were a concentration camp where we were the victims and they were the warders, the storm troopers of humanism . . .

Here Broyard satirizes the pain and pleasure found in the circumstances that evolved from what he calls "a blind date with culture [on which] anything could happen":

> We admired the German professors. We had won the fight against fascism and now, with their help, we would defeat all the dark forces

in the culture and the psyche. As a reaction to our victory, sensitive Americans had entered an apologetic phase in our national life and there was nothing the professors could say that was too much. We came out of class with dueling scars.

Surely, those "scars" were not marks of shame but of accomplishment, of having sat there and taken it straight in the face: intellectual emblems of what Faulkner said of Dilsey's people: "They endured." Those students on the blind date with European condemnation were ready to maintain a brave silence when the phantom of American society, Uncle Sam, had his mask ripped off.

Those kids at the New School were one thing, New York intellectuals were another. Broyard recognized that they were "more lost" than the Paris generation of Hemingway and Fitzgerald. His insights into Delmore Schwartz and what he represented speed right across the plate:

> While the writers of the twenties had lost only their illusions, Delmore, the typical New York intellectual of the forties, seemed to have lost the world itself. It was as if these men had been blinded by their reading. Their heads were so filled with books, fictional characters, and symbols that there was no room for the raw data of actuality. They couldn't see the small, only the large. They still thought of ordinary people as the proletariat, or the masses.
>
> I wanted to be an intellectual, too, to see life from a great height, yet I didn't want to give up my sense of connection, my intimacy with things. When I read, I always kept one eye on the world, like someone watching the clock.

The echoes of Hemingway smacking Henry James around in *Green Hills of Africa* notwithstanding, Broyard had wrestled a greasy pig to the ground. He saw how difficult it was—and still is, I might add—to get the heavens, the skyline, the feel of life, and the quality of the earth into one intellectual frame. Intelligent rhetoric and the gleam of the aesthete are sometimes so strong that we become vulnerable to theories covered with academic petroleum jelly. Such theories might leave the glimmers of their slipperiness but nothing close to thorough comprehension of the convolutions, the many moods, and the cosmopolitan bloodlines that make American life so cussedly inimitable.

Broyard, using Schwartz as an example, was looking at the complaints about the inadequacy of the perspectives of those particular Jewish intellectuals in Greenwich Village who seemed so held back by European references and preimmigration obsessions that they were incapable of getting into the surge and turmoil of American life. As Marshall McLuhan might have said, and as Barbara Solomon has examined in *Smart Hearts for the City*, Broyard was talking about those Jews who ride forward in an American car while hypnotized by the East European ghettos in the rearview mirror—whether or not they ever lived in them! The writer also recognized a personal variation on those tendencies in his own psychology, which was quite different but still walled in by the many books that he preferred to the flesh and blood of his own family and all that they represented to him.

It is his willingness to show up his own foolishness and pretension that keeps Broyard's acidic readings of his fellow bohemians from becoming self-serving or expressions of musty prejudices dusted off in an avant-garde world. He was conflicted but almost always one of them, as self-absorbed and bent on inventing a self that would remedy his background as everyone else, no matter their ethnic, class, or religious roots. His relatives of choice were authors and their words on paper:

> They were all the family I had now, all the family I wanted. With them, I could trade in my embarrassingly hypothetical life, unencumbered by memory, loyalties, or resentments. The first impulse of adolescence is to wish to be an orphan or an amnesiac. Nobody in the Village had a family. We were all sprung from our own brows, spontaneously generated the way flies were once thought to have originated.
>
> I didn't yet see the tragedy of my family: I still thought of them as a farce, my laughable past. In my new incarnation, in books I could be halfway heroic, almost tragic. I could be happy, for the first time, in my tragedy.

One of Broyard's triumphs of skill comes when he brings onomatopoeia to the fore as he describes the Latin dancing at Park Plaza,
summoning the steps and the percussion to the page:

> In Afro-Cuban dancing, one dragged the beat, like postponing or-
> gasm, witholding assent, resisting, buying time. Nobody danced on
> the beat—nothing was ever that simple. Here at Park Plaza, everyone
> skillfully toyed with the rhythm, and it was exciting to see so many
> people triumphing over time, at least for the moment. They all
> seemed competent. It was like a society with no failures.

When depicting an affair with a loony and manipulative abstract
painter named Sheri, Broyard arrives at a sexual intimacy free of the
pornographic. His descriptions of couplings contain the revelations of
personality, the psychological and emotional appetites. We also read of
the acceptance and the rejection, the questions and the oblique answers
that arrive in the sexual act, where two people come to know each other
as they can in no other way, sometimes not to their newly informed ela-
tion but to their enveloping sorrow. "Sheri understood, as we do today,
that sex belongs to depression as much as joy," he writes. "She knew that
it is a place where all sorts of expectations and illusions come to die. Two
people making love, she once said, are like one drowned person resusci-
tating the other."

He also makes other kinds of observations about sex that lift us into
another arena of contemplation, where the mystery of compacted interior
animation that we call a spirit makes itself felt:

> In *Portnoy's Complaint*, Portnoy says that underneath their skirts
> girls all have cunts. What he didn't say—and this was his trouble,
> his real complaint—was that underneath their skirts they also had
> souls. When they were undressed, I saw their souls as well as their
> cunts. They wore their souls like negligées that they never took off.
> And one man in a million knows how to make love to a soul.
>
> Sex in 1947 was like one of those complicated toys that comes
> disassembled, in one hundred pieces, and without instructions . . .

Because they didn't know how to make love, girls made gestures. They offered their idiosyncrasies as a kind of passion. In their nervousness, they brought out other, totally dissociated forms of extremity. They gave me their secret literature, their repressed poems and stories, their dances.

One of the things we've lost is the terrific *coaxing* that used to go on between men and women, the man pleading with the girl and the girl pleading with him to be patient. I remember the feeling of being incandescent with desire, blessed with it, of talking wonderfully, like singing an opera. It was a time of exaltation, this coaxing, as if I was calling up out of myself a better and more deserving man. Perhaps this is as pure a feeling as men and women ever have.

The book continually makes its way in those terms, snatching entire personalities and collective moods with a few words, musing over how many were wounded or destroyed when their interior needs ricocheted against the exterior demands of the period, and how difficult it was to communicate even the most direct emotions when the lover or the dying close friend was closed off by theories and postures. Above all else, *Kafka Was the Rage* is a tribute to New York and to writing. Only a very great city could have inspired Anatole Broyard to speak of heartbreak, death, joy, personal shortcomings, and disillusionment with such sustained and soulful clarity.

PART FIVE

Foreign Intrigue:

Some Dateline

Ganders and

Musings

Downstairs
Blues Upstairs

With all due respect for the dead, I must say that I never got it. Princess Diana was just another privileged person who received an inordinate amount of attention. But her life proved out B.B. King's observation that he had heard people say things in very high places that sounded just like the low-down dirty blues to him. The high-speed Mercedes-Benz death was a brutal tragedy, like that of any young and divorced parent trying to make something out of a messy life. Beyond that, I don't get it.

As an American, I also didn't feel that she was especially intelligent or classy or particularly attractive. We have flesh and blood women from every race, class, and religion who go far beyond her on every one of those levels. In any objective sense, there are American women in law, the arts, politics, science, business, education and whatever else, who should be considered far more aristocratic than she was. Some of them even rose from beneath the underdog to set new standards.

What Diana benefitted from was her public manipulation of an outdated concept of aristocracy, an idea of bloodline importance that I find repulsive in our time. Blood accounts for nothing. It doesn't guarantee brilliance or courage or sacrifice or anything of substance. It doesn't guarantee that you *won't* have any of those qualities either. Exceptional people are mysterious. They come from any place and every place, which is what our democratic conception fundamentally recognizes.

In England, "royalty" now means no more than palace displays of toy ritual and dull people on gold-braided welfare stumbling into the walls of life. There, in our time of talk television, Diana became more "real" than the other parasites in the palace because she resorted to airing dirty linen in a 1995 BBC interview.

That evening must have been terribly embarrassing to her two sons, whom the crocodile-teared press continues to remind us "meant more to her than anything else." Had her children actually meant so much, especially the very shy oldest son, William, the shrewd woman warrior wouldn't have submitted to the interview—or she would have cut off lines of questioning about her intimate life.

The BBC interview was a highly orchestrated power move designed as a frontal assault on the so-called royal family. She wanted her money and she wanted her titles and she intended to get them. Queen Elizabeth and everybody else had better recognize that she wasn't going quietly into that good, obscure night. Diana intended to walk in light and thunder, flashbulbs and sympathetic applause.

At that point, she was fully aware of the fact that the monarchy into which she had married was like the bloody scruff of golden fur that concludes a fox hunt. Her divorce had not ground her into nothingness. So what the ex-next Queen wanted to teach her in-laws was that in this age one might have to make do with the empire of attention that comes with celebrity. If you're going to get all the attention anyway, as she told Tina Brown of *The New Yorker*, why not shape the substance of it—or, I might add, use it to give the impression of substance. She aimed to turn the high paparazzi bounty of her image into a form of power. She wanted an empire based on the image of reverse imperialism. Instead of taking over, you bring comfort or attention, sometimes with quite splendid bravery. Then you needn't feel guilty about your privileges and the public needn't resent you for having them, which is the fate of the House of Windsor.

The strategy worked. She became "the people's princess." The masses, conditioned through overdoses of melodrama, fell for "the poor little rich girl" story ratcheted up to that of the unhappy princess in the spiritually damp castle. She touched their hearts and became ever more human.

Well, the world is a place where just as many suffer as sing. The sorrow melts upward into the air or downward into the pit. We should never be surprised when we find out that people with money or titles or celebrity or all three feel the hard blues as deeply as the poorest people on earth. After all, the truest history and the best literature have told us this as long as both have been written.

But we accept the elevation of ordinary human compassion to angelic status when a Diana shows some of it to the poor, the sick, and the mutilated. Perhaps that is because it is through actual compassion for strangers that we reenter the unblemished spirit of innocence we so often and so desperately long for. Consequently, the symbolic significance of such compassion in so jaded an age is boundless. Yet I think that we have far richer examples of what it's all about than that prize of the paparazzi who ended up one night in Paris as a poor young woman groaning her life away in a smashed up luxury car as the photographers licked her blood with their flash bulbs.

World War II
at Fifty

Tomorrow it will be a half a century since the clay idol of European fascism was sent falling and the huge sound of its crash made the noise of a defeat heard around the world. In this era, as we look at the footage from that period, it almost seems as though it was not quite real, especially when we watch the Nazi festivities those hoodlums at the top of the German government used to celebrate their mercilessly inadequate vision of civilization. The parades and the statues and the chariots exhibit the buffoon misunderstanding of heroic glamour witnessed in Klan rallies, where the sheets and symbols seem silly until one thinks of the hatred and the willingness to murder they represent.

If anything, the defeat of the Germans that ended World War II in Europe was the defeat of a kind of hatred that was defined by its advocates as the highest form of patriotism. It was a defeat made possible not only by the alliance with European nations but in partnership with a Russia that was led by a man as willing to order the murders of millions as Hitler himself: Joe Stalin.

The Russians had chewed half the legs off of the German dog of war only because their nonaggression pact with the Nazis had been betrayed by Hitler's ordering an invasion that was as fatal for the Third Reich as it had been for Napoleon more than a century before. Had Hitler and Stalin remained peaceful toward one another, winning the war against Germany would have been a much, much taller order.

As Americans, we rallied to serve the German military its canine head on a hot plate by going into an unprecedented production of weapons, by partially putting aside our racial prejudices, by allowing hordes of women into the factories and foreshadowing the changes in the work force we still see taking place.

Our movie stars, our athletes, our musicians, our media, our schools, and everything else we had—even gangsters given the order to protect the docks by an imprisoned Lucky Luciano—helped create a unified effort. In a real and ironic sense we fought for freedom against tyranny because the overall opposition—Germany, Italy, and Japan—had in common a contempt for democracy as brutal as that of our homegrown redneck terrorists in white sheets. The opposition was clear.

Of course, there are those who sneer at the war effort because of the log jams that were so obvious in our own democracy. They will cite the way Americans of Japanese descent were treated, shunted into relocation centers while their land was ripped off, tactics encouraged by rival Caucasian citrus growers in California so that competition in the world of produce would be reduced. The racism and anti-Semitism that maintained at least a low boil during that time will be put on the list, then the atrocities toward the Indians, and so on.

However true those observations might be, we have to realize that sustained motion toward a multiracial democracy is an experiment made grueling by human nature and one that maintains its own kind of blues. Learning how to be fair to those superficially—or substantially—unlike ourselves is not an easy job, however simple it might look on paper.

This half-century after the end of the war in Europe we do know a few things. None of the remarkable social changes that have taken place in this country would have been possible if the European fascists had won.

This means that our country fought not only for the freedoms that it already had but also for the invaluable latitude to struggle and expand those freedoms beyond the prejudicial barriers within our own borders.

It also means that had the Western world lost, the descendants of Stalin might well have maintained their totalitarian grip with the steel fist of mass murder. From where we sit now, that's close enough for glory and a shipload of the very finest cigars.

Hiroshima,
Mon Amour

With the fiftieth anniversary of Victory over Japan upon us, we shouldn't be surprised to hear a symphony of whining and crying over what a low-down dirty deal the Japanese got, two mushroom clouds rising over civilian populations. But Hiroshima and Nagasaki are actually examples of the tragedy that is central to the making of war.

As one who is not opposed to war and who truly believes that some can only be spoken to in the language of fire and steel, I believe that what we really have to do is face the tragic complications that are forever attached to the facts of power. It is because we do not accept the tragic elements that are connected to so much of what goes on in our lives that we too often sink down into sanctimonious cynicism.

That armchair sneering has little to do with the hard job of pushing the boulder of civilization up the greasy slope of folly, corruption, mediocrity, and incompetence. Sometimes that boulder must grind the bodies of other human beings into dead and bloody messes if civilization is to move along. That may sound cold and hard, and would be were I not talking about the facing of tragic fact. Tragic fact means heartbreak in human terms.

Perhaps the job, then, is to make sure that the stains of those crushed by our motion are neither dismissed with cavalier arrogance nor allowed to become symbols of such debilitating discussion that we lose momentum and go rolling backward, our own boulder crushing us on the way down. We then become victims of a squeamishness that has nothing to do with civilization and its complex of responsibilities.

When there is no choice other than war, when powers such as those our country fought during World War II make it clear that they, like the Confederate South, can only be spoken to in the deadly language of devastation, we must do what has to be done and face what it all means.

There will always be barbaric excesses that build upon the agreement to use the barbaric means of murder in order to take or defend territory. In short, once bloodshed is the basic unit of terrible exchange, things will not only get out of hand, they will periodically become part of a logic based less on the outcome than on the immediate possibilities for destruction of whatever the enemy values most—cities, temples, natural resources, women and children.

So slaughters of the innocent always play themselves out if the conflict is extensive enough. The real question is whether or not our own sacrifices and those we impose on the opposition add up to something that makes possible more freedom rather than less.

I don't know how many people actually believe that the United States was led by wild, ruthless pigs of war who incinerated thousands upon thousands of Japanese civilians just to make a point to the Russians. I also don't know if that was the idea, but even if it was, the overall outcome is far better than most expected once the Russians developed their own nuclear weapons.

In fifty years, we have had to make do with proxy conflicts, ruthlessly brutal struggles on the dark plains of intelligence and little wars that were largely chess games between West and East. We have sat on the cliff of universal destruction and not jumped off. In some very remarkable ways, we have had to restrain our attraction to chaos. We have been chastened by our own weaponry. In the process, democracy has made steady gains against totalitarianism.

None of this makes those many Japanese civilian deaths any less horrible, those deformed babies preserved in bottles any less terrifying, those melting sidewalks any less than symbols of civilization sinking through the sudden quicksand of mass destruction.

Our memories may forever be scarred by the images of Hiroshima and Nagasaki, but the progress of civilization up the hill of difficult opposition is made no less grand by the horrors that always arrive with the tragic blazes and casualties of war. The two mushroom clouds take a much more horrible place in the pantheon that includes ashes such as those of an Atlanta left by the march of Sherman's troops to the sea.

| Who's Sorry Now?

These fifty years later, some of us wonder why the Japanese still seem reluctant to shoulder the history of their own aggression and their own World War II atrocities. Well, they get quite a bit of help from us, among other forces. We get so queasy about those mushroom clouds rising over Hiroshima and Nagasaki that we forget the Pearl Harbor attack, the invasion of China, the atrocities of Burma, and all of the rest of the dirty doings brought off at the command of the Japanese military.

We seem to have made the atom bomb into a monstrously destructive magic that absolves the Japanese of their actions. Once the flight of the *Enola Gay* is mentioned, the Japanese suddenly become no more than victims of American racism and all discussion speeds to a close, the bloody shirt wrapped around our eyes, mouths, and ears. We are to see no evil, speak no evil, and hear no evil concerning the actions of the Japanese military during those hard years when they were bombing, invading, and murdering.

I also believe that we don't have a reasonable vision of the Japanese and the American roles in World War II because of the Nuremberg trials and the events that followed. Quite simply, what happened in Europe took a lot of heat off of the Japanese military. What Nuremberg made public was immediately recognized as an indelible and unprecedented example of the capacity for savage conduct within a highly cultivated country.

When the Nazis were brought before the world, dragging the six million Jewish civilian corpses behind them, the face of Western society was pushed down into a spiritual cesspool that nearly drowned all assumptions about the inevitable ethics and goodwill of European civilization.

We also have the fact that in 1948, the same year that we so quickly recognized Israel, Mao Zedong took the Chinese behind a thick red curtain of tailor-made Marxism. While Israel is forever a reminder of the Nazi war crimes, our policy toward communist China was to deny its existence and recognize only Taiwan.

Had Mao's China not been so brutally totalitarian, we might now see things more clearly because we would have been continually and effectively reminded of the atrocities committed by the Japanese military during World War II. As it was, the Japanese military, given a hanging or two, soon disappeared into a dark historical space as the cold war took off.

America then shifted over to worrying about the Russians and lived under one sort of Red scare or another until Gorbachev arrived. As we went through that, we also began to see a romantic image of third world revolution slowly rising into view as colonialism expired in the name of a democracy that never arrived. The underlying theme of third world liberation was the exploitation of the dark world by the white, the trampling down of communal paradises by the rapacious boots of European imperialism.

The charges were fairly accurate but they didn't take into account human nature and the fact that freedom, as we all think of it, has nothing to do with the third world. The conception of freedom behind all liberation palaver, as Harvard's Orlando Patterson has observed, was invented in the Western world. But since few understand that, it is easy for third world or non-European leaders to conveniently charge racism when they come under criticism for any of their policies—social, economic, or military.

It seems to me that the Japanese leadership has chosen to look at things that way for quite some time. That may well be their right but we also have our duty. That duty is to put as much of the truth on the table as we can find, no matter who is trying to manipulate us into forgetting the invincibly grim facts of a world history in which there is, finally, so, so little innocence.

Patty-Cake
with Blood

This past Sunday's *Daily News* included a story in which Jose Lambiet reported the details of a shocking Belgian scandal involving a pedophile gang. It should help us rethink how we handle those found guilty of sex crimes against children in America. In Belgium, ten people have been arrested, including a police inspector who covered for the gang, which was part of a network stretching throughout the kiddie porn sewers of Europe. In a country where less than 150 murders a year are reported, the facts and the confessions have put Belgium in an emotional swoon.

"The atrocities include," Lambiet wrote, "two eight-year-old girls abducted fourteen months ago, sexually abused, then starved to death in an underground dungeon; the kidnappings of four other girls, two of whom were found alive and two of whom are presumed dead; the killing of at least one accomplice, and the production of thousands of video tapes of adults having sex with the victims."

In line with what we have come to call "junk justice," the ringleader of this group of pedophiles was arrested and convicted in 1985 for kidnapping and raping twelve- to twenty-year-old females on five separate occasions. "Although he could have gotten a life sentence," Lambiet reported, "he instead was released after three years."

When the World Congress Against Commercial Sexual Exploitation of Children met in Stockholm last week for five days, 120 nations were in attendance and the Belgium case hung over the proceedings. Sweden's Queen Silvia declared these sorts of crimes a "modern form of slavery." The conference was an attempt to bring international consciousness to this problem and encourage stronger laws against child pornography and harsher penalties.

While I agree with the international community putting collective pressure on these criminal rings, stamping them out whenever and wherever possible, I think that we in America have to consider not only the rings themselves but the individual child molester who has no intention of exploiting children for gain. The bulk of those who work in the contemporary version of the slave trade are like slavers throughout the ages; they are in it purely for the money and would sell pet rocks, ice cream sticks, or bubble gum if there was equal profit. That is why we sometimes feel more hostile toward them and are anxious to see these criminals given long sentences.

On the other hand, we don't yet seem to completely understand what ought to be done with those who are not cold-hearted exploiters but constitute a menace because of their passionate, repulsive sexual feelings for children. I think we ought to prevent the reappearance in society of those convicted for child pornography or child-molesting.

While my real preference would be capital punishment, I doubt that society will go that far. So I believe we ought to put the next best thing in practice. Quite simply, sexual crimes against children should be responded to with mandatory life sentences, no possibility of parole.

I say this because we have a responsibility to the innocent and to those not so innocent. A little girl or boy who is sexually exploited in pornographic videos or who is the victim of a molester has been murdered spiritually, emotionally, and psychologically. I'm sure of this because of the difficulty children have recovering from traumatic accidents that temporarily destroy their ability to believe in security. A child who has been sexually abused may well grow up to become a functioning member of society, marry, rear children, and so on, but he or she will forever be "one of the walking wounded."

If we go back to the example of the ringleader of the pedophile ring in Belgium, had he been kept in prison for the remainder of his life it would not have stopped others from committing the same kinds of crimes but two little girls who were starved to death in his basement might never have been kidnapped. I rest my case.

Forgotten
Girl-Slave Blues

A few days ago the *Seattle Times* carried a story in which Australia's Anti-Slavery Society estimated that there are as many as 35,000 "religious" slaves in West Africa, most of them in Ghana, the others in Togo, Benin, and Nigeria. The estimate was part of a report that has not yet surfaced in America, which I found out by trying to track it down through the United Nations Human Rights Committee. The report is entitled "The Forgotten Girl-Slaves of West Africa," and was written by Paul Bravender-Coyle, who visited West Africa in November of 1995, interviewing slaves, some very old, some even as young as eight.

"Originally offered as human sacrifice to ensure success in war," the report was quoted as saying, "these girls are the helpless victims of a traditional form of slavery known locally as 'fetish slaves.' The girls are offered as slaves in order to appease the gods and to atone for wrongs committed by their relatives, usually male relations." Even these children might find themselves bullied into performing sexual acts with African holy men in order to tranquilize the gods.

It is no wonder that Afrocentric types and the civil rights establishment have yet to get heated over these kinds of issues. They have a double standard for barbaric crimes in Africa unless they are committed by white people. Believe me, if white people were at the center of this fetish-slave story, we would surely hear from them at full volume, just as we did when the freeing of Nelson Mandela and the dismantling of apartheid were the issues.

But barbarism by Africans creates problems. If you are the kind of Negro who bases your philosophy on the idea that the West is some sort of a decadent cage and traditional African identity is what you have to get back to, then the reality of Africa puts you in a world of psychological trouble.

Charles Johnson, the author of *Middle Passage*, which won the National Book Award, is very clear on this. "These Afrocentric people," he says, "are not ready to face the fact that slavery has always been a traditional part of African life. It was not introduced by Europeans and it didn't end because Africans were interested in ending it. Europeans and Americans brought an end to the international slave trade. Obviously, they didn't completely stop the trade in Africa. We just have to face the fact that there are a lot of things in Africa that we can't make excuses for."

A perfect example is the issue of female mutilation, which an international women's conference meeting in Europe tried to raise over ten years ago. This led to the members from Burkina Faso storming out at the audacity of Europeans having the nerve to question traditional African practices. I remember arguing ten years ago with an ethnic assortment of fellow *Village Voice* staff members and being told that we, as Western people, had no right to judge the traditions of other cultures.

I don't buy any of that. Universal humanism is not about a double standard. That conception, which is purely European, is behind every modern movement that responds to the idea of basic human commonality and attempts to move us closer to basic human rights.

We can't get upset when Europeans do terrible things then look the other way when Africans and other "people of color" act like anybody's worst idea of the devil. When we do that in order to limit our own disillusionment, we don't so much help ourselves as give that much more time to those who brutalize without compunction.

We need one standard of human rights. If it's good for the goose, it damn sure ought to be good enough for the gander.

Whose Business Is Our Business?

I hear and read all of the squabbling about Haiti or the Middle East. Somebody will always miss the point. Don't leave yourself out. You can even name the most irritating subject of contention, the one that drove you up the wall before we began removing Haiti's General Cedras in a gold, padded, and air-conditioned coffin of compromise. Or you can pick your least favorite involvement of American troops prior to our having to address the nut sack of dictatorial ball bearings Saddam Hussein is presently waving at Kuwait's border, an action designed to find out if we still have the grit to use our extremely expensive might and again turn the desert red with the blood of his troops and fill the sweltering air with the smell of his burning war machinery.

Whatever your selection for discussion, somebody—right, left, or center—will always assert that we should mind our own business. The words that they use, the very idea of "minding our own business," means that they don't truly understand the identity of the United States. If they think we will forever keep our nose to the grindstone of our own national difficulties, they miss the whole troubling matter that underlies the inevitable facts of American foreign policy in our age. They surely don't understand that certain kinds of problems were born alongside everything that evolved to the present version of our democratic assumptions, which is that goodness, competence, brilliance, and greatness can come from anywhere, no matter the points of social origin, no matter the superficial differences.

That Western heritage of the Enlightenment evolved because the provincial glue that had reserved every social privilege for white men was slowly and painfully unsealed. Through a good number of struggles—some of which are still going on—the whole proposition was opened up to include people of different ethnic backgrounds, religions, political beliefs, erotic plumbing, and so on. That means we don't see people as those amorphous "others" who held stationary places in the pantheon of disdain that our democracy has worked against over the decades, slowly pulling itself out of the old, gooey skins of accumulated prejudice.

It was impossible to enrich our social policy through our willingness to hear more and more domestic charges of bad marks in the area of fairness—yet be surprised that we are always caught up in somebody else's mess sooner or later. We are who we are precisely because one group after another has proven far beyond a reasonable doubt that it, too, has a right to try and climb up after the gold and silver apples of the tree of life. Each group, too, however superficially different, includes our brothers and sisters, some unbelievably far below even the flimsiest mediocrity and others so high above average that we recognize them as the incomparably gifted. Embracing these proofs of universal human possibility brought us to the problem of our not being able to mind our own business.

That is because a central part of democracy is evangelical humanism. We not only sooner or later believe everybody is human, we act on what their human rights mean to us. It all goes back to the evangelical beginnings of Christianity and the knocking down of the idea of a chosen people. The evangelical impulse seeped quite understandably and quite uncomfortably into the secular world of domestic and foreign policy. Our sense of human rights sends us out investigating things and leads to our screaming about another set of causes. We end up worrying about the welfare of children internationally, about world health standards, about the genital mutilation of female children, and the rest of it. That's who we are.

We'll never change, especially in our world of international mass media. As long as we take human suffering seriously, we'll be in somebody else's business. Our principles make us self-righteous, make us dupes, pull us into catastrophic blunders, and cost us too much money. They even give foundation to the ruthless blunders of our espionage units. We become insufferably pompous as we speak from the right or the left, howling—rightfully or wrongly—about some atrocity we should redress. The evangelical high-mindedness represented by a troop ship or one filled with medicine, blankets, and food is who we are. Such are the inevitable and unwieldy burdens of greatness.

Trouble
in the East

Four choruses of blues changes, and a coda, for Sarajevo.

1.

It is in a bottomless pitch-blackness that the hard blues is played. In Bosnia, the snow falls. Its cold flakes heat no sweet sentiment. In Bosnia, the corpses are stacking up, but they lack the gruesome hysteria achieved by the cinematic grand guignol of our popular entertainments. In Bosnia, winter rises up and eases on out, but death still uses the thin blue blades of its nails with no distinctions as to health or frailty. In some distinct way, all of this connects us to the immemorial times that startle like a well of blood gushing from the ground. A moral eclipse is in place and there is darkness bloating the spirits that flop so stickily in the soul-catching buckets carried underground by the rabid moles of war.

2.

What should always haunt the soul are the circumstances of death; the circumstances determine the distance between stoicism and the dog-whistle-high rage at betrayal. In a novel I am writing, one of the characters observes that Jesus Christ is the greatest of all tragic heroes because even he, who knows without a doubt that he will soon be at his Father's side, finds it so hard to face the finality of human death that he cries out on the cross, "Father, Why Hast Thou Forsaken Me?"

In that very cry, perhaps better than in any other tale, we are told what death really is—something that terrifies even the gods if they dare take on human form. In the case of Jesus, he knew well and long before the grit and gore of Golgotha that he was to be sacrificed. Yet he trembled so mightily that his teeth nearly shook from his jaw as he asked that the bitter cup of sacrificial demise pass his lips. Permission denied.

Was Jesus undone by the expanding pain of death or did his hard blues rise up from the hot blade of betrayal? Was it the condition of being tormented by the soldiers of a brawny civilization and forced to drag the weighty structure upon which he would be crucified? Or was it the sense that a greater disengaged force was looking on as he suffered every stroke of a whip, every thorn into his flesh, every splinter as he dragged his cross, every sharp stone under his feet, each swing of a hammer against the spikes, each second of agony on the meat rack of crucifixion? Both bitter passions in the sun on that not yet rugged cross were probably fused in the bubbling gruel of blood and flesh.

3.

That gruel is served over and over. It is standard fare on the menu every second of the twelve months of the year that are the twelve bars of the blues we hear sung, either in some kind of words or in some kind of mumbles: Oh, Lord, why do I have to know that on some certain morning or down there on a particular afternoon or standing quiet in a night wind too peculiar to help you lose these blues, Oh, Lord: in the spring, summer, fall, or winter, everyone we know or have ever heard of will slip on the invisible nightshirt of eternity. Starting off as casket passengers to the bone orchard of the burying ground, all will, forever, as my grandmother described it, "have breakfast with the moles."

In this eclipse, in this darkness on the delta, with the moles of war rabid and reproducing themselves through infection, we must ask ourselves where we are in this geography of spiritual dimness, where standing still is suicidal, where walking is dangerous, and where running almost guarantees the crippling fall that precedes being devoured or infected.

Looking on, it is quite easy, at this long, long distance, to sip—not with our mouths but with our eyes and ears—the statistical gruel of blood and flesh, our stoicism in a high, articulate place.

In the night wind up here that sweeps away no blues, it is far, far too easy to accept the spiritual bedsores that come of winding the tattered sheets of Rip Van Winkle strategies around our souls until they become comatose. Seems like that to me.

Perhaps the blue steel fact, as always, is the blood-encrusted morality of daybreak. It begins with what seems a bright and falling star, in the hard blues air, but is actually the terrible and murderous descent of a moral but bludgeoning stop sign.

Coda: Rescue Me

In some equally applicable dream:
The ones who become the rescued
sob the tears and snot of joy
as that falling light showers down
those fantasy deaths that slide
so, so quickly into a new and pitch-dark appetite,
one equal to the fidgeting rabid moles,
greasy soul buckets at the ready,
drooling for their very own grand guignol,
demanding that it be erected in symbols of revenge:
stench-ridden, flat, broken, hardening, twisting,
in the hard blues air, twisting
across this brand new winter of the heart,

telling all of us the weight of time on our souls,
corpse by corpse by corpse by corpse.

1993/November 29;
finished: 1997/January 12

PART SIX

Up from the Grim:

Transitional Speculation,

Ron Brown, and a

Christmas Card

Who Will Enjoy
the Shadow of
Whom?

*Mr. McLuhan says that the whole world is going Oriental, and
that no one will be able to retain his or her identity, not even the
Orientals. And of course we travel around the world a lot, and in
the last five or six years we, too, have noticed this thing to be
true. So as a result, we have done a sort of thing, a parallel or
something, and we'd like to play a little piece of it for you. In this
particular segment, ladies and gentlemen, we have adjusted our
perspective to that of the kangeroo and the didjeridoo. This automatically throws us either Down Under and/or Out Back. And
from this point of view it's most improbable that anyone will ever
know exactly who is enjoying the shadow of whom.*
Duke Ellington, introducing *Chinoiserie*, 1971

Even though error, chance, and ambition are at the
nub of the human future, I'm fairly sure that race as we presently obsess
over it will cease to mean as much 100 years from today. The reasons are
very basic, some technological, others cultural. We all know that electronic media has broken down many barriers; it was even central to the fall
of the Soviet Empire because satellite dishes made it impossible for the
government to control the images and the ideas about the external world.
The totalitarian distortions were battered to their reality of pulp fiction
and the people began to realize how far behind the rest of the modern
world they actually were, no matter what their leaders told them. That national and international flow of images and information will continue to
make for a greater and greater swirl of influence, back and forth, in circles,
triangles, figure eights, and so on. It will increasingly change life on the

220   UP FROM THE GRIM

globe but it will also change our American sense of race. In that regard, the steady march toward greater recognition of human commonality will maintain itself, however much we become more and more aware of the many ways in which people handle the problems of food, shelter, romance, parenthood, income, entertainment, religion, and whatever else. Where travel used to broaden us beyond our provincialism, electronic media will continue to do the trick a century from now, furthered by the space flights into an endless universe that will probably give us another perspective altogether. Such flights will not make us less human but they should help make us less narcissistic. That is an improvement devoutly to be wished.

For all of our American prejudices on the planes of race, we have a very long history of absorbing whatever we could from one another, consciously or not. I thought about this another way when I was recently talking with the exceptional writer and thinker Sally Helgesen. Helgesen is from Michigan and said something about the current film *Fargo* which nobody else has. Assessing a tale where comedy and murderous horror are woven together brilliantly, Helgesen observed that one of the scenes in which an Indian criminal is interrogated by a female Minnesota cop made her realize how the stoic character of the Northern Europeans who had settled out there blended together with the indigenous people for a particular aspect of American character. It influenced their facial expressions, the way they spoke, their gestures, and the way they walked. They had miscegenated culturally, whether or not the necessary bodily fluids had been exchanged for the rearrangement of bloodlines.

I would suggest that this is something that has been going on for a very long time in America, from sea to shining sea, border to border. But in our present love of the mutually exclusive, our pretense that we are something less than a culturally miscegenated people, we forget our American tendency to seek out the unique or the exotic until it becomes a basic cultural taste, like Chinese food or sushi or the growing national popularity of Mexican food. This is what guarantees that those who live on this soil a century from now will see, experience, and accept many, many manifestations of cultural mixings, blendings, and additions. I do not think that the question of race will disappear or that we will be closing in on some paradise in which color means absolutely nothing, but I do think that we will become far and away more comfortable with human commonality and variety than we are now. This, of course, will be a reiteration of the most high-minded ideas of the civil rights movement. In other words, before we assume that race will go the way of the dinosaur, we should remember, as Americans, that slavery lasted a long, long time in our magnificent and bedeviling country. But neither slavery nor racism stopped the cultural mixings. They just kept on keeping on.

While most American writers miss these things by country miles if, indeed, they even think about them, somebody always knows. In her 1992 novel, *Smart Hearts for the City*, Barbara Probst Solomon superbly examined the mixtures of our identity over a period of almost sixty years, from about 1930 to the middle 1980s. Of the subject of this essay, she says,

> We will probably find ourselves going the way of the Latin countries. In those places, miscegenated identity is, quite simply, *the* identity of the culture. The Spanish and the Portugese came here, they didn't have women, they wanted them, and so it began that way. Whether or not all of the circumstances were pleasant is not the point. That is how they started becoming what they are. This passes all through the writing, the literature. In order to be interesting in those places as a writer, you have to display your knowledge of the cultural complexity of Latin American, of South America—the things from the Iberian Penisula, from the Indians, the Africans. All of these things are taken for granted the farther south you travel in this Hemispere. I believe our future is the same.

In that future, definition by racial, ethnic, and sexual groups will most probably have ceased to function as the foundation for the commodity of special interest power that we so often see now, when ethnic and sexual alienation are academically and politically huckstered. Ten decades up the road, few should take seriously, accept, or submit to any form of segregation marching under the intellectually ragged banner of "diversity." More emphasis on individual choice will rise into the social vision. The idea that one's background should determine one's occupation, one's taste, one's romantic preferences, or any other thing will dissolve in favor of identity by class, occupation, taste, and so on. Just as it is not unusual for us to now go and see a play in which nontraditional casting allows directors to assign family roles purely on the basis of skill, not racial compatibility, we should expect those kinds of things to move further and further into our society. With the increasing reality of the half-caste and, just as often, the poly-caste, Americans of the future will find themselves surrounded in every direction by people who are part Asian, part Latin, part African, part European, part American Indian. What such people will look like is beyond my imagination, but the sweep of body types, combinations of facial features, hair textures, and colors of eyes in what are now unexpected skin tones will be far more common, primarily because our traditional paranoia over mixed marriage is now decreasing and should by then be largely a superstition of the past.

In his extraordinary essay, "The Little Man at Chehaw Station," Ralph Ellison describes a youthful "light-skinned, blue-eyed, Afro-American-featured individual who could have been taken for anything from a sun-tinged white Anglo-Saxon, an Egyptian, or a mixed-breed American Indian to a strayed member of certain tribes of Jews." He used the young man as an example of what Ellison realized was our central problem—"the challenge of arriving at an adequate definition of American cultural identity goes unanswered." The youth drove a car that was itself miscegenated visually—"a shiny new blue Volkswagen Beetle decked out with a gleaming Rolls Royce radiator." While his feet and legs were covered by riding boots and breeches and he held a riding crop in his hand, he wore a multicolored dashiki, and "a black homburg hat tilted at a jaunty angle floated majestically on the crest of his huge Afro-coiffed head." For Ellison, "his clashing of styles nevertheless sounded an integrative, vernacular tone, an American compulsion to improvise upon the given."

The vernacular tone Ellison wrote of is what fumbles up all those who would wish to keep race in its irrational place. It is what makes us improvise upon whatever we actually like about each other, no matter how we might pretend we feel about those superficially different. We have been working out these dissonances or celebrating the ways in which they jangle convention for at least as many years as Americans have realized that this country is one thing, Europe another. Further, the social movements of minorities and women have greatly aided our getting beyond the always culturally inaccurate idea that the United States is "a white man's country."

That is why I think we can understand another aspect of where the society is headed by the fact that so many Republicans were passionately supportive of Colin Powell going on the road and seeking the presidential nomination for their party. Before Powell backed away from what might have been a grand moment in American politics, one life-long Republican told this writer that the unbeatable ticket would be the general and New Jersey governor Christy Todd Whitman. A good-looking Negro and a good-looking white woman raising their clasped hands on the podium at the Republican Convention would have revolutionized our sense of political reality, whether or not they had won. So it is easy to imagine that a century from now American politics will have opened up all the way to the top in exactly the same way that American sports have, where we can see complete audience respect and adulation for championship men and women of almost every racial background, from Michael Jordan to Michael Chang. Though the words were probably written by someone like Peggy Noonan, Ronald Reagan said of the 1984 Olympics that the American team included athletes who looked like the people from all the other nations. As Americans, they had the faces, the colors, and the bodies of the world. He was right about that one.

While this country cannot become more of an ongoing mix than it already is, once what Barbara Solomon deduced becomes an accepted reality, people will be much more at ease with the fact that we are a nation of mutts, that we have been miscegenated by blood and taste for a few hundred years. We sometimes tend to forget how much the Pilgrims learned from the Indians, or look at that learning in only the dullest terms of exploitation, not as a fundamental aspect of our American identity. We look at so-called assimilation as some form of oppression, some loss of identity, even a way of selling out. In certain cases and at certain times, that may have been more than somewhat true. If you didn't speak with a particular command of the language—or at a subdued volume—you might have been dismissed as crude. If you hadn't been educated in what were considered the right places, you were seen as some sort of a peasant. And on it went.

But that is only one side of the story. We forget that by the time James Fenimore Cooper was inventing his backwoodsmen there was the easily recognized phenomenon of the white man who had lived so closely to the land and the Indian that he was, often quite proudly, a cultural mulatto. He was a white man without precedent, from the fine-tuning of his hunter's senses to the buckskin shirts, jackets, pants, and boots that his European ancestors never wore. We forget that we could not have had the cowboy without the Mexican vaquero. We don't know that our most original art music, jazz, is a combination of elements African, European, and Latin. Few are aware of the fact that when the Swiss psychoanalyst Carl Jung came to this country he observed that white people walked, talked, and laughed like Negroes. He also reported that the two dominant figures in the dreams of his white American patients were the Negro and the American Indian. Black and red were on their minds.

One aspect of what Jung meant about American talk can be experienced whenever one listens to broadcast recordings from the 1930s that contain the sound of Benny Goodman's voice, which was unaffectedly Negroid. That is a perfect example of cultural miscegenation. As with such things American, it led to what must have been oddly discontinuous but democratic moments. When Goodman, a Chicago Jew and a giant of the jazz clarinet, married into the Vanderbilt family, one could imagine how unusual the exchanges must have sounded when those who were both descendants of Northern European Christian wealth and products of upper-class Eastern Seaboard manners found themselves talking with a man whose bloodline reached back to Eastern Europe and whose skin was white but whose voice had the sidewalk timbre and rhythm of a Southside Chicago Negro.

It goes the other way as well, which anybody from far enough outside of New York City can tell you. Upon arriving in Manhattan, one immediately notices a predominant accent that seems thoroughly Jewish, which leads to confusion when speaking to people over the phone. *Everybody* sounds Jewish, even if they're talking about how much they don't like Jews. After a bit, however, the ear begins to make out the black, Latin, Italian, and Irish variations on that sound, which is itself some goulash of inflections, at least half from Eastern Europe. This is equally true when Northerners new to the South find themselves trying to determine the racial identity of the person on the other end of the phone. This is America. Culturally speaking, the bagel has become as ubiquitous as the hamburger, the taco as familiar as the hot dog. There are middle-income

Americans of every stripe, descended from a tradition of overcooked meat, who can put their feet under the table of a Japanese restaurant and have themselves a fine time eating raw fish. They'll never get their parents and grandparents into those joints.

What will fall away over the coming decades is our present tendency to mistake something borrowed for something ethnically "authentic." A few years ago, I had an experience that was a personal variation on what Ellison noted in "The Little Man at Chehaw Station." I was a speaker here in New York at one of those Pan-African conferences, which always turn out to be dominated by combinations of sanctimonious self-pity, race worship, trickle-down Marxism, colonial West Indian perspectives inappropriately applied to the discussion of American life, and whatever academic convention of French thinking has been trendily bootlegged into the obfuscation. I found myself talking with a tall, wide-beamed young man whose freckled skin tone was somewhere between the color of a banana and a tangerine. He was asking me why I didn't have much time for the latest version of "black identity." I didn't argue that there isn't something of the sort, but it is only an ethnic variation on the national feeling for life and style. As Americans, we are always mutating into recastings of one another.

Irritated, the young man said I didn't recognize the cultural insularity of race as he shifted back and forth in his bandana, his dark plaid shirt, his baggy pants, and combat boots. I told him that the look he had picked up from rap videos that he thought obscured his middle-class background in favor of the style of the black street thug was actually the way Mexican kids in East Los Angeles had been dressing for over thirty years. The real and fake Compton gangsters he was imitating had picked it up from them. They hadn't invented it any more than the white musicians attracted to the blues have created the music that they know most perfectly expresses the way they feel about the world, even if they hail from the kind of lily-land where Mark Fuhrman would feel most comfortable.

I went on to say that anyone who has observed the dressing, speaking, and dancing styles of Americans since 1960 can easily recognize the sometimes startling influences that run from the top to the bottom, the bottom to the top. This phenomenon includes descriptions of spiritual appetites and states of being that have come into our lives, sometimes clumsily or pretentiously, through forms of worship from the Middle East and the Far East. Further, it is not even vaguely unusual to hear educated people of whatever color or ethnic group use a diction that includes slang and terms scooped out of the disciplines of psychology, economics, art criticism, and so on. In fact, one of the few interesting things about the rap idiom is that some of the rappers pull together a much richer vocabulary than has ever existed in black pop music while peppering it to extremes with repulsive vulgarity. They did not pick up those words in the street, where inarticulate monosyllables, shrugs, hand signals, and overly burdened cursing define the discourse, or whatever passes for it.

Nothing I know of gives the impression that we are destined to become one bland nation of interchangeables from coast to coast. While the inevitable social demons of folly, corruption, mediocrity, and incompetence will continue to appear and reappear, regions will remain regions and within them we will find what we always find: variations on the overall style and pulsation. As the density of cross-influences progresses, we will get far beyond the troubles the Census Bureau now has with racial categories, which are growing because we are presently so hung up on the barbed wire of tribalism, fearing absorption, or "assimilation." One hundred years from today, Americans will look back on the ethnic difficulties of our time as quizzically as we do on earlier periods of human history when misapprehension defined the reality. They will still be squabbling and those supposedly speaking in the interests of one group or another will hector the gullible into some kind of self-obsession that will influence the local and national dialogue. But those squabbles are basic to upward mobility and competition. Yet it is the very nature of upward mobility and competition that eases away superficial distinctions in the interests of getting the job done. We already see that in the integration of the workplace, in the rise of women, in the large corporations that grant spousal equivalent benefits to homosexuals and lesbians because they want to keep their best workers, no matter what they privately do as consenting adults. In the undaunted march of the world economy, the imbalances that result from hysterical xenophobia will largely melt away because the Americans will be far too busy standing up to the challenges of getting as many international customers for their wares as they can. That is, if they're lucky.

Meditation
on Ron Brown,
in Two Parts

1. *In the Rain, into the Hillside*

We know that ours is a time, like all times, that has its special serving of trouble. The lack of confidence in the finest ideas about human freedom and democratic society has created the kind of uneasiness in a number of quarters that demagogues lie in wait for. The troubles in the world of work that are being wrought by our swifter and swifter technological refinements and innovations rattle even the middle class. At the bottom, too many have forgotten that learning—not glib disdain for the hard work of getting a good education—best puts one in a position to shape the dimensions of fate.

On this Easter weekend, it seems to me that the illuminating life and tragic death of Harlem's Ron Brown, the Secretary of Commerce, were connected to the idea of serious democratic resurrection in the world

227

of politics. Though the media has chosen to recycle its urban version of bootstrap Negro mythology, Brown started out literally at the top, a penthouse apartment in the Hotel Theresa, which his father managed. He did not rise into the political heaven of great influence from anywhere near the bottom, sitting on his welfare mammy's knee. Brown went to private school and to college in Vermont, served in the military, and earned his degree as a lawyer.

Ron Brown represented the solid Negro American middle class that is usually best prepared to change the national game once the rabble-rousing, marching, and anarchy are out of the way. While such public spectacles might draw well-needed attention to problems, serious and insightful vision put into the nuts and bolts of policy is what brings about actual shifts in the quality of life. Truly getting into the sweat and grime of the work increases our respect for others—be they friends or enemies—across the simple-minded divisions of race, sex, and class.

Ron Brown was the next step after Adam Clayton Powell. For all his shrewdness, Powell was taken down as much by his egotistical nose-thumbing as he was by the racial double standards of his time as they played themselves out in Washington. When he pulled down his pants to the world of his detractors, Powell got a stiff, stiff kick, not the kisses he asked for. He lost everything.

Brown was the other side of that. He became increasingly powerful and was crossing lines that had never been crossed in his time. The progression was steady. Smooth as spring drizzle on a window pane, always perfectly dressed, even when casual, Brown marched his way to glory, never being any less than a number one himself, not a number two somebody else. He was able to work in black New York radio for Percy Sutton's WLIB, move on to the Urban League, head Ted Kennedy's staff, marshall Jesse Jackson's 1984 presidential campaign, use his office as the national chairman to almost miraculously rebuild a shattered Democratic Party, play a key role in Bill Clinton's election, and innovate relationships between the federal government and the business sector that were realistic responses to the full court press of politics and corporations nations such as Japan bring to world market competition.

When he went down in that military airplane, the sound of the wind and rain singing a wet tune of death, Brown may well have had his head full of figures rolling out to the billions, maybe the trillions. He was surrounded by corporate executives whom he had organized for the purposes of scouting out business opportunities in rebuilding Croatia. Brown's phrase in our rhyming time was "trade, not aid." Business executives who were accustomed to battling total alliances between foreign governments and their private sectors found themselves startled when Brown moved to put Washington behind American business and fight for bringing more jobs into this country. He was in the vanguard. He knew where the war was—in the world market.

When our best ideas and hopes seem to have been crucified and shut off in a cave behind boulders of cynicism and demagoguery, we are quite lucky to have people like Ron Brown step forward and begin excavating the will and the soul of our nation. They prove that all of the complaints about race, about "glass ceilings," and so on, while they might be true in a number of cases, are not the only facts. In his poise, brilliance, wit, and recognition of compromise as the lubricant of democratic politics, Ron Brown was a man whose flesh and blood achievements can easily resurrect optimism. We should all be proud of him, for he set a high standard in a sometimes appalling age.

2. Soaring Home

Over the years since the death of John Kennedy, we have seen many funerals of public figures and have mourned many who were felled in the middle of their duty. Martin Luther King was even elevated to the position of a social saint, a crusader against injustice whose goal was to influence politics toward fairness. But King's martyrdom was only part of the monumental process that led to all we learned from the reactions to the death of Secretary of Commerce Ronald Harmon Brown.

The celebrations, the mourning, and the funeral of Ron Brown put the most richly complex aspects of the national soul on display with a grace that was surely one of the high points in our American history. Never before had there been a Negro who worked at the top of the system in the way Ron Brown did, reinvigorating the Democratic Party as national chairman, then mastering the technology for fundraising and the coordinated campaign techniques that together sent Bill Clinton to the White House. Acknowledged as an innovative strategist in world trade and competition, he was a tree-shaker *and* a jelly-maker.

In death, Brown was eulogized by such an epic range of people that it was ennobling to watch the ceremonies. We were allowed to see not only which way we are going but what truly important Afro-Americans can do and *are* doing. By showing everything, C-Span provided us with a superb rejoinder to a media too often addicted to black geeks. This wasn't the celebration of a rabble-rouser, a hate-monger, a political buffoon draped in coy outrage, lunatic theories of racial origin, and paranoid wrongheadedness.

None of this is to say that there were not times when Ron Brown may well have worked the dubious end of the street, making shady deals here and there, but that in the overall picture he was a man whose accomplishments brought far, far more light than fog. In an age such as this one, our nation needs to see something quite real about our possibilities. The demagogues, the nut militias, the mad bombers, and the politicians too stuck in ideology to do the inevitably compromising work of government give many of us a democratic migraine.

The night of praise before the funeral in Washington's National Cathedral detailed our democracy at its best. It brought out our political and commercial aristocracy of achievement, and in each reminiscence of Ron Brown we felt the weight of an intelligence, a wit, a courage, and a willingness to find human commonality across barriers. He was remembered with real feeling by Christians, by Jews, by men, by women. Brown had touched their minds and their souls and they weren't reluctant to say so.

When we saw all of those magnificent Americans and representatives of foreign countries speak about this man or come to mourn him, our society was given a public set of rituals that was reinvigorating. The varied range of speaking voices, from the thick refinement of Pamela Harriman to the pulpit fire and lyricism of Jesse Jackson, the humorous recollections of Kwesi Mfume, and Bill Clinton's memory of playing basketball in South Central Los Angeles against Brown and some street kids, gave us a picture of a man made even more complete by his son's eulogy.

The spiritual depth of the music in the National Cathedral made gravely majestic by death was capped by the solo trumpet of Wynton Marsalis playing "Flee as a Bird." That clarion trumpet reminded us of the vital mulatto mix that rose into jazz from New Orleans. That mix touched the world in just the way that Ron Brown wanted to in his part of the arena. Jazz said that the Negro sense of life could speak for humanity at large. As the funeral ceremony ended in Arlington National Cemetery, the reaffirmation of our common humanity that had risen into full view made the tragedy of Ron Brown's death seem an act of harsh providence that let us know, once more, just who we Americans are.

| Spirits Spun in Gold

There is almost always a surprise in the South. When my wife and I went down to Charlottesville, Virginia, this past weekend, we saw a perfect preview of the humanity beneath the meaning of the Christmas spirit. The event we attended, however, was much rarer than Christmas celebrations. We had been invited by Nathan and Charlotte Scott to celebrate their golden wedding anniversary.

I first met Nathan Scott at Ralph Ellison's funeral, where he delivered the final words of prayer and scripture as the great writer's remains were sealed in a wall not far from the uptown New York home he had lived in for decades. I got to know Scott better as we talked at parties, Ellison memorials, and over the phone. Educated first in the public schools of Detroit and later a recipient of degrees from universities, Scott is a stately brown-skinned man in his middle seventies and a highly regarded scholar of twentieth-century literature and theology. His unforced bearing and that voice, covered with the dark pitch of the Negro pulpit and given to the acute stresses of the academy, make it obvious that Nathan Scott Jr. is one of those men who commanded respect as he made his way in the world.

His Charlotte is a creamy beauty from Yonkers who probably could have crossed the line into so-called white America and lived a very different life if she had been of that mind. Charlotte Scott, however, was far too soulful for that. She has the knowing eye and the certitude, the graciousness and humor, that have long defined a certain sort of earthy American aristocracy, no matter the color, the class, or the religion. She is a pioneer woman with a high degree of unpretentious polish, a gourmet dish with a chitlin spirit.

The Scotts lived in that truly windy city for twenty-one years when Nathan taught at the University of Chicago. He then accepted an invitation to teach at the University of Virginia, and the two have lived in Charlottesville for twenty years now.

The banquet room chosen to celebrate the golden wedding anniversary was filled with between eighty and one hundred people—Negroes, whites, Asians. Nathan and Charlotte's son and daughter-in-law, Nathan III and his wife, Carol, have two lively sons. Their daughter Leslie, the widow of her Yoruba husband, lives in Charlottesville with her four children—three daughters and one son.

My wife and I were seated at the table with Nathan and Charlotte, but I had no idea what I was going to hear. The poet Michael Harper had come down and he started off the statements of praise, which were picked up by this one and that one. But when Nathan Scott stood up, a mist of emotion wetting his eyes, he went on to tell the story of his meeting Charlotte fifty years ago in New York.

It was a simple story of two well-educated young Negroes meeting through a mutual friend and continuing to meet, day after day, until they decided to marry ten days later. What made the story so special was the feeling of romance, of awe, and humble gratitude for such luck. I had never sat next to a man who spoke of a woman with that kind of feeling in a public situation. In times as vulgar and overstated as ours, it seemed like a miracle.

The Christmas story is the story of a miracle, but I would say that the truest miracles in its wake are those possessing the kind of human feeling that maintains such a marriage, begets such children and produces grand-children who possess a balance and a dignity unsmeared by the filth of the period. Henceforth, when I think of Christmas, I will always think about Nathan and Charlotte Scott and the magnificent line that their un-daunted love produced.

PART SEVEN

Images of Light in Dark Rooms:

Some Cinematic

Achievements

I am as disturbed as the next person by some of the technological gore fests that update the spectacles movies have presented from the olden days of heavy ketchup to the exploding heads of our moment, but my real interest is in how hard facts and high fun sometimes come together in one work or form the basis for two different kinds of efforts. I say this because our collective American autobiography is tragic, is comic, is both, and is sometimes too ambivalent to be understood as anything other than the blues. While the commercial dictates of Hollywood remain constant, we do have actors, seasoned and rising, as fine as any who have ever appeared within the borders of the shining screen in the dark room—Bill Cobbs, Gene Hackman, Morgan Freeman, Robert Duvall, Robert De Niro, Nick Nolte, Tommy Lee Jones, Jeff Bridges, Mary Alice, Diane Keaton, Glenn Close, Michelle Pfeiffer, Anjelica Huston,

Blair Brown, Denzel Washington, Sean Penn, Lawrence Fishburne, Regina Taylor, and Tim Roth, as a short list of examples. We also have growing directorial talents as different as John Sayles, Tim Robbins, the Hughes brothers, the Coen brothers, Carl Franklin, Quentin Tarantino, and Tim Burton. The achievements of masters such as Robert Altman and Martin Scorsese have not been in vain.

It is also interesting to notice that we see a new kind of cinema now, one that reflects either how much America has changed or what America really is. There is a serious attempt to bring our many human forms and faces and backgrounds into human contours. This has been struggling along for at least thirty years, the first high point reached not in film but in television with *Hill Street Blues,* which made possible the vision realized in the recent *Heat,* where no single ethnic was required to represent the exotic or be a composite of the group: characters were varied in their sensibilities, regardless of race. I say this for one reason. From my perspective, no matter how much I appreciate the great works of the golden age of Hollywood, I am almost always irritated when I realize an America full of black people doing all sorts of things other than working in positions of service missed the silver screen during the 1930s and the 1940s. That America didn't get there in the 1950s either. Spilled milk or lost black gold, we can't do anything about that now. But it is important to know that we missed something. If we know that, we might, as some are trying to do, regain the past as only the arts can because they work in that arena where fact and myth are made interchangeable by imagination and the mysteries of human feeling.

Our USA story, which has never been small, is so big now that we need epic visions to stand tall against the mirror-licking of this narcissistic era. Sometimes, again, television even takes the lead. With the exception of *Lonesome Dove,* nothing has so successfully appeared on the epic scale of *The Godfather* and *Godfather II,* which means that the miniseries may be where television can most effectively push its chest against the silver screen. Where we are now, as the nation redefines itself, is at another edge of fresh recognition. That is why I include the following pieces about American film. They either remake and expand something beyond what we might have considered its limits, or they tell us things about the wages of stability and change as we stand in the middle of this tumultuous winding down of the twentieth century. At this time, we find ourselves moving far beyond the stereotypes that have held us in prejudicial check for so long, while newly terrorized by unpredictable violence and ever observing those willing to refashion any sort of minstrelsy if the bucks are large enough.

We're still in front, for all that. As I observed in an essay written for *American Enterprise* magazine,

> The very development of heroic figures from the worlds so stereotyped by Hollywood proves that American life is far from the closed book of atrocities our country's most stern critics seem to believe it is. In one way or another, we have seen our legendary dream machine shift its sympathies and elevate the downtrodden and the excluded, usually in the same heavy-handed fashion customized for the old popular images the new ones repudiated. Minorities and women continue to move into fresher areas of characterization, functioning so often in narrative positions of complexity and authority that people new to America are convinced that the country is truly a multiracial enterprise in which the sexes stride closer and closer to equality. That is not hard to believe in our real world, where so many black mayors and women executives and minority intellectuals, experts, and advisors are seen on the news discussing and analyzing far more things than race, sex, or social prejudice.
>
> The democratization of the matinee idol and the sex symbol has always been in motion and is now far from an enclosed idea of refined looks. The position of star or sex symbol eventually included people such as Woody Allen, Spike Lee, Barbra Streisand, Madonna, and Whoopi Goldberg, none of whom have traditional good looks or would even be considered attractive within the parameters of their own ethnic backgrounds. But they have somehow hooked into the national appetite for different sorts of charisma—from intellectual wit to bad boy racial posturing to Brooklyn schmaltz to bimbo brazenness to the idol-smacking and dirty-mouthed hot mama from the other side of town. A poll taken some ten years ago revealed that

most American families, if they couldn't have their actual fathers, would choose Bill Cosby! In a recent survey, American teenagers said that the woman they respected most after their mothers was Oprah Winfrey and the man Denzel Washington. While these polling phenomena represent the fluctuating penetration of high quality or mediocrity or trash, they are all aspects of the unexpected democratic evolutions basic to the social intercourse and development of our society.

That just about lays it down.

Two Out of Three:
Reinventing Americana

Some years ago, *An American Werewolf in London* turned its part of the horror genre around by making the man who became a beast under the light of the full moon a young Jewish guy from Long Island. He brought to the British Isles his nightmares about Nazis, his neuroses, his outsider paranoia, and full servings of his guilt, all of which were counterpointed by the parodic twists of urban Jewish wit. The film had successfully done something that Ishmael Reed once claimed: familiar genres can be renewed by using an ethnic point of view. The best Afro-American films often do just that. They invent fresh ways of experiencing the stories and the situations that give narrative form to the human condition in American terms.

Three new films give us a chance to look at different aspects of the phenomenon. Because Spike Lee's *Clockers* is a move forward for the diminutive director but does nothing to enrich American cinematic artistry, I want to first discuss Carl Franklin's *Devil in a Blue Dress* and Allen and Albert Hughes's *Dead Presidents;* they refresh the detective story and the tale of the heist while either reclaiming the Afro-American humanity of the past or giving the street pressure of the black criminal world its ominous due.

There are very obvious reasons for the success of Franklin and the Hughes brothers. The physical styles of Negroes, the contrasting body of rhythms, intonations, and accents they bring to English, their slang, the facial expressions, the slick to gutbucket approaches to sexuality, and the panorama of skin tones open up truly American tales with elements that are both particular and universal. We have long heard this in the best of our American music and oratory, seen it in our dance and our athletic games, and laughed at how it applies to standup comedy. When the Negro arrives with more going than the accident of color and wooly hair, with real talent and imagination, Americana is enriched in the very same way that is has been deepened and broadened by the best of the Irish, the Jews, the Italians, and so on.

This rarely happens in our cinema and we have lost golden ages of Negroid Americana because the conventions of minstrelsy held sway for so, so long. In our own century, when Hollywood was going about the business of creating an American mythology that spoke to and for the world, the vitality and the drama of the Afro-American life that gave so much to the culture and the meaning of the nation were largely reduced to no more than well-meaning liberal propaganda focused on how bad it was for the colored people to live under the caustic reign of the white folks. Though there have been exceptions over the years such as *Halleluyah, Carmen Jones, Nothing but a Man, Claudine, Cooley High,* and *To Sleep with Anger*—to name a few of the very few—the complexity and the range of rural and urban Negro life in the worlds of work, play, romance, family, politics, adolescence, religion, crime, and everything else in which humanity most powerfully and subtly makes itself either clear or mysterious are largely absent. From the flip side, there was the blaxploitation craze of the 1970s, which was the cinematic forerunner of rap. Its cardboard celebration of dope dealers, pimps, whores, guttersnipes, derangement of the senses, and anarchy was a phenomenon worthy of James Baldwin's phrase "Uncle Tom turned inside out."

Devil in a Blue Dress is so good at reinventing the feeling of a genre that its cinematic craft makes a blaxploitation film like *Shaft* seem even more heavy-handed than it did twenty-five years ago. That should not surprise us, given what its director, Carl Franklin, did in *One False Move*, his first film and a splendid reworking of the chase with racial, regional, and class nuances. What Carl Franklin has achieved in his second film, with no small help from Denzel Washington and the rest of the cast, is a feeling for urban American life in a Negroid mode that neither points at itself with ethnic pomposity nor fails to use the detective story for the revelations about the nature of our civilization that is its most ambitious task. Brilliantly adapted by Franklin from Walter Mosley's novel, the film takes us down into the social sewers that are always revealed by the explosions of violence, that subterranean world of perversion and respectable people who are exposed as no more than fat rats in power.

The substructure of Los Angeles in the 1940s, which was where Philip Marlowe had his adventures and learned more about the proportions of sludge than he wished to, is now the daunting tunnel of large question marks that Easy Rawlins is tested by as mystery upon mystery pulls the World War II veteran into the squish and stench of spiritual dung. Because Rawlins is a Negro, when he goes where he goes and suffers the insults, beatings, and threats that are basic to the detective story, there are other dimensions put into the tale. His meetings with politicians, knuckleheads, the rich, and the police have racial elements that intensify the class prejudices and the brutal uses of power the traditional detective encounters in hard-boiled situations. Body position, flashes of the eyes, and facial expressions are quite important because much of what happens is played between the words, with assumed or rebuked privilege the wire carrying the electricity. To the film's credit, all of those situations have a very natural feeling, with only a brief voice-over near the end coming off as an inappropriately pompous race editorial.

Equally good is the feeling of the Negro world that Rawlins lives in. The life that blues and jazz musicians were putting into their music comes forward with a confidence, a lush sensuality, a camaraderie, and a wit that adds another layer to the gallows humor we refer to as "black comedy" in a nonracial sense. Relaxed community, buoyance, and harshness are superbly balanced, creating nothing like heaven but something quite akin to the sense of vitality at odds with tragic darkness and absurdity that was central to John Ford's vision. When Rawlins needs support and calls in his fellow Texas buddy, the murderous Mouse, we also see a turn on Ford's understanding that good men, in order to bring about something close to justice, must sometimes make use of those who are loyal, callous, and absolutely ruthless.

As Easy Rawlins, Denzel Washington gives us his finest performance on film. He achieves what only the very best of remarkably handsome actors can, an exceptional range of feeling that either intensifies his looks or neutralizes them so that the weights and nuances of passion are liberated. We can see the emotion flitting across the actor's face and hear its various meanings coloring his speech. One of the best of Washington's many splendid moments comes when we notice that his eyes have suddenly gone wet after he pounds a bar with a hammer because he realizes that someone he truly considered a friend has betrayed him. Let us hope that Washington and Carl Franklin find the right scripts and work together many more times.

Just about the whole acting gang is extremely good, but the one other than Washington who will startle with his invention is Don Cheadle as Mouse. The actor slips the potential noose of the cartoon and makes his character a small package of thoroughly human anarchy. The orchestration of the devil in Mouse's soul is as fresh as the interpretation James Cagney brought to Tom Powers in *Public Enemy*. Rarely does anything this original reach our theater screens.

The broad, unsentimental understanding of community and the tragic wit of its morality are some of the reasons why this film will be remembered as another signal victory in our struggle to artistically realize the universal potential of our ethnic particulars. Able to intoxicate through the many ingredients of its artistry, *Devil in a Blue Dress* is a truly new down-home brew in an old and favorite bottle.

The Hughes brothers are going places at a hot pace. While they zipped past *Boyz N the Hood* with the severe and unapologetic accuracy of their first film, the 1993 *Menace II Society*, *Dead Presidents* goes far beyond that effort in its ambition. This time, consciously or not, they have rung some new changes on the theme of *The Roaring Twenties*. In the 1939 gangster classic, Cagney played a World War I veteran who returns to Manhattan and can't get the kind of a life he wants outside of crime. The central character of *Dead Presidents* comes home from Vietnam to a New York community in which he finds himself unemployed and, after hard luck and trouble, decides to better things by getting together an older crime mentor, a female black radical, and some fellow war veterans for a big stickup.

The Hughes brothers have a special gift for capturing grit and counterpointing it with humor that is either smooth or prickly. Though in their early twenties, they have done quite a job of bringing back to life the world of the late 1960s and the early 1970s that was grist for so much blaxploitation. Where the sense of place and the vision of life in those films were just so much chocolate-coated ham, *Dead Presidents* has the soul and complexity of motive all narrative art must possess if it is to touch its source and communicate beyond it. For all their brashness, the Hughes brothers are in pursuit of the sticky, unpredictable manifestations of humanity, the moments of tenderness and clumsiness between young lovers, the bitterness that seeps into the spirit as the hard blues of life in our time throws its withering body punches and smacks one's head until it rings like a big cathedral bell.

Theirs is a gift for moving forward by fast or slow blackout, a technique they used in *Menace II Society*. This is the old, classic way to control the passage of time. The individual episode in the new film is like a chorus in jazz music, an improvisation on a theme. We are given a wide scope of emotional states and reactions as the film goes its tragic way. The Hughes brothers want to show how the kind of nice young men who are both attracted to the streets and want some kind of adventure can become embroiled in social scenes where either furious or ice-cold violence is the bloody coin of the realm. The directing twins also understand just how trouble and combative politics can drain a lot of the sweetness from certain kinds of women.

As their themes develop, we see variation given to recurring images

and situations. The delivery truck that takes three of the central characters on a milk route foreshadows the armored one the same three will try
to rob near the end. The rooms and the relationships change. When we
are returned to pool halls, automobiles, dining rooms, and street corners,
something else is inserted, a twist of feeling or a chance for revenge or
deeper romantic passion or gloomy recognition. The image of the main
character running in his girlfriend's neighborhood is picked up in Vietnam and later follows the robbery. The black face paint of jungle battle
becomes the white mime masks of the robbers. The Hughes brothers also
know how to make violent situations move beyond shock and take on different meanings—comic, terrifying, exhilarating, humiliating, and heart-
breaking.

What reviewers have missed in terms of character development is
the obsession with manhood of Larenz Tate's Anthony, the lead role. Not
listening closely enough, they don't comprehend his evolution from a
good-natured high school kid all the way over to the planner of a heist.
The belief that his masculinity must entail coming to terms with extremely tough situations is what attracts him to running numbers and
hanging around with pool hall thugs as a teenager, then draws him into
the Marines and volunteering for the toughest unit in Vietnam. When his
family is shocked by his decision to reject college for the military, Anthony reminds his father how he had told his sons that going into the
service "made you a man."

It is that same concern with manhood that prods Anthony into violent criminality. When he finds himself in a situation where his wife and
a cuckolding drug dealer contemptuously scoff at him for "not being a
man," the angry desire to stand equal to the well-off criminal and become
a provider underlies the decision that dooms his future. A proud and frustrated young man who becomes irrationally impatient when faced with
difficulty, Anthony chooses to do something that is bold and military and
carries with it a skewed commentary on the political fate of Negro Americans. As with Hughes characters in *Menace II Society*, Anthony's politics
are essentially vague, no more than slogans soaked in his rage. He is attracted to Black Power rhetoric because of its assertiveness, not because of
what it says.

Larenz Tate, whose humanization of foolhardiness and violence in the first Hughes brothers film was so impressive, stretches out and proves himself perhaps today's most talented young American actor other than John Leguizamo. The course from naiveté to fury is negotiated with so many turns of feeling that we witness an easygoing but mischievous young guy develop into a professional soldier, a diligent father, a confused drunk, and an unemployed man ready to die rather than submit to the deadly force of a hustler who sticks a pistol in his face. The wholeness of his humanity is another high mark in our contemporary art. Keith David, Rose Jackson, and Clifton Powell are equally marvelous. Quite good are Chris Tucker and Bokeem Woodbine.

Where the film fails is in its not making the Black Power sections sufficiently charismatic. No matter what we might think about such political pulp, it needed to be delivered with more force—enough to let us believe it might get Anthony's attention. There is a lot of wit in the way black pop tunes from the period are used, for instance, James Brown chanting "payback" just before Anthony explodes on a bully. Overall, this is a very srong effort and one that takes on the subject of the difficulties young men of this nation have often had when they go to war looking for manhood and glory but return home to unemployment, a different world, and the humiliations that result from a lack of skills. It is a story as American as that of Frank and Jesse James.

Clockers is another confounding example of the incomplete talent that is Spike Lee. Surely blessed with the ability to quickly absorb cinematic techniques, he is almost always at a loss for the human understanding that would move his work into fullness. The little filmmaker's problem is that he suffers from what Ralph Ellison recognized when observing that the self-aware satirist is usually a sentimentalist who uses ridiculing humor as a device to protect his or her work from the mush that destroys artistry. Lee is not self-aware enough to recognize that about himself and realize that comedy brings out his strengths. A black nationalist version of the comedy director in *Sullivan's Travels* who wants to make "big statements," the pretentious Brooklyn mighty mite is not up to the demands of dramatic development, which is why his efforts outside the mode of satire always sink down into long, virtuosic videos periodically bellowing out obvious messages.

Only Lee could make a film about the blood-spattered world of drug dealing and announce that it would be the nail in the coffin of the genre. That is his way of submitting to convention while pretending to spurn it. But because Lee and Richard Price wrote the script from Price's novel, and because the director has such brilliant actors as Harvey Keitel, Delroy Lindo, John Turturro, and Regina Taylor, there is much more success than one would expect of something solely conceived and scripted by the filmmaker.

While making an unflinching connection between the street anarchy of the crack business and the visions that come out of gangster rap, the film repeatedly shows how much stronger adults are than children, even those who are armed and ready to go buck wild at any moment. When these street punks have to stand up to enraged men or women, they fold up or hide behind the foul-mouthed sullenness that is a form of retreat in the face of greater opponents. If Lee is saying that the rat dung of gangster rap is an influence that helps reduce human beings to spiritual rodents, he might well be right. But since one of the kids advocates the Afro-fascist simplemindedness of Chuck D and Public Enemy as an alternative, Lee remains in a political muddle.

There are also real problems of perspective because Lee doesn't arrive at the "Shakespearean achievement," which is making us recognize the humanity of people with whom we don't identify, something the Hughes brothers did so well in *Menace II Society*. These young crack dealers, who work on Brooklyn project benches in *Clockers*, remain so distant that they come off as some suborder of mammalian life. Mekhi Phifer's performance as Strike, the dealer whose soul we are supposed to see volleying back and forth between good and evil, shows so little acting skill that he can do nothing with the extremely limited emotional scope of the character. He is probably most interesting for the attentive movie fan because, even with his dark, dark skin, Phifer looks so much like Billy Halop of the Dead End Kids—an unintentional comment on the difference between American faces and the divisions of the races.

However boldly Lee flirts with the kind of wild, thematic crosscutting Godard brought to his political period, there is no structural command. While the scenes with the cops are very, very good, there are also unbelievable moments, such as an older drug dealer savagely and systematically destroying a boy's car right across the street from the police station! Each surge forward is followed by something that drains away drama or nullifies credibility; and, as usual, Lee is never one to avoid stopping his film to give the audience a lecture on doing the right thing.

When one thankfully gets to the end, the feeling of having gone nowhere is mixed with a deep appreciation for the work of the best of the actors and the director's undeniable technique. Who is to say that Spike Lee might not someday bring it all together, equaling his cinematic facility with a true sense of the human heart and the ability to realize the originality of narrative form he has yet to find? Perhaps all our Brooklyn Napoleon has to do is spend some time seriously studying the films of Carl Franklin and the Hughes brothers. They are already bound for glory.

Blues at the
Gallows Pole

Though our New York governor George Pataki re-
cently turned the capital punishment juice back on, many are still at
odds over the question of legalized human destruction. This question
will surely heat up again with the recent release of *Dead Man Walking*, a
remarkable film written and directed by the equally remarkable Tim
Robbins.

In a time when we expect so little of American film, especially when
it comes to deep human matters such as death, grief, compassion, and redemption, Robbins has shaped a work of stunning heartbreak and harsh,
empathetic lyricism. If only in terms of its epic humanity, *Dead Man Walking* is a transcendent moment in our art. Two young lovers are killed only
because they are in a remote place after dark; one of their killers is executed because he didn't have the money for a better lawyer. By shrewdly

orchestrating the depth and variety of the responses to both the crime and the sentencing, Robbins gives his film the flip-flopping insights of the blues.

In her role as a lively contemporary nun who has to endure condescension and contempt while meeting the spiritual needs of a convicted murderer, Susan Sarandon is superbly weathered, humorous, terrified, and determined. As Sarandon's nun wills herself up to the love at the center of her religion, we see the mighty power of engaged humility.

The murderer breathes through Sean Penn, who has a protean capacity for nuance. This performance makes the idea of "originality" inadequate. His is the acute gift for becoming somebody else, not displaying a novel style. Understanding perfectly the rhythms of the human heart in conflict with itself, Penn stands quite tall in the small, magic circle of those who bravely command their greatness.

If Robbins is against capital punishment, he doesn't punk out by making things slogan-simple. The grieving family members who want the murderer executed—and the people who do the cold prison work of execution—are as purely human as the murderer's family, the nun, the murderer, and those who are fighting to save him. Such a range of human feeling across lines of conflict doesn't allow the audience to become smug or disengaged.

As Sarandon's nun explores the murders, allows her heart to withstand the emotions of the families, and confronts the killer himself, we are shown that true compassion requires the constant regeneration of courage. Her spiritual duty demands that she seek out the human soul in a despicable piece of murdering white trash, one whose racism and disdain for authority mask the kind of cowardice that knuckles under to totalitarian anarchy.

When that soul is found, he remains, for all the heart revealed as he trembles before the imminence of his death, a man who killed in nothing less than cold blood. As this evolution achieves a masterful shattering, the empathy magnetized by the experience ennobles and deepens the humanity of the audience.

One of the film's largest achievements is that it makes those who believe in capital punishment, as I do, endure its brutal facts. It also allows us to remember that the condemned are executed not because they are monsters or animals, but because they are human beings who have committed irreparably monstrous acts.

Robbins, perhaps unintentionally, makes this clear by juxtaposing the horrific details of the murders with the killer's execution. It is also true that the kind of man Penn brings to such palpable, imposing life might never come to know his own humanity were he not faced with the finality of his execution.

Civilization is a thing filled with discontent, but we fail to truly comprehend our own duty to the recognition of hard human tragedy if we cannot face the savage means of institutionalized execution. It is through those actions that we express the deadly moral weight of our compassion for the slaughtered. With quite uncomfortable resolve, we sacrifice the murderers to justice just as they sacrificed their victims to chaos.

John Henry Versus the Minstrel Machine

The inordinate success, both personal and corporate, in one part of our society and the social failures in the areas of integration, public education, and cultural quality make the theme of redemption inevitable. So much has changed for the better and so much has yet to be done. Redemption, even so, is central to our national vision because the social contract under which we live allows us to redeem ourselves anytime we truly face up to short-sighted, prejudicial, and corrupt policies. When government gives us the blues, we use government to blow the blues away. So it is quite understandable that two recent American films, Spike Lee's *He Got Game* and Warren Beatty's *Bulworth*, take on the subjects of redemption, corruption, and selling out. One has the all-American goods in a renewed set of brilliantly layered variations; the other is good old boy radical-left paternalism, a reshaping of the Tarzan spirit in ski cap, gutter rhymes, and dark glasses.

Lee's tale is rooted in our biblical tradition, our folk myths, and our inevitable American questions about how we relate to the marketplace and to ourselves. It is an inventive, dramatic, and witty allegory. This new work outstrips a career that began with bumptious satire and often lost itself in the agit-prop narrows of a cinematic black nationalism that guaranteed ebony and ivory were always at odds in very obvious and cardboard ways. In fact, the decision to involve Denzel Washington's character in an interracial romance that is not sneered at by the material itself may well have cost the filmmaker success at the box office, since so many black women across the country shouted at the screen in outrage and apparently discouraged others from seeing the film.

Beatty's film exhibits no actual courage at all. Touted over and over by the critical establishment as some kind of political breakthrough, *Bulworth*, for all its topical references, is in the long line of thirty years of American films in which we are told that the CIA is a diabolus ex machina, that Washington is an auction block parading one whorish politician after another, no matter the party, and that big business will murder to keep its hustle going. These "insights" are spouted by a California senator named Jay Bulworth who rises from the ashes of his incinerated integrity by hanging out with some black people and getting crude-oil soul injections—a politicized update of all those westerns and jungle and South Sea Island movies about a mighty, mighty white man who is inducted into the tribe of embattled natives and ends up becoming not just their spokesman but their chief, even outdoing the young tribesmen at their own stuff and sweeping up the prettiest native maiden along the way. Going native nowadays means Bulworth must take on the dress and manner of a rapper in order to get his point across. He is so able to "keep it real," as the cornball "street brothers" say, that when Bulworth repeats facile things that black people have told him they themselves are amazed and act as though what they said must actually mean something now that a famous white man is saying them on television! Bulworth converts even the dope-dealing blacks with their own words. What a friend they have in their self-made Jesus.

Though Beatty's contrived dip in the tar bucket has been praised as proof of his revitalization, Lee is the one who has not only extended himself but also vastly increased the breadth of his evocative powers. With *Do the Right Thing* far behind him, Lee no longer revels in the major social tragedy of the last thirty years—the corrupting and coarsening of Negro American popular culture through the mass media celebration of the most crude and ignorant black people as the truly "authentic." Like the slave trade, the culprits are black and white but the victims are overwhelmingly black. From the blaxploitation films of the seventies to the rap videos that equally glorify ruthless materialism, mindless hedonism, and self-debasement of one sort or another, too many black people have been programmed to willfully underplay their intellectual abilities and display as much rudeness as possible in order to avoid "acting white."

Unlike Beatty, who so wants his hero to become a messianic "wigger" that he cannot challenge any of that reductive "blackness," only pander to it, Lee is looking to regenerate recognition of the charismatic influence that unbrutalized Afro-Americans have long had on our national popular culture, on our way of taking ideas and transforming them into richer ways of living. Traditionally, the Negro has mediated between the raw and the refined levels of our culture, reinterpreting and remaking, helping supply the country with better and better means of recognizing its own vernacular uniqueness and flexibility, usually through an imaginative, improvised vitality, a sense of the individual and the collective; a pliant ritual of down-home awareness, majesty, and humbling spirituality.

He Got Game uses basketball to symbolize the elastic possibilities of the democratic proposition—the individual, the team, the individual. The enormous amounts of money, privilege, and fame that surround the sport raise the ongoing issue facing the nature of civilization in our society, which is whether or not we will continually fight to bring morality, ethics, and the profit motive together. That is what Jesus Shuttleworth has to learn how to do. The kid can go for the gold that symbolizes all of the expensive consumer addictions to prominence through brand-name surfaces; or he can first seek out the development of the inner life represented by a college education and its connection to forgiving his father for the accidental killing of the athlete's mother.

The film opens with a thematic and spiritual overture: a montage of American kids, black and white, rural and urban, either playing alone or on teams. The railroads that once connected us have been replaced by a rubber ball bouncing on concrete, on wood, and dropping through the metal hoop and the cloth net. The loneliness and isolation of practice is preparation for the very best that one can do within the mutating force of the collective. The visual overture's music is Aaron Copland's "John Henry," giving an epic dimension and setting the narrative in the arena of myth, the American tale of a contemporary Negro superhero whose ability to drive to the hoop must face the automated challenge of a hammering machine of celebrity. As the camera settles on the bronze statue of Michael Jordan in flight in front of Chicago's importantly titled United Center, and Copland's powerhouse dissonance rings out, Lee is letting us know that the greatest basketball player of all time is our contemporary John Henry and that our country needs flesh-and-blood heroes, they whose mythic deeds enlarge the frame of our ideals through pure human achievement, improvisation within the parameters of the rules, each hero a succeeding Icarus who rises toward the sun of objective recognition with the whole world in his hand.

Using the exceptional palette of techniques that make him the grand virtuoso of his generation, Lee is able to more successfully combine drama and satire than he ever has before, counterpointing the humanity of his central characters—from children to adults—with the comic and ominous gargoyles that tempt and threaten them in the wilderness of Coney Island, a crumbling dreamworld where Jesus attends Abraham Lincoln High School and becomes nationally famous on its basketball team, the Rail-Splitters. The open opportunity associated with Copland's music pulls the big sky of the western and the heartland, the sorrow and the glory of the country, onto those basketball courts. The rapping Public Enemy—its enormous artistic and technical limitations appropriately embarrassing in contrast to Copland's—supplies the crabbed, hostile yammering of the streets.

Human or demon, the characters and caricatures surrounding Jesus are black, white, Italian, and Hispanic. They arrive from the college and professional worlds of big money sports; they are family, friends, and lovers, most of them trying to manipulate Jesus for their own economic benefit. Support or betrayal can come from anywhere. Pulling timeless power up from the past is an antidote to the sullied compromises and trends that function as parasites, sucking away the blood of one's human-

ity. Consequently, the many references to teaching, to learning fundamentals, and the emphasis on a college education are both allusions to
how Lincoln the common man distinguished himself, and reiterations of
the Negro American tradition of uplift from the inside out. The emphatic, loving, demanding, and cruel taskmaster that was Jesus's father
when he taught him the game of basketball is also Negro history itself, a
thing of inspiration and horror, magic and disillusionment, compassion
and sadism—the source from which the individual must pick the most
profound forces and avoid the soul shriveling that comes of hysterical self-
pity, cynicism, and bitterness. Discipline, wariness, compassion, and good
judgment are of absolute importance.

   None of that is important to Beatty or to his film. What he wants to
do is show just how willing he is to accept black people as "they are."
Somehow, they are always down there below Bulworth and below the entire supposed white world. A couple of colored folks show up in media but
there are no black people who are the equals of the senator. After all, if
they were, he couldn't save them. He couldn't be the white man so capable of leading them to the promised land that they can shout, almost
down on one collective knee, "Bulworth, you my nigger." I guess that's a
"gender-bending" political update of "Bess, You Is My Woman Now."

   Beatty's conception of his black characters is rooted in the dehu-
manizations of videos and sitcoms, but one of the shocks of He Got Game
is what Ray Allen, an actual basketball star, does under Lee's direction.
He creates a young man so complex and given to such a subtle range of responses that Jesus, so full of conflicting ideas and feelings, is an antidote to
the cardboard "inner city" cutouts we get in Bulworth. Lee's Jesus is a
young man who personally knows the world of the flesh and the devil. So
his integrity in the face of temptation doesn't read as that of a candy box
goody-goody. He has bent the rules, encouraged his girlfriend to get an
abortion, uses foul language, and dips into a decadent bacchanal. Jesus,
like his father, Jake, is what historian Stephen Ambrose says Americans
have sought in the wake of Watergate, the imperfect hero like Meriwether
Lewis, the one who stands up, finally, and gets the challenging job done,
against all odds.

   From Denzel Washington—as Jake, the father of Jesus—Lee draws

one of the great performances of the last decade, something quite different but equal to the startlingly original job this actor did in Carl Franklin's
Devil in a Blue Dress. Pathetic, arrogant, insecure, stoic, brutish, tender,
suspicious, disciplined, sadistic, fatherly, and choking with the desire for
his son to forgive him, this character has classic American dimensions,
wide like the country but intensified by the laser precision of an ethnic authority so fundamentally human that it bores through all walls of class and
social division. When Jake says to Jesus, "You better get that hatred out of
your heart, boy, or you'll end up just another nigger, like your father," he
means something far deeper than what Bulworth is called with affection.
He is telling his son that part of becoming a man is learning to accept your
pain and calling upon the courage to redeem yourself from bitterness
through forgiveness. In a time as splintered as ours, there could be no
more powerful statement.

Where Warren Beatty has taken us backwards, Spike Lee has
brought us up to date. In deciding to create a coalition with Aaron Copland, the Brooklyn Jew who set the tone for the cinematic sound of America, Lee has stepped beyond what we expect of him and brought all of us
back into the tragic, sacrificial myths of John Henry and Abraham Lincoln as well as into the fierce, bruised optimism that equally defines our
nation. Lee is as surprising right now as Lyndon Johnson was when he,
who had once run on a segregated ticket, became the greatest chief executive of civil-rights legislation since Lincoln. Let us hope that Lee's box
office failure doesn't push him into a Vietnam of dismay.

The Radio Play Goes Public as the Sit-down Raises Up

I thought I had said my say on American film for this collection when David Hare's British film of Wallace Shawn's American play The Designated Mourner *opened in Manhattan. Hare had directed it on stage at the National Theater in London and, according to Stanley Kauffmann, filmed it on weekends during the run. That gives the film sort of a miscegenated identity, which is American enough for this writer, especially since I couldn't imagine it being written by anyone other than an American, however universal its contemporary concerns.*

The Designated Mourner *thrilled me so much that I went to see it four or five times near the end of its run and would have continued to look at it in theaters—as well as organize more viewing parties—if it hadn't closed. The film was a tonic in our time of so many special effects replacing dramatic revelation and so many breathtaking technical displays of stage craft in expensive productions offering the same combination of the elaborate and the empty.* The Designated Mourner *bet on the actor and the word. I had the same feeling watching it that I did when I saw Kenneth Branagh's uncompromised* Hamlet: *Some people, like the Bard himself, know that the image of a human face or body might be given far more meaning by a thousand words.*

Samuel Beckett's theater was about the feeling of placelessness that arrived when God was chased from the spiritual horizon by science and technology, leaving only the mystery of birth and the inevitability of death. Action meant nothing; ultimately, impotence was all. As his work progressed, if we can describe what happened with such a word, actors ended up to their necks inside urns. It was no longer about the combination of flesh and action. For all the bubbling fuss, experience left one with no more than a voice: connection to the external world of mammalian life was scratched out. For those who believed him, Beckett had expressed something as innately tragic as the Pol Pot schools where children were taught to draw Xs through chalkboard images of people and villages (after all, there are only so many ways to get back to the year 1). So, as Beckett would have it, words were what made you human, no matter how oddly they were used, and all you did, finally, was say something—to others, to yourself, to the very agony that resulted from the pointlessness of existence and the terror of death. (Given the easy observation that Beckett was eventually working on a theater in which acting was stripped down to the manipulation of the voice, it is equally easy to imagine that either slides of images and words projected onto a wall, or the black screen with the white letters of the old silent films, might have been the absolute finale, since each work of an artist is an end in progress.)

In David Hare's film of *The Designated Mourner*, Wallace Shawn's words and vision take Beckett up the road quite a bit. The stripped-down reenters the world. His three characters—Jack, Judy, and Howard—almost always remain seated at tables as they talk to the audience and to each other. But what they have to say, however complex and contradictory, is direct, lyrical, comic, erotic, sullen, and, finally, for all the actual sadness, quite ominous. The question of God doesn't come up because all of that has already been settled.* What human beings do to

*This is not true of Farrar, Straus and Giroux's published version of the play, which contains references to God, some self-explanation that is too explicit, and a few other devices that were, rightly, cut from the script that was filmed.

themselves and to others is all there is, good or bad. There are no other subjects.

Within this frame Shawn has accomplished something rather remarkable: a tragic farce that is politically focused yet quite free of the ideological stodginess so characteristic of our grim while bountiful age. His political tale is essentially poetic; the issues are the martial ways in which any hierarchical social system defends itself once some form of disagreement within traditional policy has been defined as an order of extreme. So somebody up there doesn't like those below and will do whatever is necessary to keep them in their place. If the threat is sufficiently real—or sufficiently imagined on a paranoid express—maintaining order may well include snuffing out or remaking those among the privileged who, while neither violent nor activist, are rebelliously empathetic. Attacking the rebellious among the privileged for their effete snootiness is a technique used by those who have to destroy their own individuality and grovel in mediocrity in order to make sense of their cowardice.

As in Beckett's theater, we have no idea where these people live and distinctions are arrived at through adjectives that almost magically bring specificity, which allows a Shawn phrase as simple as "a delicious sandwich on a white dish" to remove the world of the characters from that of too much abstraction. Somehow, we seem to see all of the particulars of the sandwich. Or we feel as though we know the place when Jack says, "And then a few weeks later I ran into her again, late at night by the lake in that park in that little alley of trees where they used to hang those enormous paper lanterns." It is a way for Shawn to free himself from exactly the poetic silhouettes he has used to avoid the kind of detail that makes most political works so boring or, in their self-righteous obviousness, so condescending. There is also a point to the allusions the characters make to folktales and fairy tales. They imply that this play is meant to serve the very same purpose as those stories set in mythical, once-upon-a-time lands: to let us in on some truth about how the world works or how we might or might not act at moments of serious decision. This could also be the sound of the town crier amplifying his statement by ringing out the blues on the bell in the center of the village.

Shawn's once-upon-a-time world is, doubtless, our own, and through it he examines what highly civilized people and those not so civilized do within a supposedly liberated human universe. That universe has replaced the once dominant Judeo-Christian cosmos in which a Supreme Initiator supplied form and meaning to existence, giving high or low marks for moral performance. It is not, mind you, a world lacking universal creation from above, however far below heaven above happens to be these days. Every so often, the cabinet of the regime changes and there are new color combinations worn by those in power, new restaurants, and new styles of cooking, not to mention the organizing of parades in which new breeds of dogs for sale are shown off. Fashion and commerce renew the society. New entertainments and new creature comforts are new reasons for living.

Yet there actually remains a parallel to the Western religious tale, but it seems meant to let us feel how smugly our spiritual needs have been secularized. The chosen people of the Old Testament are now intellectuals like Howard, whom Jack satirizes by saying, "How should I begin to tell you about this remarkable man who responded so sensitively to the most obscure verses and also to the cries of the miserable and the downtrodden, sometimes virtually at the same instant, without ever leaving his breakfast table?"

The chosen Howards are so tuned up to French academic flatulence that any attempt at comparative objectivity is scorned as a cover for prejudice and condescension. Dismissing the shenanigans of authority with satirical observations laced up in smirks, they consider themselves engaged in emotionally supporting the liberation of those at the bottom, "the dirt eaters." (Though now an elder statesman and a patriarch of refinement, Howard discovered the humanity of those at the bottom when he was a young man and made the fatal mistake of writing about them in an essay called "The Enemy.") Year after year, Howard, the Moses of his crew, remains under observation and is suspected of being a traitor by lowbrow philistines in government. As Judy says of Howard, who is her father, had he not switched from essays to poetry, had his work been clearly understood by the numbskulls in power, he would not be "allowed to exist."

There are collaborators below, like Jack, whose marriage to Judy brought him into the circle of the cultured elite but, incapable of appreciating and responding to refinement, he feels such hateful envy of the cho-

sen Howards that he wishes them destroyed, or at least given their comeuppance. Jack is tired of his father-in-law making him play the idiot, of being asked by Judy about his position on the downtrodden, and being
criticized for not taking sides against those in power. He would rather re-
lax and get along. After all, things are what they are and they always have
been. The simpler the better. The hell with it.

The play's themes and conflicts are orchestrated with musical skill
through variations on motifs in which the excluding and destructive uses
of power are mirrored in the drama, the mystery, and the comedy of sex—
the class and the ass struggle. While some are rejected for their lack of
politics, others are sexually rejected or become sexually alienated; the
intellectually incompetent are also bad lovers whose performances are ap-
plauded only by those who know nothing of sex; the intellectually superior obsessively think of death and have fantasies in which their privates
are quite skillfully massaged by cold-handed lovers; the sexual fumblers
write columns about sex. The play progresses through their tales, arguments, theories, admissions of resentment, lust, voyeurism, and the private thoughts of romantic desperation, fatigue, rage, loneliness, and
defeat symbolized by masturbation. In fact, one might ask if meditation,
explanation, justification, and masturbation are but different versions,
when it comes to these characters, of the same Dagwood sandwich and
the same sticky dish.

In a sense, the play is a cat and a mouse game. The president of the
country, some sort of totalitarian, is described as a cat, while the people
below him are referred to, insultingly or affectionately, as mice, rats, and
rodents. As we know, once a cat has clawed and battered a captured
mouse into a daze, it playfully tortures the wounded prey until hunger or
boredom overcomes interest in the sadistic game. Then, in one savage
move, the cat tears off the mouse's head. That is exactly what happens in
The Designated Mourner. One by one, the dissidents are assassinated—
or jailed, then assassinated after release, or reimprisoned and officially
executed.

The violence starts outside in the dark world, comes through the
window as a rock, and eventually arrives with a knock at the front door.
Images of being struck or Judy's nightmares about being clubbed or Jack's

fantasies of murdering Judy with a croquet mallet evolve into an anony-
mous old man actually having his head bashed in by thugs of the regime
just outside of Howard's house. The question of refined means of execution coyly mentioned by Judy in the overture of monologues and discussions develops into colored tubes pushed down the throats of the
condemned, killing them softly. Bedclothes, prepared meat, animals,
birds, coldness, wetness, buttocks, rectums, urine, and feces are among the
objects, images, textures, sensations, body parts, and the leavings of ex-
pelling functions mentioned in the overture by one or another of the
characters then developed for linguistic and dramatic form throughout.

The dominant character is Jack. The play begins and ends with him
talking. Jack's tale is a series of tremendously long monologues that put
him in the present and the past as narrator and participant. Actually, he
is in the present sitting at a table telling us his story just as he would in a
coffee bar after the smoke of battle has cleared and society is back to going about its business. Jack is the survivor. Everybody else is dead, speaking to us from a place in the past of Jack's mind. Jack, in the quite reduced
ritual circumstances of a café, announces that his purpose as the designated mourner is to tell us of a way of life that only he remembers.

Through an odd and brilliant alchemy, Shawn creates in Jack an
original fusion of the narcissistic and all-purpose self-loathing type only
our jaded circumstances could have produced. Jack has heard all of the
theories and the complaints. He's been educated. The sort of people he
knows are leaning rather heavily against the walls behind which the elite
thinkers live, all hoping to get inside. As mentioned above, Jack painfully
fails to meet the standards of the society of liberal intellectuals like his
wife and father-in-law. In this circle, fine art, as in the writing of John
Donne, has a timeless power to communicate through the ages and, as for
societal concerns, anyone who fails to become outraged by the treatment
of the poor is perceived as some sort of a slug suffering from spiritual
Alzheimer's.

Jack feels excluded, both by the art itself and by those, like Howard,
who refuse to teach him how to fall in love with great writing, how to get
it to let him in. He knocks and knocks at the door but gets no answer.
This experience parallels his growing distance from Judy with whom he

has a wonderful love life until the two of them move into Howard's house so that Judy can minister to a rather vague illness of her father's. Once there, they have to submit to Howard's monumental ego and essentially volunteer to carry his opinions around pinned to their hearts. Jack withstands it all until the handwriting on the wall becomes obvious: Howard, Judy, and their supercilious group—"the readers of poetry"—have only so much time left before they get it in the neck. Jack's hatred of Howard extends over to his feeling for Judy, who now seems as erotically far from him as his own attitudes and abilities are from Howard's: "I kiss you, and it's as if my kiss goes hurtling off a cliff. You take off your clothes but you're not naked." He's got the ice cold blues and, like Howard's lady friend Joan, leaves the sinking ship as soon as one steadily afloat comes close enough.

A genial monster of compromise, Jack belongs to what Susan Sontag wrote of in an introduction to Machado de Assis's *Epitaph of a Small Winner:* "That tradition of narrative buffoonery—the talkative first-person voice attempting to ingratiate itself with readers, . . . chatty, meandering, compulsively speculative, eccentric . . . reclusive (by choice or by vocation); prone to futile obsessions and fanciful theories and comically designed efforts of the will; often an autodidact; not quite a crank; though sometimes driven by lust, and at least one time by love, unable to mate; usually elderly; invariably male."

If we think about what Sontag wrote, we realize that Shawn has made Jack a character much more readily expected in fiction, someone whose stretch of tale in the mouth normally comes to us from the narrator of a short story or a novella, which is almost how the play can be read. But it *is* a play. Some of the technical devices are as old as King Willie's *Othello*, where Iago steps in and out of the story, narrating and performing, setting up the action, the strategy, and the conflicts in the addresses to the audience that precede his strolling in among the other characters to do the low-down dirty stuff that leaves the stage so covered with blood. Then, in the art of fiction itself, *Moby Dick* is so wide open that Ishmael moves from first to third person or supplies other characters with first-person or interior monologues, making us wonder, if we want to follow any kind of logic, whether or not the narrator has made the whole thing up in the first place.

An aesthetic miscegenator of forms and a symphonic developer of symbols and motifs, Melville appropriated anything he needed in order to make his fish story work and is, therefore, an all-American forefather of *The Designated Mourner*, which seeks the freedom necessary to perfectly capture its world—the radio play with the actors seated onstage instead of in the studio, the stand-up routine delivered sitting down, the monologue, and so on. No matter its European avant-garde theater precedents, the play is as deeply American as it is an internally complicated response to what has happened to the stage outside of this country. Consequently, there is a deceptively bare order to this terrible little tale that Jack tells us about his fall from grand aspirations to ordinariness, to compliance with a totalitarian order, to his finally moving beyond the big issues, the cold murders, and the difficulties of struggling with incomprehensibles such as the now forgotten John Donne. In Jack's shrunken cosmos, where even his prized pornographic magazines have ceased to move him, appreciating the early evening breeze will do.

I did not see David Hare's London production of the play that featured Mike Nichols as Jack, Miranda Richardson as Judy, and David de Keyser as Howard. All have the same roles in the film, which works very well in this era of the talking head and of C-SPAN, where drama can surge forward from panel discussions in which none of the participants rise to their feet but the heat moves up through the ceiling. Hare has been criticized here and there for making use of some colored gels every so often but those criticisms are irrelevant when we consider the very high quality of the acting, especially that of Nichols, which amounts to one of the most original performances ever captured on film.

Nichols is familiar at the same time that he is brand new, his performance an innovation of nuance, rhythm, inflection, and tempo that gives Jack a startling vitality. The emotions are quite varied and the dimensions given to them create a wholeness that rises into shape on the wings of a protean resentment of any significance that moves beyond the personal or that asks one to consider anything other than immediate pleasures and concerns. Nichols initially pulls the audience in through his humor, setting up punch lines masterfully. His vast command of the expressive allows Nichols to make Jack shy at one point, belligerent at another, brimming with hate then in need of the richest tenderness, full of self-deprecation but capable of murderous outrage, jaded as well as naïve, as appreciatively admiring as steaming with jealousy, hateful of high culture's metaphors but able to experience how they come about when he feels love for a woman other than Judy, and so on and on. His control of the text, which is as full of the vernacular as the poetic, allows us to experience a man's spiritual suicide, and the pathos that results from it. But our human identification with this extraordinary performance is smacked by the fact that part of its grand accomplishment is effortlessly making us realize that Jack is much like Andre Gromyko, who was the protean man of totalitarianism, surely the greatest manipulator of shifting regimes the second half of this century has seen. Jack is that most facile of collaborators, the sort who will survive because he realizes that he is a rat and that a rat "will do what it needs to do throughout its life to stay sleek, fat, and healthy, which is the beautifully invariable destiny of the rat."

Jack's identity as a masturbator (so wittily punned as he fondles himself in a *tool* shed) is symbolic of his refusal to move out beyond himself. That is why he is incapable of sex with Judy after she and Howard have served five years in prison and Howard has been killed shortly after release. In order "to make the best of a bad situation," Jack has had to destroy himself, do away with his previous personality, his conscience, and the murmurings of his individual spirit. The destruction is described in terms of the murder of an apparition, something close to an internal force whom he finally sees: "I went up to the figure, the unpleasant little self, and sort of pulled it by the arm in the fading light, and I spun it around toward me. And then I threw it on its back and kicked it smartly in the face, and then I sat on top of it, grabbed its neck, and choked it and strangled it and bashed its skull against the floor until it stopped squealing, stopped howling, gasped, and was gone."

Through Nichols we believe Jack's joy at the freedom to drop free of the clothes made heavy and slippery by his failed attempts at holding onto the thickly greased pig of high culture, but when he urinates and then defecates on a book of poetry we realize, as we always should, that products of culture are not forces in themselves; they are protected and passed on. No matter how much went into the making of them, they are easily defiled and forgotten. We also believe the tears of his grief in face of Judy's execution, which prove that the murmuring and fretful little consciousness he killed has resurrected itself. Jack, as in some ancient tribe where a boy is chosen to mourn in memory the passing of an order and wail before "a magnificent sacred fire," finds himself in the debased position of burning "a bit of paper" in a café, the flame moving slowly because of the sticky crumbs left from the eaten piece of cake that had rested on it. Jack, as much a murderer as those who literally did away with the chosen Howards, wanders off, a brokenhearted philistine who will go back to nature in order to satiate his needs with the beautiful colors of the evening light.

However stuffy and self-satisfied, however effete and pretentious upper-class radicals like Howard, Judy, and their friends might be, they have the right idea: We should do what we can to help those who are systematically thwarted from rising to the position of choosing among the better things that human beings have preserved. Deciding to confuse the messengers with the message is perhaps the last resort of the coward confronted by the unfairness of life. As with everything else in our world so overpopulated with observations, we have heard it all before. And, as in all works of art that are actual and exceptional, the common has been made uncommonly new. LeRoi Jones wrote that about John Coltrane and he could just as easily have been writing of *The Designated Mourner* and those who helped make Wallace Shawn's words achieve a poetic politics so far beyond propaganda.

The Nutty Professor

T*he Nutty Professor*, a new vehicle for Eddie Murphy, is more than just a highly successful comedy that exceeds its source, a Jerry Lewis variation on the Jekyll and Hyde tale. It suggests that while the blood and gore of films dominated by special effects are slurped up by millions, something profound is also happening in pop culture. Quality is slowly coming back.

In a CNBC interview with Al Roker, Murphy spoke of how his marriage and his children have changed his perspective. He described a home off-limits to friends from his wild nights in the fastest lane. The comedian told Roker that he was after deeper experiences and wanted to show, in his new movie, that he was just as vulnerable as the next guy.

What *The Nutty Professor* adds up to is more than that. Murphy's performance as a 400-pound man exhibits a much richer scope of feeling than we are accustomed to getting from him. He also plays a breath-taking range of characters, male, female, young, old, white, black. In cultural terms, the movie powerfully rejects the ruthless vulgarity of his 1987 *Raw*, which remains at the very bottom of the slimiest show business barrel. I wonder how he'll someday explain that one to his children.

Murphy largely set the precedent for demeaning rituals of the sort presented by rap production mogul Russell Simmons week after week on *Def Comedy Jam*. In *Raw*, he went beyond even the worst of Richard Pryor, who put the word "nigger" into popular entertainment. When Pryor brilliantly extended upon his first influence, Jonathan Winters, by hilariously portraying a wide range of people, no matter the race, he displayed the originality of genius. But the dark side of Pryor used the street-corner level of vulgarity that, in show business retrospect, is no more than minstrelsy with dirty words. Uncle Tom cursing his way to the bank.

Murphy proved on *Saturday Night Live* that he could also emulate people of various races and classes; but when he discovered that there was a market for the most repulsive monologues possible, the comedian sold out to hard-core filth. Along the millionaire road, he lost his way, setting aside his gift for impersonation and losing his audience.

Still an original, Murphy has now reentered the Bill Cosby universe that he had worked in so successfully in *Coming to America*, which benefited from makeup so refined that the comedian was able to portray both black and white characters on a visual level equal to his vocal mimicry. What Cosby did and continues to do stands above the encrusted grime of popular culture, satirizing while affirming the best of common values.

Though there are a few heavy-handed moments of crude humor, Murphy uses *The Nutty Professor* to reject the worst of his own past in favor of the explorations of the human heart that Pryor—at his twisting, unpredictable best—delivered with a pathos no other comedian of our time has challenged. The Murphy vehicle also nukes the *Def Comedy Jam* level of buffoonery, which is quite interesting, since Russell Simmons is one of the producers behind *The Nutty Professor*.

Who knows, maybe Simmons, the ringmaster of the new coon shows, will turn a corner himself. All is possible, since Simmons will surely go where the most money is. If so, we will witness another example of a public taste for higher quality in the market elevating the very nature of the product. It has already happened in rhythm and blues because women got tired of hearing themselves called bitches and whores. *The Nutty Professor* shows that you can keep the sting without losing the soul.

Bull Feeney
Plays the Blues:
John Ford and the
Meaning of Democracy*

Intro in Autobiography and Aesthetics

As an American formed of cosmopolitan bloodlines—African, Choctaw Indian, and Irish (from an Atlanta, Georgia, plantation on my father's side)—I want to talk about the relationship between jazz and John Ford (who was born John Augustine Feeney Jr.). My intention is to first address the music, that art of the invisible. Then I will look at how the man whose emulation of a human battering ram in high school football games led to his being called Bull Feeney. It is highly probable that Ford—whose art was that of the moving and two-dimensionally visible—said more about the narrative drama and the glory of American

*Somewhat differently, this was delivered as the 1996 Saint Patrick's Day address at the American Irish Historical Society in New York.

democracy in epic and mythic terms than anyone else, stretching from the Revolutionary War to the last hurrah of an Irish mayor who made his way from beneath the seat of society all the way to the wheel of power.

Having grown up in a home where Louis Armstrong and Duke Ellington were as popular as the Western movie, I found myself absorbing the meanings of jazz at the very same time that I was being drawn into John Ford's art through the popularity of John Wayne. Armstrong and Ellington were the symbols of genius expressing itself with virtuosity, satire, comic flamboyance, lyricism, and the elegant colors harmonically voiced in the American orchestra of the jazz band. As Albert Murray observes in *Stomping the Blues*, Armstrong—Papa Dip—was the brown Prometheus who set fire to American music. Papa Dip taught everyone how to swing and improvised with such confident style and emotional flexibility that he gave innumerable artists options that had never quite existed in Western music. Armstrong the progenitor had much in common with Ford because his sensibility and his art rose from a huge camp in which the buffoonish met the lyrical, bravado moved arm in arm with romance, and the sense of duty was made luminous through the grandeur of human endurance and personal sacrifice. Ellington was the D.W. Griffith of jazz, the grand master who best organized the relationship of the solo improvisation (which is the musical equivalent of the cinematic close-up) to the call-and-response of the arrangement (which is the parallel of cross-cutting).

Listening to their recordings and learning, over the years, what they meant to the history of American expression, I was eventually to see just how much what they did had in common with the vision John Ford brought to his finest films. It is important here to remember what Ellington said of the blues, something which I have often quoted and always will:

> The blues is the accompaniment to the world's greatest
> duet,
> A man and a woman going steady
> And if neither one of them feels like singing 'em, the blues
> just vamps 'til ready.

Another quite important part of my life as a young Negro lad was repeatedly seeing Ford's *How Green Was My Valley*. I watched it whenever I
could because there was something in the tale that spoke to the world surrounding me even though the people, superficially, were so different. The
cinematic depth gave me one of my earliest experiences of the meaning of
the universal achieved through aesthetic form. The actors portraying the
community of a coal-mining valley didn't look like the people of my
neighborhood—except for those who were light, light and damn near
white—and they didn't sing or dress like them, but, boy, did they speak to
what I was trying to understand and what I already sensed about the nature of life. I got excited whenever I knew that movie was scheduled to appear on the screen of the electronic box out of which light and images
projected the life of the world, trivial to profound.

While I couldn't have said then why *How Green Was My Valley*
touched me so, I can now. It took the experiences of a boy growing up in
a Welsh family and used them to address how the smoldering dreams of
childhood can be doused by the ice cold fluid of tragedy, the heartbreaking facts that freeze and drown, one by one, those hopes that once seemed
on the path of the inevitable, if only because of the sturdy ways in which
families functioned and because of the steady camaraderie that a small
mining community expressed through song, humor, concern for the sick,
and so on. None of those things turn out to be stable, however, for there
is rebellion within that splits the family, disasters that diminish it, and
conflicts with the community that lead to stones being hurled through the
window of its home. Disillusionment, heartbreak, and disaster did their
usual mauling and slaying. In other words, John Ford recognized, as did all
true jazz musicians, that the tragic blues looms in wait and that we are all
destined to be dipped in their coldness, no matter where we start, no matter who we are, but that our humanity, our willingness to dream and to attempt to do right by our world and by our fellow human beings is what
raises a warm sword of heroic light against the cold, wet, black blackness
of gloom. Like Ellington, Ford knew that the blues perpetually vamp until you are ready to sing them.

It was also, in those years of obsessively playing cowboys and Indians, a pleasure to see how Ford brought together the spit-and-polish blue

jackets of the cavalry with the buckskin outfits of the scouts and trackers. He seemed to feel the American West more deeply than anyone else and was able to give as much understanding to the destructive intensity of battle as he was to the way the women looked on the arms of the white-gloved horse soldiers as they paired off and then danced on the shiny floors or were seen through the windows and lace curtains that symbolized the arrival of refinement. Duty was something Ford believed in, even though he knew that it might cost almost more than one could bear or demand more than one would survive.

As a member of a *blues*-collar community, I found Ford's women quite familiar. Tough as they were fickle, stoic as they were shy, vain to the gills but possessed of immeasurable understanding, they might have nostalgic memories one moment and find themselves ready to heckle or fight the next. In those ways, they were counterparts of the blues and jazz singers whose searing lyricism, wit, and independence filled out the erotic poise of the blues beat with the kind of confidence that easily outdistanced the images of coy ice princesses or pompous busybodies bloated with hot air and condescension. Maureen O'Hara, who might well have been the most beautiful Irish woman ever captured on film, inspired whopper-sized fantasies—her eyes so tender or so wild, her voice timid or obstinately frisky-tailed or brassy with rage, her spiritual profile a combination of innocence and sensuality, stubbornness and depthless compassion. Through Ford, all of those qualities were brought to the full-fledged human condition in which we understand just what kinds of women, in every place, in every race, inspired the poetic exaggerations that led to the conception of the mud-spattered goddess, she for whom the bath was so important because all dirt was inevitable.

As a member of a hot-headed family ever ready to splinter into feuds, I can attest to the many sides of domestic life that the director had the ability to express with superb penetration. When we observe the middle-aged couple played by Donald Crisp and Sara Allgood in *How Green Was My Valley*, we wonder who better than Ford could give flesh and image to those unpredictable moments when the very real masks, mutually soaked in piss and vinegar, are subtly pulled down by the spontaneous arrival of a romantic feeling far too durable to be denied? Was there

ever a father more complex than Crisp in that same film or more a patriarch of the uncivilized than Walter Brennan in *My Darling Clementine* or
Walter Kemper in *Wagon Master*? Was there ever a filmmaker who did a
better job of moving, unit by unit, from the individual to the couple to the
family to the community to the national sense of honor and the tragedy
that draws so much blood and leaves such a train of corpses in the wake of
almost all expansion, of every dream, of any serious attempt at building a
country and making sense of the contradictions and the conflicts?

1. Victory of the Common

*The following section of this essay is adapted from some program
notes for a concert presented by Jazz at Lincoln Center, which
were later slightly reworked for the liner copy of a compact disc
called* Jazz at Lincoln Center Presents: The Fire of the Fundamentals. *I use them here because this was the first place where
I began working on the relationship of John Ford to jazz and jazz
to him.*

What the jazz musician most truly represents is the
victory of the common citizen, or the uncommon citizen from common
circumstances. That is why the story of jazz is one of the grand tales of do-
it-yourself invention evolving into a set of fundamentals that met the
standards of artistic majesty by absorbing and extending all useful information, no matter how basic or complex. This music rose from a variety of closed social circumstances to international recognition and took
prominence as an art of a technological age, one in which the individual
was in danger of being swallowed or enslaved by machinery. Through the
symbolic perfection of human being and machine that we hear in the best
performances, when the human spirit is projected through the machinery
of an instrument, jazz musicians proved over and over that the soul was
capable of making its way even in times so unprecedented, so filled with
new challenges, in a century and a culture that needed an art perpetually
rooted in the earth but capable of traveling into the universe of sophistication. Jazz pulled together things that were superficially at odds.

Blues, ballads, 4/4 swing, and Afro-Hispanic rhythms are the central elements that distinguish jazz from other musics, and through those fundamentals great talents and innovators have always had their say, sustaining and extending our most democratic art, bringing the dreams of our most enlightened social propositions into the active arena of aesthetic vibrance. In jazz, the democratic imperatives of talent determine success, nothing else—not who your father or mother might be, what your sex is, where you come from, what you worship, how much you have in the bank or stand to inherit or have lost. Though a professional can easily sit at the piano and play jazz alone, what we are almost always talking about when we discuss the music is the fact that you have to be able to take a song and invent upon it within an ensemble. You have to develop your own sound and your own style, which expresses itself most powerfully when it achieves improvisations so sensitive that they enhance the creations of others, just as the creations of others enrich yours. In essence, this is a democratic form in which the individual and the mass reinforce each other. That is what jazz musicians mean when they say of a group's members that "They really play *together*."

In more than a few ways, the techniques of jazz represent the kind of mediation that John Ford saw between literal policy and the practical policy that was improvised. As Peter Stowell observes in *John Ford*, "In film after film Ford demonstrated that the march of civilization is epitomized by tensions engendered in the spirit versus the letter of the law. Mediators are needed to bring the two into harmony." Jazz musicians are such mediators. Their art allows the letter of the law that is composition made in the past to meet the spirit that is improvisation made in the present. They bring into harmony the past and the present, the known and the unknown, the familiar and the unexpected, the exotic flowers of the swamp and the universal crown of the stars.

We can better understand what jazz is within the context of our civilization by also looking at the way Ford used Will Rogers, the part-Indian actor from Oklahoma, an American of homespun intelligence and satire. Ford saw in Rogers a man who could express the elements of this country in his own style and thereby embody the sort of Adam a new Eden needed if it were not to succumb to the decadent overcivilizing of Europe. By overcivilizing I mean nothing other than the ritualized behavior, manner, and social vision that expressed not enriching discipline but decadent, prejudiced restriction. Stowell writes of Will Rogers and the myth of the American West: ". . . he was a wanderer with a strong feeling for family and home; he believed in progress and traditional values; his comedy was serious, though he took nothing too seriously . . . He made people smile during the Depression, gave them faith in their youthful energy, got them to laugh at themselves, taught them to take nothing for granted, coached them in the joys of the vernacular . . . He wielded power without making it seem sordid."

Stowell could just as easily have been writing of Louis Armstrong, whose beginnings in New Orleans put him in the cultural gumbo out of which so many different strains of Americana rose. Armstrong, as well as Rogers, could have been the subject when Stowell wrote of the actor and comedian:

> He seemed to have the freedom, space, spirit of equality, and opportunity to become truly the American Adam, not an eastern and warmed-over European model . . . Mass communication allowed Rogers to become the only Adam to present himself as he was . . . Whatever the medium, he was always himself. Everything about Will Rogers signified emergence, freshness, and innocence. But he also embodied the contradictions of polarity. He was a mediator. He was the uncommon common man, the eternal boy with the wisdom of the ages, the skeptical optimist, the natural man who charmed the sophisticates, the folk philosopher who manipulated the media, the friend to every man with a deep reservoir of loneliness . . . He lived during America's entry into the technological and information age. He did not become a hero through the always-tainted heroism of war. He expressed America's most positive values. He was just innocent enough to express them sincerely and just wry and sly enough not to make people gag on them.

All of those observations are equally true of the great instrumentalist and singer whose message was spread through the precision engineering of the trumpet, the electronic destroyer of distances that was the radio, the entertainment and study guides that were recordings, and the retainer of moving images and sound that film became. As the first unarguably great jazz improviser, Armstrong's influence cannot be separated from the innovative mediation that he brought to the letter of the law that was the written composition and the spirit of the law that his improvisations constituted. Armstrong never reminded his audience and his fellow musicians of anyone other than himself, no matter the context in which he appeared—recording, public performance, radio broadcast, film. Papa Dip, the New Orleans Prometheus, became famous for his ability to change the maudlin popular song into a work of art through bending it, leaving some notes out and adding others, slyly and wryly making fun of the mushy lyrics in his verbal asides or gargling them in his throat then spewing out percussive, wordless flights of pulsation that suddenly tore out the heart as they became transcendently lyrical. Armstrong turned something like *Sweethearts on Parade* into a three-part miniature concerto for horn and voice in which each of his statements is distinctly different but creates a meditative to sweltering whole so glorious in its conclusion that the uncommon common man—free of all well-meant but condescending, polemical sentimentality—rises to inspirational victory. Papa Dip's individual art, like jazz itself, resolves the relationship between the individual and the community. Through Armstrong, we recognize that jazz is the work of both the comic and the tragedian. Sometimes, we hear a musical counterpart to the disruptive anarchy of the slapstick comedy given transport by the physical genius of Buster Keaton. We witness the lyric acrobat whose daring sense of balance is equaled by the range of aesthetically realized passion.

As capable of charming the illiterate as the sophisticated, Armstrong can take our breath away and elevate our spirits. No matter how bad the surroundings might be, Armstrong, like the cowboy hero, comes swing-galloping over the hill just as it seems that the bad guys devoted to stodgy rhythm and the dissemination of mush are about to win the day. In no time, he brings inspired, charismatically pulsating form to the deadening circumstances of sallow feeling. In the wake of Papa Dip, the artistically successful jazz musician wields power that is nether melodramatic nor obnoxious, achieving individuality through the collective affirmation of the swinging band, now and again meditating on the moment while alone at the piano keyboard, seated and orchestrating the individual consciousness through the paces of blues and swing. While Will Rogers might well be the perfect Adam within the context of John Ford, it can easily be argued *and* proven that Louis Armstrong is an Adam of much greater import and influence.

2. I Make Westerns

In the westerns of John Ford, Stowell writes, "The frontier is always a place of struggle and mediation set as it must be on the ever-changing cusp between the positive and negative qualities of the wilderness and the positive and negative qualities of civilization. On the frontier the American dream avoids banality because it is tested and challenged in the crucible of change, struggle, and mediation." Ford's art allows us to see the same kinds of crucibles represented by jazz musicians, they who collectively solve the problems of giving form to performance through improvisation. Like the exponents of blues and swing, Ford's people have to work things out, as often as not in unconventional ways, ways that call for their improvising solutions to the disasters that arrive through willful opposition of the sort that always comes with war, whether with Indians or with the outlaws and anarchic cowboys who pose threats to the motion of American civilization or aim to reduce communities to no more than citizens cowering in fear of arbitrary force. In order to more clearly make my point, I must use another longish quote from Stowell, which sets up the perfect frame for my own observations about John Ford:

> In this myth of American civilization the Civil War and the subsequent forty years represent the pivotal era of American history, for it signaled a rebirth structured on division and unification. The post–Civil War West became the most potent frontier because from a twentieth-century perspective one could see the confrontation

between a true wilderness and *modern* civilization. In this respect, both the time and the place made for a truly unique frontier. Out of this frontier there emerged frontiersmen who successfully mediated or unsuccessfully attempted to mediate the extremes of civilization and wilderness, man and nature, East and West, individual and community. The heroes of these romances were the cowboys, outlaws, cavalrymen, gamblers, stage drivers, adventurers, lawmen, Indians, farmers, wives, and prostitutes of the frontier who transcended the trivialities of safe, secure lives by forging precarious existences beyond the reaches of respectable, civilized societies.

The western frontier was the vessel into which the American dream could be poured, mixed, and separated: egalitarian yet individualistic, pragmatic yet idealistic, vast yet restrictive, just yet intolerant, agrarian yet mercantile, friendly yet dangerous, self-reliant yet cooperative. If the evolution of the western frontier stood as a microcosmic model for the development of American civilization, and since America has been conceived as the New World, then the story of the West could be read as the story of world civilization. From the perspective of America's first frontier stage, Europe was the decadent civilization, but in the post–Civil War West the American East took Europe's place. Only in the West could all people be free, live as equals, own land, move at will, make a fresh start, draw strength and moral purity from unspoiled nature. Southerners could regain their dignity, blacks could coexist, and immigrants could fit in. But since the frontier also tested these precepts, man's physical, psychological, moral, and ethical limits were stretched to the breaking point. As the frontier myth has it, the whole of human history can be played out in this mythically compressed and highly charged era.

But what one loves about the way Bull Feeney cinematically plays the blues is his understanding of how Americans, no matter their initial opposition, eventually merge into what the writer William D. Piersen calls "a new cultural alloy." In his films, we also see an evolution in which the images of Indians and Negroes move further and further away from tools of comic relief or dread until they reach the tragic complexity and human recognition elemental to the Americana of our epic. When the flag is raised at the end of *Drums Along the Mohawk*, which takes place during the Revolutionary War, we see that those looking up at it are not only male and female but white, black, and Indian, the three human strains that Constance Rourke recognized as the central ingredients of the composite we call the American. *My Darling Clementine*, Ford's mythic reading of the Gunfight at the O.K. Corral, brings together the Mexican and the white American as well as Wyatt Earp the lawman and Doc Holliday the killer, all eventually working toward bringing order to Tombstone. In *Fort Apache*, an equally mythic but broad and stinging meditation on Custer's Last Stand, Ford shows how the racist attitudes of one Colonel Thursday led to his destruction because the spit-and-polish leader was incapable of accepting the idea that Cochise was a warrior who understood the deceptions of strategy well enough to dupe an arrogant Eastern cavalry officer. In short, condescension and prejudice can make you look like a fool in one instance and lull you into literally losing your scalp in another.

As we know, *The Searchers* is one of the most resonant of all American films for it looks at the race war that was the battle against the Indian and maps out the labyrinths of literal and cultural miscegenation that were as true to that part of our history as they are to our moment. The evolution of the tale shows the West with its mask pulled off, acknowledging the parallel savagery of the whites and the Indians, slaughters of the innocent abounding on either side. We also see that human virtue, like human repugnance, knows no special point of origin. Throughout, Ford makes it clear that even the most charming and gritty people of the frontier can have the serpents of racism hissing inside their hearts—their bitterness over the losses of loved ones and their own fears of being destroyed work together, building not on hearsay but upon fact, ever deepening the pockets of irrational poison within their personalities. This is directed and executed with absolute subtlety and power in the character of Laurie Jorgenson, born of Swedish and American parents (a miscegenation of nationalities).

Vera Miles gives the frontier girl a beguiling combination of shit, grit, and mother wit, but stops far short of melodrama as she is called upon to voice a racist anger that has suppurated in Laurie since her brother and his fiancée were killed by the Comanches early in the film. When Laurie stands looking like somebody's grown-up angel child in her white wedding dress and says, in words of cold fire, that the slain mother of a girl kidnapped by the Comanches would have wanted a bullet fired into her daughter's head once she had slept with Indian "bucks," we see something more than the spiritual silt of hatred. We also understand that racism maintains itself, not because everyone surrounding a racist is equally twisted, but because that very racist may also have so many winning aspects of personality that his or her prejudice is too easily forgiven—one of the very worst examples of the power of the "lovable rogue."

The Searchers is given narrative form by the wandering effort, year after year, to find little Debbie. By the time Debbie is returned to her community, she has grown into young womanhood and slept as a wife with Scar, the polygamous Comanche chief who led the murder raid that killed off her brother and sister, her mother and father, leaving her the sole survivor. Even in a xenophobic climate wrought by what Churchill called "the havoc of war," her sexual involvement across race—and the cultural experience that has made her identity partially Indian—must, finally and in the name of true democratic community, be accepted and Laurie's hysteria rejected. Debbie represents both of the warring factions and, having known both the bitter and the sweet in the worlds of the white and the red, she is now everybody's angel child. We cannot change the tragedy of the past, Ford seems to be saying, but we truly realize our democratic selves—our history, our heartbreak, and our achievements—only when we are able to accept the many forms of humanity that we have absorbed. Miscegenation as mediation.

With *Sergeant Rutledge*, Ford, who was always strongly aware of the tonal colors of the voices of his players, arrives at the dramatic power of the Negro timbre. Using a sound as deep as the blues, Woody Strode shoots for the moon on the witness stand and becomes the revelatory hero whose own pain and sacrifice encapsulate the story of the man, of his people, and of the nation itself, a country which can only achieve its self-respect by standing up to the difficulties its democratic variety presents with ceaseless inevitability. With his head shaved smooth as a cue ball,

Strode's horse soldier supplies a compelling fortitude that counterpoints the previously barbered baldness of Stepin Fetchit's character in the 1937 *Steamboat Round the Bend*, itself an argument with the limitations of minstrel obsequiousness. Yet we would also do well to know that Fetchit was fond of telling other black performers that he got the idea for his cunning buffoon from a cat that once came into the middle of a situation where he was working. The feline creature stopped everything and subserviently meowed at those trying to shoo him away—but held its position, going *nowhere*. Even further, we who look closely at Ford's films should know that the director understood this quite well himself, since the excessively groveling colonized servant in *Wee Willie Winkie* turns out to be a spy intent on freeing rebellious prisoners and helping to overthrow the British rule of India, perhaps one aspect of the director's recognition of both espionage tactics and the wiles of Uriah Heep in another context.

Essentially, *Sergeant Rutledge* is a remarkable variation on the theme that played itself out in *Fort Apache*. A buffalo soldier, a Negro cavalryman named Braxton Rutledge, is accused of raping and killing a young white woman, then murdering her father who discovers him just after her death. In a number of flashbacks, Ford impresses upon us the importance of interracial cooperation to the winning of the West and to solving our problems, whether on the battlefield or in the courts, where Rutledge is defended by an admiring white officer and the audience is given another variation on Ford's sense of the tension between improvisational mediation and stilted formality.

By the end we find that the Negro is innocent, nearly martyred for a white culprit. "As in *The Sun Shines Bright*, a black has been made the scapegoat for the sickness of white society," Joseph McBride and Michael Wilmington wrote in their *John Ford*, a good observation but not deep enough, for we also learn that the father was, in fact, killed by the buffalo soldier—in self-defense. This also goes beyond the 1953 Ford work cited by McBride and Wilmington because the slain white man, coming upon a Negro kneeling over a dead white woman, immediately shot the highly respected black cavalryman, assuming guilt on the spot, no questions asked. All that Rutledge had achieved as an exemplary soldier was set aside as the dark history of xenophobic presumption rose up in the father, gun blazing with the force of his hysteria. Here we see that the false read-

ings determined by ingrained prejudice, once again, can result in decisions that lead to one's own death.

We see more than that when we recall that there was a similar situation in *Young Mr. Lincoln*, where there had been a struggle between the
accused and the murder victim but another person had secretly done the
killing. There is also something of what Faulkner was looking at in *Intruder in the Dust*, his own tale of the wrongly accused Negro in which Lucas Beauchamp sails so far above segregated society that one character
says of him, "We got to make him a nigger first. He's got to admit he's a
nigger. Then maybe we will accept him as he seems to intend to be accepted." Similar attitudes, less crudely expressed, are muttered about the
familiarity of Rutledge and his friend, the young white woman who is later
raped and murdered.

Then there is the 1964 *Cheyenne Autumn*, a late Bull Feeney western in which he looks at genocide and makes it clear that the Indians have
been dealt to from the bottom of the deck. Still profound for all its flaws,
the film goes to the other side of historical self-flagellation because Ford is
too much of a bluesman to pretend that all is well when the white folks,
finally, get the hell out of the way. The Indians have fled their reservation
and are chased by the cavalry, captured, and nearly exterminated by the
German-American commander of a fort, the European death camps obviously resonating against an earlier ethnic conflict. But when the Indians
win out and are left to themselves, Ford lets us have it full blast. A hot-
headed young warrior who had taken one of the wives of a tribal elder is
suddenly shot dead by the older man, which is Bull Feeney's way of saying
that the problems of our humanity are there, always there, no matter
whether we find ourselves in war or in peace, in situations of mixed ancestry or among our own. The blues, always the blues, just vamps until
ready.

3. The Ellingtonian Dimension

*In writing an essay about Duke Ellington, I compared the
uses he made of his players to what John Ford did with his actors, ending that
part of the discussion of the bandleading maestro's organization with an allusion*

to Ford's smacking Henry Fonda on the set: "[Ellington's band] was also his version of the John Ford stock company, which used the faces, voices, bodies, and talents of performers such as John Wayne, Henry Fonda, Maureen O'Hara, Victor McLaglen, Donald Crisp, John Carradine, Ben Johnson, and lesser known actors as often as possible. As with those actors, Ellington musicians like Johnny Hodges, Lawrence Brown, Ray Nance, Jimmy Hamilton, and Paul Gonsalves did their best work in the bandleader's stock company, the contexts he provided for them far more inventive, varied in mood and challenging than anything they—or anybody else—could create to suit them so perfectly. As composer, arranger, coach, and rhythm section accompanist, Ellington was also the master scriptwriter, director, lighting technician, dialect expert, head of wardrobe, set-designer, manipulator of special effects, and makeup man. While his legendary patience with his stars of sound was such that he could ignore a fist-fight in a German hotel lobby between his son, Mercer, and a veteran band member, asking only if his suite was ready, Ellington could also explode, once ragefully slugging a drunkard to the floor because he had been embarrassing on stage one time too many. Yes, beyond extending, elaborating, and refining his themes and the talents of his players, he and John Ford had more than a bit in common."

She Wore a Yellow Ribbon is the film in which Ford got from John Wayne the superb performance as Nathan Brittles, a silver-haired horse soldier nearing retirement. In one of the best Western scenes ever filmed, Brittles meets an equally aged Indian friend and they talk of how old men who have known war should try to prevent it whenever they can. Here we note that no one understood John Wayne's voice better than Ford and no one could make more of it. In this scene, the timbres and the emotions of his and the Indian's voices allow us to rethink Ford's films in terms of the accents, the registers, and the tonal qualities his actors use when delivering their lines, giving another meaning to the term "horse opera."

We suddenly realize how precisely Ford orchestrated the many accents, dialects, and kinds of talk in his films, ranging from the refined to the crude and elaborating on his concern for music. This made many of his works cinematic extensions of what Melville did so brilliantly in Moby Dick, which is fundamentally, as was Huckleberry Finn later, about the breadth of the American voice, and is also the point Duke Ellington made about the Negro American musical voice in *Black, Brown, and Beige*. For his westerns, as an example, Ford would orchestrate accents that come from the Midwest, the South, Oklahoma, Ireland, Sweden, and Mexico. He knew which actors to cast for their particular gifts at delivering specific styles of speech with authority and scope. In that respect, Ford is also akin to Ellington, who voiced his chords according to the different ways in which the instrumental tones of his highly individual musicians could make given notes sound. Ellington said that when he heard a note in a given register he then had to decide whose note it would be, resulting in a timbral harmony of exquisite precision.

There are nearly as many examples as there are sound films made by Ford. Here are some. Listen to Henry Fonda, whose basic vocal tone is used so differently in *The Grapes of Wrath* as opposed to *Young Mr. Lincoln* as opposed to *My Darling Clementine* as opposed to *Fort Apache*. When Ford directed James Stewart as the marshal in *Two Rode Together* (a varia-tion—though less good—on *The Searchers*), comedy, avarice, virtue, and rage were woven together so well that Stewart's famous sound was put to uses outside of what we normally expect of that purely American actor in the cowboy context. One of the film's best moments—as Tag Gallagher points out in his intimidatingly marvelous *John Ford: The Man and His Films*—resulted from Ford tricking Stewart and Richard Widmark into improvising a remarkable scene near a river. As they discuss women and marriage, what is essentially Stewart's monologue is slyly and wittily countered by Widmark, whose interjections have the parodic spirit of a jazz piano player perfectly accompanying a soloist while making subtle fun of what he improvises.

Ford is well known for the use of song in his work but there is per-haps no more startling depiction of beauty *in* the beast than the moment in *The Searchers* when Ken Curtis, as the smitten bumpkin who speaks with an extremely crude accent, picks up a guitar and sings to his strong-willed lady love in a luminous and bewitching voice. Ford is telling us that when we see such headstrong women in the company of yokels, some-thing may exist in the men far different from what we are superficially able to recognize. Within the context of the film, we understand perfectly why

Laurie Jorgenson, this super fine-looking Texas girl, decides to marry him and temporarily abandon the torch she carries for another. Like the audience, she has been absolutely charmed.

4. The Machinery of Democracy

Though he once said of himself, "My name is John Ford and I make westerns," the director was precisely attuned to his own era. He well understood what the technology symbolized in his historical films by weapons, books, trains, the printing press, and the telegraph meant to the modern age. We should expect such awareness from a man who, like Armstrong and Ellington, had grown up with this century. Some of his most profound thinking appears when the relationship of the machine to the individual, to the age, and to democracy come together.

The Wings of Eagles is the story of Spig Wead, flying ace and naval air force innovator. It includes one of John Wayne's finest efforts, a performance in which we see him age and become frail, reflective, and sad in the face of what his self-centeredness has cost him in the intimate world away from public triumph. Wayne had evolved under Ford into one of the great film actors, an original who could stretch a much wider range of expression than he is usually credited for, which included a very fine talent for comedy that Ford plumbed in *She Wore a Yellow Ribbon* and Wayne himself extended under other directors in such films as *Rio Bravo*, *North to Alaska*, and *True Grit*.

In *The Wings of Eagles*, we are initially fooled by the first half hour, which is a tribute to the slapstick anarchy of the silent era, when American comedy took the form of successive collisions, building from one chaotic situation to the next, something Ford does again in the middle of the later *Cheyenne Autumn*. We are also given to believe that Spig Wead is, essentially, invincible. Bulky and arrogant, he crashes a plane at an officers' picnic, wins aviation races, survives riotous brawls. He is the American Adam become Samson, slayer of expected limitations.

Then, on the very night that he returns to the wife and family he has always neglected in favor of the duty and adventure which are fused in the machinery of aviation, Wead is awakened on the second floor when he thinks he hears one of his children cry out. The big man stumbles and falls the length of the stairs, ending up paralyzed from the neck down. This is the beginning of a series of tragedies and disappointments. After a long re- covery, he remains crippled in both legs and moves about with two canes, his wife and family pushed from his life because he now sees himself as a burden too great for them to bear. Later, however, it is made clear that Wead is so self-centered that what seemed some sort of nobility was actu- ally a way of easing his own responsibilities. A terribly negligent husband and father when he had everything working for him, the egocentric naval hero could not have stood the limitations of home in a diminished capacity.

Wead leaves the service to become a successful screenwriter and playwright, his physical prowess replaced by his ability to create vehicles of action for others. Then, as he and his wife are about to get back to- gether, World War II begins and Wead joins up, now a man whose impor- tance comes from thinking, not acting. In this respect he becomes a symbol of the way power asserts itself in a civilization, perhaps first in a do-it-yourself manner, then through the inventive wisdom of those inca- pable of manifesting the overt force itself but quite able to conceive how it will function. Wead develops some innovative aircraft carriers but, al- most as soon as they prove their worth in battle, he suffers from a heart at- tack and must retire from the service.

Wayne's character resonates against the democratic image of Franklin Roosevelt, who didn't become a great politician until he devel- oped polio. Spig Wead is representative of how those who might only have been cripples in earlier periods find places for themselves within our democracy because, like the hayseed singer in *The Searchers*, they only need instruments to release and accompany the gracefulness of their hu- man passion and imagination. Wead made his marks actively in the first part of his life, then moved on to become a creator, just as Roosevelt in- vented the vast bureaucracy that was a necessary response to the demands of the Industrial Age and the Depression and went on to improvise the quality of leadership adequate for the requirements presented by the al- liances and the massive battle theaters of World War II.

Perhaps Ford's most profound look at the relationship of technology to our contemporary world displays itself in 1958's *The Last Hurrah*. The film is surely a lament for the old Hollywood, since its cast is dominated by veterans beyond middle age, such as Donald Crisp (whose career reached all the way back to *Broken Blossoms*, D.W. Griffith's tragic drama of interracial romance, prejudice, and murder, a clear rejection of *Birth of a Nation*, the director's innovative masterpiece made problematical and disheartening by its xenophobia), Pat O'Brien, John Carradine, James Gleason, Basil Rathbone, and Ed Brophy. The film says its piece through a gloomily comic acknowledgment of the fact that the traditional political machine of flesh and blood would be replaced by the real machines of the media.

What a number have taken as no more than a parody of Nixon's "Checkers speech" (which amounted to a perversion of Roosevelt's "fireside chats") is actually something far more impressive. Ford was commenting equally on the gimmickry and the potboilers of Hollywood—the wider and wider screens, the "casts of thousands," and the quite popular films set in the ancient world so that they could include scenes as nearly-nude-as-possible within the conventions of the time. As an example of an artist at war with the contrivances of excess, *The Last Hurrah* speaks directly to our very own moment, when so many films substitute special effects and gore-shock for human drama. (But ours is also a moment when the Fordian power that comes of character, ritual, and the hilarious weight of the unpredictable—all moving back and forth between satire—underlies the rebellion against formula and gimmickry we see in films as different as *Pulp Fiction*, *Dead Man Walking*, and *Fargo*.)

Ford also uses *The Last Hurrah* to take another look at the variations of xenophobia that are older facts than the social contract. The descendants of the Pilgrims hate the immigrant political power represented by Spencer Tracy's Mayor Frank Skeffington and look with unmuted disdain upon the poor and their needs. The intention of the Yankee blue bloods is to stop Skeffington from being elected for a fourth term, and the airheaded candidate they choose to back is a comment on how the contempt of the rich and the malleability of the stooges who do their bidding lead to reactionary alliances that calculatedly diminish the reach of democratic consciousness and policy. But we also realize that Ford is creating a drama of symbolic racial integration when the descendants of the lower-class Irish and the upper-class British talk of their children going to the same schools and "intermarrying." This extends upon his own many repudiations of *Birth of a Nation* in which the future director galloped on horseback in a hooded robe as one of the heroically depicted Ku Klux Klansmen. As they say, we all start somewhere.

The Last Hurrah is periodically blunted for at least half of its length by Spencer Tracey's tipsiness, resulting in more than a few of his lines coming out in muffled slurs. But, from the scenes in which defeat is imminent, Tracy rises to such stoic recognition and spiritual ache that the film takes on a dark lyricism in which the way loss is handled tells us that Skeffington is, in fact, a people's hero whose cunning and willingness to play dirty has less to do with solidifying his own power than with allowing him the flexibility to sustain the elements necessary for democratic realization. This is in perfect keeping with Ford's *Young Mr. Lincoln*, where the future president manages to have just about all of the qualities that Stowell used to describe Will Rogers—and isn't above being the trickster who will cheat to win a tug of war, or the eloquent down-home foe of anarchy who can talk the rage out of a lynch mob. Mediation with the feeling of the blues.

Coda

On any evening, in any American place, I might turn on the television and see a film of John Ford's, maybe something like *The Fugitive*, which is perhaps the most beautiful black and white film ever made, or I might be swept by the images of another into that house at 1239 East 28th Street in Los Angeles, where I began studying film through the *Million Dollar Movie*, a television offering that ran one film night after night for the entire week, sometimes with matinees on Saturday and Sunday. Then you could memorize the dialogue and begin to learn things about camera position, lighting, cross-cutting, and scores, none of which you realized you were being taught through the obsessional combination of appetite and repetition.

Just as easily I can hear certain performances by Louis Armstrong or Duke Ellington and return to the home now burned down and that world vaporized by time. I can see my younger brother whom I both loved and hated and who, before he could read, was able to somehow pick the tunes my mother wanted to hear from stacks upon stacks of 78-rpm records. That street and those people, some of whom are now gone (my brother from the complications of a gunshot wound to the stomach he received years earlier, my mother cremated in Houston, Texas, after her 1992 death on Bloomsday), rise into asphalt, concrete, fences, lawns, bricks, homes, and life once more, crossing the dark breech of eternity. I am back there just as the boy was in *How Green Was My Valley* and nothing is dead, nothing gone, all is made perpetual through the regeneration of memory.

These are the sorts of things that men such as John Ford, Louis Armstrong, and Duke Ellington do. They say who they are with complete individuality but who each of them might be is so at ease within the reverberations of humanity that he expands our experience with new things and reminds us of older, ancient, more timeless elements, such as the moments our primordial ancestors learned they could put something that was far, far inside themselves all the way outside and that its clarity of form seemed to speak not only of their own perspectives but for all of those whom they knew and that the ones who were particularly moved by the objective scratchings left on a wall or in the dirt or the invisible touch of this song in the evening when the sun went down *might* say something back, with just a little bit of soul, now, just a little bit. That little bit was always enough because it had the spark of regeneration, the central achievement shared by Ford, Armstrong, and Ellington, three godfathers who made even grander the mighty essences of American culture and the symbolic meanings of democracy as artistically revealed in sound and image, rhythm and tune.

PART EIGHT

Coming From Strength

Miles Davis in the Fever of Spring, 1961

I wear Brooks clothes and white shoes all the time
I wear Brooks clothes and white shoes all the time
Get three C's a D and think checks from home sublime

I don't keep dogs or women in my room
But I love my Vincent baby until the day of doom

Rhinehart, Rhinehart, I'm a most indifferent guy
Rhinehart, Rhinehart, I'm a most indifferent guy
But I love my Vincent, baby, that's no Harvard lie
—"Harvard Blues"

So much was behind him on the Manhattan night of May 19 when he walked on that world-famous stage in 1961 and heard the applause of a full house. The audience was about half black and half white, ranging from sidewalk types to high society in the close rows and the boxes. What happened is now on *Miles Davis at Carnegie Hall*, the double compact disc containing the first full release of all the material played on that evening in its exact sequence. A signal moment in jazz took place, one in which so many aspects of American culture, stardom, personality, politics, and ethnic complexity were put on display or implied. The evening was a benefit for the Flying Doctors of East Africa, a humanitarian organization founded in 1957 by three plastic surgeons, one American and two British. Based in Kenya, the Flying Doctors provided medical assistance, surgery, and training to populations suffering from disease, deformities, and wounds brought about by accidents or violence. Outside the concert hall was an ambulance, newly purchased for the organization, that those attending the benefit could see and examine.

During that first spring of the youthful and doomed Jack Kennedy administration, there was a national feeling of invincible optimism undercut by the shock and despair that came from the country witnessing the barbaric Southern responses to the Civil Rights Movement, which was perceived by some Negroes as no more than one aspect of an international problem with race and colonialism that connected all black people. In that context, Davis would sum up all that had happened for him since he had made his comeback from drug addiction at the Newport Jazz Festival in 1955, perhaps all that had happened since he had begun playing with Charlie Parker ten years before that.

Now was his time, nobody else's. The trumpeter was ahead of the curve, holding a position that was much larger than the sound of anybody's music. His attire was under as much awed scrutiny as the notes he chose to play. He had been setting styles among Negro musicians and others for at least six years, defining what was hip and what was not. Philadelphia drummer Rashied Ali remembered how an album cover of the middle fifties with Davis in seersucker jacket, no shirt, and cap had kicked off a trend. Trumpeter Ted Curson observed how musicians laughed at white buck shoes until Davis wore a pair and let them know that those, too, were theirs for the having. Opening the way was his business. The attitude with which he carried himself, a chastening kind of arrogance, exuded something that made it possible for him, as trumpeter Bill Dixon recalled, to enter and change the context of a room as thoroughly as Duke Ellington and Thelonious Monk did, two other Negro men whose power took on a palpable condition in the atmosphere as soon as they came through the door. Davis didn't announce songs and he never seemed too happy to be *anywhere*. Geniality was verboten. Were his attitude reduced to one question, it would have been, "So?"

Some speculated that the nastiness of his attitude had been picked up from his hanging around with the dismissive and monumentally egotistical Sugar Ray Robinson, the greatest prizefighter of all time and one of the champion boxers who might be seen in the audience on any of the nights when the pugs decided to go downtown and hear their buddy blow his horn. Davis was surely quite impressed by Robinson's public demeanor, which was low-keyed, articulate, and matter of fact, even playful. Yet he was never caught wiping shit off his imperial grin. There was not the slightest hint of inferiority or intimidation in his manner. Quite the reverse: he was a king among men. The fighter was also highly regarded in the world of sports and show business for his powers as a negotiator of contracts, his smoothness, the fact that he demanded percentages of gates and the profits from radio and television or—with the fans in the seats and ready for the battle to start—Robinson would sit in the dressing room still in his street clothes ready to go home if the promoters didn't bend his way and put up some more money.

Robinson owned a number of businesses in Harlem, and one of them, Sugar Ray's, was the hottest bar uptown, where every black somebody who was *truly* somebody came to drink, talk, and be inside the black rhythm on its hippest tip. When the great boxer walked into his club, everything went his way and the energy shifted because the emperor of the evening had brought greater power to the night. Miles Davis noticed that, just as he had seen it with Charlie Parker and Duke Ellington. On an athletic level, the trumpeter so admired pugilists that he studied the high art of fisticuffs among them, loving the various punching bags as well as the jabs, punches, and feints training gave destructive accuracy. He eventually had a boxing gym built in the basement of his home. There was sophistication in his soul and a taste for blood.

This small man with the big influence, he who would turn his back on his audience and walk off stage, gave the impression that the conventions of the entertainment business had never entered his mind and evolved into his own Sugar Ray. When sustained attention came his way, Davis was ready to hold power over others. He did this in a number of ways and for a number of reasons. Davis used his rasp of a voice at such a low volume that people had to pay close attention to understand what he was saying. They had to lean into a land of whispers. He made anybody, black or white, feel that nothing about him or her was automatically important or worthy of respect. You could be treated like mud no matter who you were. Yet another part of the awe musicians felt for him came from the fact that Davis had, as Dizzy Gillespie observed, revolutionized working conditions when he forced club owners to accept three sets a night, not the forty minutes on and twenty minutes off that began either at nine or ten and continued until closing time, which could be, in Manhattan, 4:00 in the morning. The silly kinds of album covers art directors conceived with no images of Negroes weren't for him and he made this obvious when the cover of *Someday My Prince Will Come* had a head shot of his beautiful wife, Frances Taylor. Musicians had deep respect for his highly intelligent sense of overall musical engagement, which brooked no racial lines and went far outside of jazz in pursuit of scales and forms he could adapt to his music. One musician recalled noticing two things:

> Miles was always surrounded by a lot of white people whenever I went over his house. They were giving him music and he was analyzing it with them. Once, now, I walked in on him talking to them whities and his voice was straight and normal, just like anybody. Loud. I heard it! Then when he saw me, he went back down into that frog voice everybody was used to. He thought that was hip. Made him seem like a gangster or something. That wasn't all of it either. I found out that another thing he was doing was he would be hanging with Gunther Schuller, John Lewis, and George Russell. They would be looking into some different stuff and discussing another whole level of music. These guys were into conceptions, not just how to play some hip notes on some chords everybody else played. Miles, John, and George, those Negroes were standing toe to toe with them whities, *intellectually*, and they were bringing home some *serious* bacon.

As handsome, jet black matinee idol, the trumpeter was also—along with Nat Cole and Sidney Poitier—breaking down the color restrictions of sex appeal among Negroes and whites. He stood shoulder to shoulder on the plane of pretty boys with Billy Eckstine or Harry Belafonte, each the traditional, light-skinned version of an attractive Negro, a heartthrob palatable to the white and the black. Now, with cool Miles Davis, an extra look was added to those that raised bushfires below the navels of American women. The skin tone yoke of "if you're white you're all right; if you're brown stick around; if you're black stay back," was slipping off. To those yellow-loving Negro women who once said of men his color, "I've already got me one shadow, I don't need two," Miles Davis was starting to seem kind of sexy. Black motherfucker. For the white women, rich and famous, or rich and unknown, or just pretty and curious, or not pretty but still attracted, the black guy with the trumpet and the dark glasses became an embodiment of the primitive and the cultivated in one package. That stuff crosses the street: There is also the fact that extremely dark Negroes with superior abilities can put the white and the black under a spell, each group feeling that it is in the presence of something aboriginal. Wow-wow from back before way back. That, too, worked for cool Miles Davis. Oh, he had it going on.

His trumpet style, as deeply steeped in the Negro tradition as possible, was all his own, a cool mist or blast of blue flame full of insinuation, sensuality, remorse, and melancholy. That style was not the sound of a man walking on eggshells, as someone had described it. Saxophonist Jackie McLean reckons it more to that of a man sitting on a slowly floating block of ice at the North Pole, encircled by nothing but water as far as the eye can see, and unflinchingly telling his Harmon-muted story and the story of all he knows. Whatever the image his sound inspired, by 1961 Columbia Records, in its ads and through its record club, had promoted him in such a way that one could not feel *truly* sophisticated unless a recording or two of his work was in the collection. Moody and romantic, sailing up over the beat of his subtle to extremely swinging small group, or expanding the emotional range of his art in concerto situations devised by the trumpeter in conjunction with Gil Evans, the Miles Davis horn not only helped define the very best of American life; it helped purify our conception of what quality was possible within the arena of the popular. In that respect, he was a miniature Duke Ellington of his moment.

Though born in 1926 and but a week shy of his thirty-fifth birthday on that May night at Carnegie Hall, Davis had the knowledge of a man much older than he actually was. He had come up the privileged way and he had come up the hard way. His father was a quite-well-to-do dentist in

East St. Louis and a gentleman farmer who raised prizewinning swine. The high life and the low life were equally familiar to the trumpeter and he now had democratic contempt for the pale, blue-veined wealthy who thought some line back to the *Mayflower* kept them from being sad, boring, pompous, unwitty pains in the booty; he had disdain for the immigrants who ran show business, and there was nothing in his heart but a feeling of rancor toward those Negroes struggling below who had allowed dissipation to tear them down from the proud glory of their talent.

In New York, Davis had learned about the lack of communication, the decadence, and the perversion that attended more than enough of the long-term wealthy and the nouveau riche. He looked somewhat askance when they appeared around him. Given his complexity, there was still an ease he had always shown toward these people, from the forties forward, when he might talk with them about horses, golf, hunting, the latest fashions for men and women, as well as the various painters and sculptors who were at the centers of discussion when the innovations of the century came into the conversation. Inky, as he was sometimes called by those Negroes ready to chide him, knew how to make the upper-class white people look up to him. The trumpeter was far from an anti-Semite or a bigot of any sort, but Davis knew that if America weren't so racist Jewish entrepreneurs wouldn't have been able to corner so much of the market and move back and forth between the darkies in the basement and the white folks in the office buildings that nearly touched the sky. The Negro provided the fault line that allowed plenty of despised Europeans of whatever religious backgrounds to stand in with the white crowd, to even carry themselves as though they knew more about the United States than black Americans and could serve as their guides into the greater society. They could kiss his ass at high noon on the steps of City Hall. He enjoyed frustrating them and playing hard to get, negotiating with the same sort of toughness Sugar Ray was known for, letting it be known that he didn't really enjoy performing that much and wanted to stay off the scene in order to investigate his other interests. If there was going to be any begging connected to gigs, it wasn't going to be on his part.

Once a shameless heroin addict himself, Davis would use the harshest terms to describe those still pinned to the cotton by syringes. They were barely above filth, even if they were his friends. He could knowingly describe to outsiders exactly how drug deals went down on the Manhattan avenues where the dope was bought and the dope was sold. Anytime some friend who was still tied up came by his swank home and borrowed money for heroin, Davis would note "for drugs" on the remaining stub after writing the check and tearing it out of its book. The trumpeter became so opposed to anything pharmaceutical that he boasted of not even using aspirin. But every now and then he wavered and the neighborhood druggist had to slip him some pills to handle his troubles. According to Philly Joe Jones, Davis's drummer in the classic quintet of the fifties, the bandleader would, here and there, use some heroin. After throwing up like a beginner, Davis would go up on the bandstand and, emboldened by the drug, take chances of a taller order than usual, bringing them off only because he had done all the laborious technical homework necessary to capture and give compelling logic to a spontaneous and formidable fantasy. Nothing, however, took him off of the career path he was on once he got a true sense of where he wanted to go.

By the late fifties, polish and the good life were essentially what he was after but Davis had no intention of automatically accepting anybody else's definition of what either of those two things meant. Clothes, food, cars, and whatever else went with feeling the sheen of absorbed quality just under the skin were what he wanted, first and foremost, when he wasn't only obsessing over extending his musical abilities. Davis was a gourmet cook who lived on the Upper West Side of Manhattan and would instruct the women in his building on just how to prepare succulent meals, step by step. If they got in jams, his door would either be knocked on in a panic or he would get a frantic phone call. Then, in his signal rasp, the trumpeter would talk them through the culinary crisis. Once, when preparing his legendary chili, Davis realized that something was wrong; it didn't yet have that perfect taste. Eventually, he took two teaspoons of water from the tap, stirred them in, tasted the chili, and announced to his friends that the offering had now crossed into the territory of the delicious. Davis had begun driving sports cars during the middle fifties after walking past a showroom window and seeing one of the small automobiles conspiratorially winking at him. The trumpeter stopped, paused, turned around, and saw, once more, the car wink. He knew then that there was no choice other than to buy it. What else could he do? The car wanted *him*.

At least that was what he told his friend Jean Bach, a beauty of the Grace Kelly visual strain who had been running around with Negroes and anybody else she damn well pleased for almost twenty years. Her sweet man as the Depression wound down was the musically combative trumpet giant Roy Eldridge. She rode around Chicago with the medium brown, slick-haired bantam flamethrower in his car when such things certainly were not done by upper-class cutie pies groomed for positions of significance in what was then the certified, snow white aristocracy of this land. Bach, a Vassar girl from Chicago, was also palsy with Duke Ellington and knew her way around the Manhattan she had migrated to and in which she found her own success in radio. She was an insider when she started to learn the ways of Davis in the middle fifties.

"Miles was very different from other jazz musicians I knew," Bach recalls. "When I met him at a party in Boston, he surprised me because he was such a good dancer. Very, very good. He knew all of the steps and was very graceful. This guy didn't step on your feet and stagger around. Oh, no. Completely at ease on the ballroom floor. Most musicians can't dance, of course, but he sure could. Miles knew how to lead and all he wanted to talk about at the time was Grace Kelly. He was fascinated by her, which might have been one of the reasons why we became close. I believe he liked my look and I was from that kind of background.

"His own look was very important and he explained to me that because he was very dark he picked all of his clothes quite carefully. He never wore white dress shirts, for instance, only off-whites, like eggshell and different shades of blue that complemented his skin. Details were important to him. Some of them were odd and some of them weren't. His star was on the rise and he had an absolutely charming balance of the cocky and the elfish in his humor. The things he would say. Oh, he was just such an *imp*. He wasn't funny; he was witty. But his wit could put you on the floor, I tell you. There was always an unusual angle to what he said and what he saw. He was sort of a handsome leprechaun. Small, beautifully built, and full of mischief. Things were panning out for him and he intended to enjoy himself. But there was always this kind of sadness about him. It was there and very penetrating. You knew he had been hurt by something or was sunk in some kind of deep melancholy. Miles could withdraw into his sadness and it could seem as if he wouldn't be able to come out of it. His unhappiness could trap him and hold him down. It really could. Depression was one of his struggles."

Davis was also struggling with his dislike of women, which began with his mother, whom he almost never brought into a conversation with Bach for any purpose other than to make fun of, or to serve as the wicked queen at the center of some bitter anecdote from his childhood. He wasn't very thrilled by black women and made them the butts of jokes for their lack of education or their bad taste or their huffy pretension or their provincialism or their palatial rumps. One Negro woman thrown out of his house nude and covered with cigarette burns made her way into the acidic cup of gossip that was passed around during those years. White women could be criticized for their hair clogging up the drain in his bathroom. In one case, after he had visited a young white woman in the hospital, reading Paul Lawrence Dunbar and James Baldwin aloud so she could get an equal black dose of rural and city feeling, her miscarriage of the child she carried by Davis was described as a clear example of her ineptitude: "Oh, she can never do *anything* right."

Conversely, there could be no more courtly man and no one more capable of expressing transcendent romantic emotion through his horn. As trumpeter Freddie Hubbard recalls: "That Negro was slick harmonically. He caught something playing with Bird. Charlie Parker taught him something. He learned it and he *edited* it. There was some hip, inside-the-chord stuff he worked out that let him make his statement with less notes. Then he had a *tone*. You hear me: a *tone*. It could touch anybody but it could do something different to women. Miles would hit a low note with that Harmon mute in his horn and the girls would move their legs like they had just got too hot to keep their thighs together."

Davis began learning from Charlie Parker when he was working on Fifty-second Street with him in the middle forties. The trumpeter had arrived in 1944 from East St. Louis with a suitcase of Brooks Brothers suits and plans to study at Juilliard and in the streets of jazz. Charlie Parker was the man Davis sought and he spent his first weeks in town looking for the alto saxophonist. Davis had heard Parker when he came through St. Louis with singer Billy Eckstine's band, which had needed a substitute trumpet player and hired the dark young man. In that band a new music was in the process of being made. It was soon known as bebop or rebop or bop. The style was far more intricate than normal and its texture was leaner, even abrasive, devoid of the lush vibrato that distinguished earlier schools. Essentially, Parker was its fountainhead. He was a phenomenon possessed of such magical muscle memory that he could teach his body to do almost anything at extreme velocities—throw with great accuracy, shoot pool, play golf, do card and coin tricks, assume very difficult yoga positions. That ability had allowed him to learn the saxophone far faster than even his legend had it. At seventeen, in 1937, he could barely play at all. In three years, he was a top-flight young alto player. In seven years, his abilities made the majority of jazz saxophone players want to hide under the bed. Davis knew from the first time that he heard Parker what kind of playing he wanted to do himself. He was equally taken by Dizzy Gillespie, who was the organizer of the style and a trumpet virtuoso to end virtuosi in jazz. While his tone was thin, Gillespie played with such slithering rhythmic daring and harmonic complexity that he, like Parker, redefined his instrument. Gillespie, who would one day look like a wind demon with his enormously puffed-out cheeks, also taught those anxious to know just how to play the new bebop style, including not only the brass and reed players but also the piano players, the bass players, the drummers. Parker had the language but Gillespie ran the homemade conservatory.

Davis found Parker in Harlem that fall of 1944. He was ragged and homeless, high on heroin, but always ready to live life his way, which came down to two words: *me first.* They roomed together for a bit and Davis studied what Parker and Gillespie did while taking classes at Juilliard. Sometimes, when the music coming from the many clubs on Fifty-second Street was at an end, he and the trombonist J. J. Johnson would sit in Grand Central Station and study the scores of twentieth-century composers that Davis had gotten from Juilliard's music library—Stravinsky, Ravel, Debussy, Bartók. That intellectual curiosity never left him. At the time, as Vernon Davis remembers his brother, "Miles was like Jack

Armstrong on the radio, the All-American boy. He was sweet as pie. Do anything for you. My brother was cocky now. He got that on his *own*, not from my daddy, not from my mother, not from *anybody*. That came with him; that was his own thing. But he was still the sweetest kind of boy. Charlie Parker, New York, women, and all those kinds of things changed that over the years."

In essence, the 1944 Davis was then a country boy and would remain so for the rest of his life—regardless of how much he came to know, both intimately and conceptually. He was also another of the many spoiled, middle-class Negroes who had brought so much to jazz and had long been battering the one-dimensional stereotype of the impoverished, bare-footed darkie wailing his woes from behind a stack of cotton bales. Duke Ellington, Coleman Hawkins, and Fletcher Henderson were men of his ilk, innovators all, each reared in comfort and thoroughly modern in taste and deportment. Davis, whose grandfather on his mother's side was an American Indian who wore his hair in two long braids, had been served by a maid in his father's Southern-style mansion on two hundred acres, where he learned to ride horses, fish, and hunt.

For all that, the ethnic skin game still revealed itself. As Vernon Davis recalls, "We lived in those times when it was all crazy. It was supposed to be segregated, but that was some shit. In the Negro school named after Abraham Lincoln we already had integration, you know. We had the blondes and the redheads and the ones with the blue eyes and the green eyes and the hazel eyes and the hair running all the way down their back and that sort of thing. They weren't considered white because they had people who looked like us in their families *some*place. So in the white schools, you had just white people. But *we*, you understand, had *everybody*. Once you saw all of that and you met people in your family looked as white as anybody in the movies, you knew this whole thing was fake. Color didn't mean anything. My brother didn't need to get to New York to find out a damn thing about that. He liked who you were. He didn't care what color you were. Miles didn't look up to you to look down on you. You had to show him something. Then he made up his mind whether the two of you could hang out or you could go to hell."

In the bandstand sweatshop of high-velocity music-making that

Charlie Parker preferred, the world swiftly moving by in glinting details, Davis got his first New York notice, sometimes struggling with the music, eventually finding his own way to fill in all the spaces. But he was soon looking for something of his own to play, a compressed breather from the cascading triplets that characterized Parker and his followers, no matter their instruments. Lester Young, Billie Holiday, and Louis Armstrong gave him strong clues. Each of them were whittlers. They cut things down and they sailed. Their music was whimsical, melancholy, spiritually weather-beaten, full of brave and gutter humor but, finally, dreamy and majestic in a decided manner. Davis liked what they did and learned from Thelonious Monk how to use stark materials that could, in their simplicity, create an inverse kind of dissonance against complex chords. If, as saxophonist, bandleader, and scholar Loren Shoenberg observes, the harmony itself is harsh, then a direct consonant melodic invention is dissonant. Uh oh.

His own first recording date as a leader, in 1947, used Parker on tenor, and Davis was heard moving in his own smooth direction. He was also in the process of working out what would become known as "cool jazz," an approach to sound that seemed "white" to a number of Negro musicians but, in its most popularized and deracinated version, might best be called suburban, soft and fluffy, rather light and flat in the ass. With a short-lived nine-piece band that used the tuba and the French horn, Davis helped spread into greater prominence the clouds of color that were identifiably central to the work of the white bandleader Claude Thornhill. The nonet used those musical tints and textures with what the trumpeter had learned from Parker and Gillespie. In that sense, the importance of what Davis was doing had a meaning beyond the notes that were being written, harmonized, and improvised.

The whole effort symbolized an interracial cooperation that had no real precedent in jazz history. White musicians had been influenced by many black musicians and Negroes had been influenced by a few white musicians; they had all jammed together on hundreds upon hundreds of nights; beginning with Benny Goodman's Quartet, featuring Lionel Hampton and Teddy Wilson, they had started working together in public; but close collaboration of the sort Davis and John Lewis had with Gerry Mulligan, Gil Evans, and Johnny Carisi had not happened before. Black and white musicians tended to pick up from each other what they picked up, or Negroes ghost-wrote material for white bands or, like impassioned extras, supplied "hot" features in white bands. The mutual attempt to consciously draw upon the evolving blues and swing-based Negro American tradition as well as the art music of Europe was new; it was a kind of integration devoutly to be wished by many Americans, in and out of music.

Since Davis had gone to Juilliard, it was quite understandable that such a possibility would mean something to him. What he in particular sought was the seriously urbane, which, as Negro men like Benny Carter and Ellington had proven, could cross all lines of ethnicity and class. The goal was the profoundly sophisticated as opposed to the highly polished but depthless. Then a vital understanding of the rough-and-tumble streets could artistically coexist with the more subtle, the less obvious, the view from the top of the park; thus creating a much broader palette of human expression. This was equally symbolized by Negroes such as Billy Eckstine crossing over into the territory of the romantic balladeer, which had once been the exclusive domain of the alabaster pink-faced matinee idol, so much so that white record producers usually spurned the idea of Afro-American men singing anything other than the blues.

In "the quarter of the Negroes," as Langston Hughes called it, being "cool, calm, and collected" was also a form of protest against the rough and the unready, not only in racial terms but in the terms of living life itself. It rejected the overheated and the hysterical. For Negroes, cool had a very special aspect of ambitious rejection. It meant, when most realized, having the ability and the inclination to whip out the down-home grinds and bumps and all of their steamy traces at the drop of a hat, but the equal ability to move on out beyond the uneducated and the vociferous, lifting off free of the minstrel mask and the brutal, anti-intellectual elements Americans of all colors always found themselves threatened by, from within and from without. Cool in being and cool in music were about the Negro making off with what James Baldwin called "the sacred fire," the differentiations of flame that warmed the cultural penthouses of Western civilization as opposed to the oil drums full of flickering trash before which those without a clue to the broader doings of life warmed themselves. But in the hands of the least imaginative, the low-keyed style was the Lester Young extension squeezed out of the blues and, as things may happen, the cool movement soon supplanted the biting and more tumbling style one side of Parker and Gillespie represented. Correctly called pipe-and-slippers jazz, that kind of cool approach moved as far as possible from the feeling of the Negro and turned the tables on those who had measured the art by its heat, its rocking or sensually delicious swing, its updated Elizabethan depths of emotion. The know the white will of cool jazz at its fullest was to know a wisp.

Oddly, Davis was soon bumped out of something he had helped start and was scrounging around New York looking for dope. When he got jobs he was often too high to play as well as he could and he began to look the part of the addict, so much so that Billy Eckstine, as Jackie McLean remembers, once took Davis off the street and gave him a beautiful overcoat to replace the filthy piece of garbage that he was wearing. At that time in the early fifties, Davis was getting with the Harlem Sugar Hill crowd that included McLean, Sonny Rollins, and Art Taylor, all fellow talents, all fellow addicts, all destined to make their names known and respected. He was ascending in the music though sinking in his life. Swinging hard was on the trumpeter's mind but contrasted with a pliant lyricism. He wanted to bring the burning and the soothing together. All he had to do was get off the drugs and something strong would start to rise up out of him. But those years of drug addiction were quite a battle. The whole trouble with heroin began shortly after he returned to New York from a brief but successful trip to Paris in 1949 and found himself unemployed, bored, and frustrated. Since he couldn't free himself of the dope, one wealthy white woman from Detroit got him a psychiatrist, which didn't work. Nothing did the job until the trumpeter had been shamed, when his father made it clear that he knew his son was on drugs. Then, on a visit to his father's house, the trumpeter went through withdrawal, later telling Jean Bach that his entire body felt the way he did when his foot went to sleep: the sensation was a convergence of numbness and pins and needles.

By 1954, as Davis liberated himself from the hook of heroin addiction, he became the insider's truest post-bop trumpet player. Dizzy Gillespie was then less concerned with first-class bands and had expanded the entertainment side of his presentation, though he and Davis both did in Chet Baker when the dark blond supposed wonder from the West Coast was brought to New York. Baker got top billing at Birdland over Gillespie one week and over Davis the next. Musically speaking, the two put the white hope's head in a bag and turned the bag flat, red, and sticky. Davis was especially angry because he saw Baker, whom he had so heavily influenced, as no more than another example of how some white guy could bite a chunk out of the neck of a Negro's style and set up residence in the bank, the blood from the chunk of meat in his mouth dripping a puddle that turned to gold at his feet. Downtown in 1956 at the Cafe Bohemia in Greenwich Village, Davis told one Harlem friend over drinks at the bar that he intended to "bust all of this up. Miles said that they had stopped him as long as they could and now he was coming for their ass and coming with his own kind of thunder." That might explain his unpredictable attitude toward white musicians. He could talk of Gil Evans as his best friend but might, given his mood, ask a white musician wanting to sit in with him, "Do you see anybody up here who looks like you?" When Stan Getz headed for his bandstand, Davis would tell this great player to leave or he would call Sonny Stitt in order to make sure that his ass got eaten up. These sorts of things made him aloof and caused white musicians and writers to feel they had achieved a victory if Davis spoke to them or gave the indication that he had any respect for what they did. Where Negro musicians had traditionally been accessible, Miles Dewey Davis was not.

In 1955, at the Newport Jazz Festival, Davis had made what was considered a comeback. It actually was not, since the trumpeter was getting very good reviews for public performances in 1954 and had them coming out to hear him when he performed at Manhattan record stores and night clubs. At Newport, Rhode Island, what actually happened was that a large number of people went ape wild for him as he played a set with Thelonious Monk, Gerry Mulligan, Zoot Sims, Percy Heath, and Connie Kay. The bootleg recording of that performance is neither particularly impressive nor the sound good enough to give us an impression of what kind of nuance was at work. Whatever the music actually sounded like, Davis was then cleaned up and ready to move out toward stardom. He convinced producer George Avakian that it was time to sign him to Columbia

Records, devising a brilliant plan that would get him out of his contract with Prestige, where he had already made a number of now-classic all-star recordings. Davis wanted Avakian to approach Prestige with the idea that if the trumpeter signed with Columbia and made a small-group recording, the attention would shoot up the sales of the three or four small-group recordings he still had to do for Prestige in order to finish out his contract. Prestige went for it and Davis did a marathon session before the taping microphones with his great quintet of the time, which included John Coltrane, Red Garland, Paul Chambers, and Philly Joe Jones.

It all changed for him when 'Round About Midnight came out on Columbia. The pink-and-blue jacket showed Davis in dark glasses holding his horn, looking removed, unapproachable, a contemplatively hip man in his own world, one who had no time for entertainment, an elegant piece of coal squeezed into a diamond by the pressure of the times. The music is perfect, track to track, the band performing with superb locomotion and indisputable lyricism. Davis was now on board the gravy train and it was starting up for him. Avakian got the trumpeter a good manager in Jack Whittemore, who kept the band working so that Davis would have stable personnel and the latitude to keep the sound of the group developing. Avakian took Debbie Ishlon of the promotion department to hear him at the Cafe Bohemia. Ishlon had been responsible for getting Dave Brubeck on the cover of Time magazine. According to Avakian, Ishlon's experience of hearing and seeing Davis was pivotal:

> Debbie flipped out and saw him as a new super-cool image. She was responsible for getting the editors of Town and Country interested in Miles. Otherwise, they would never have done anything with jazz, I'm sure. And it was during the Cafe Bohemia period that he started to do two things. He blew more and more solos with the mute right on top of the microphone, and then he would turn his back to the audience and even walk off. That got a lot of talk. Let's face it, Debbie helped exploit that with the image of the artiste who is all for his music, and the audience doesn't matter. But the main thing is that she got Miles into areas that no jazz artist had ever been in before, and that helped build him up quite rapidly.

The other thing is that we started a record club, and nobody knew how big that became. There were no record clubs at the time except the old Book of the Month Club deal with Victor Red Seal, which was for classical music only. So we ended up having a total monopoly on a phase of the business which nobody knew was really big. That was the secret behind people like Miles suddenly becoming big stars.

The next Columbia recordings couldn't be with small groups because Prestige was pushing out the quintet records the trumpeter made in order to complete his contract. Those Prestige recordings were very popular and Bill Cosby said at a New York memorial for the trumpeter that one could be considered extremely hip in Philadelphia during the fifties by just walking around with a Miles Davis quintet album under one's arm. In a shrewd attempt to avoid being lost in a glut of small-band product, Avakian knew Columbia had to go for big. As part of that strategy, Davis then hooked up again with Gil Evans, spurning Avakian's suggestion that he use Gunther Schuller to write and conduct long works for him. Davis had already participated in Columbia recording experiments under the direction of Schuller, performing on pieces written by John Lewis and J. J. Johnson. He wanted something else and got it. Evans put Davis in the kind of context that almost all superior jazz musicians, beginning with Louis Armstrong, evolve toward, which is the concerto in idiomatic terms. What begins in small bands is almost always taken into a larger environment. This was true of Gillespie in his big bands and the longer works he commissioned during the bebop era of the late forties; with varying success, Charlie Parker had agreed to appear in formats broader than his quintets and quartets and wanted to perform with orchestras; Clifford Brown had recorded with strings. Davis, expanding upon his *Birth of the Cool* context, was in there again, ten years gone by and all kinds of fresh information and ideas behind his forehead.

The brilliantly promoted and highly successful *Miles Ahead, Porgy and Bess,* and *Sketches of Spain* are signal examples of his powers. The recordings were inclined toward the pallid textures that resulted from the impressionistic influences on Evans and from the disavowal of the varied

Negro vocal inflections that had meant so much to the richest instrumental timbres of the idiom. Usually, when this was not the ongoing
obsession with getting a pass into the European party of aesthetic seriousness, it was a psychological assertion on the part of white musicians
who became fed up or bored with the assumption that they were less than
authentically equal artists because of how far removed their cultural roots
were from the Negro origins of the craft.

But that didn't really matter, finally, when it came to the collaborations between the little man from East St. Louis with the trumpet and the
long, tall Canadian with the arranger's pen. Regardless of how indistinct
some of the arrangements might have made jazz seem, Davis himself had
those things in his playing and was never—even at his most puckish—
very far from the stink and the grease of the gutbucket at the center of the
art. From one perspective, we hear something like the suave, country-boy
Negro in Harvard Yard, surrounded by all kinds of refined knowledge and
pulling together the stuff with an equally refined angle that surprisingly
aligns the conventionally astute and the down-home for yet another tri-
umphant level of Americana. In fact, one could say that where Davis
moved away from the cool school was in his grasp of the *blues* and all its
myriad meanings, something that he also played with far greater authority
than either of his most prominent trumpet rivals during the fifties, Gillespie and Clifford Brown. In fact, as the *Portrait of Duke Ellington* proves,
Davis's collaborations with Evans had reawakened Gillespie, his former
mentor, who was seeking to reach the levels of emotional depth, subtlety,
and large-ensemble context that Davis was so good at expressing and
devising with his best friend. Even Louis Armstrong approached Evans
about writing something for him after he had heard *Porgy and Bess.* The
Davis style, his sound, and the settings he chose for his horn were touching even the ambitions of his idols.

Style was one thing, band leading another. His intelligence and his
charisma made Davis one of the very greatest leaders in his peak years and
his bands were some of the most hard-swinging units in the music. Some
had included Jackie McLean, who played the alto saxophone like a blow
torch; Horace Silver, a pianist and composer who was a foot-stomping
brigadier general in the war against tepid, West Coast jazz; Kenny Clarke

and Art Blakey, two of the most innovative drummers in jazz history; Sonny Rollins and John Coltrane, the freshest tenor saxophonists of the day; Garland, Chambers, and Jones, the most highly regarded rhythm section; Bill Evans, the man who would become one of the most influential pianists of the last forty years. Davis also, with *Kind of Blue*, made the strongest case for the modal movement of limited harmony and scalar manipulation that maintains affecting sway even to this moment.

Beginning with the classic band of the middle fifties that included Coltrane, Davis started to impose a perfect combination of the loose and the prepared. He didn't like music that sounded thrown together and wasn't very fond of the jam session context, where personality was reduced purely to improvisation and never expressed itself in overall shape. His popularity was connected to that sense of order and to his awareness of the nature of the public ear as well as some advice he had been given by his mother. Slow songs, medium-tempoed pieces, and bouncing numbers are usually what the public likes most. Extremely fast performances of the sort Charlie Parker loved were never popular. At one point, Vernon Davis remembers, the trumpeter's mother told him that if he wanted people to listen to what he was doing he needed to slow down and give them tunes that they could hum, some references, something that stuck in their minds, something that didn't just fly by like a succession of fastballs that struck out the audience's attention and its affection. Davis took heed. His repertoire still included quick-stepping bop tunes and all kinds of blues but was soon dominated by popular songs of the day, or older popular songs like "Bye, Bye Blackbird." Like the straw-hatted white woman in the yacht race on the cover of *Miles Ahead*, he was leaving spray in the faces of the other racers.

But Davis knew that there was always color trouble to be had, even if one wasn't looking for it. In 1959, while he was taking a break outside Birdland, a white cop saw him put a pink lady in a cab and told the trumpeter to move along. Davis, beautifully dressed as always, wanted to know why he was supposed to move along. The cop told him because he said so. Davis refused, saying he was just standing there getting some air. The cop threatened to get a little heavy. Davis told this representative of law enforcement that he was working downstairs with his band and that, if the

cop looked, he could see that the picture on the wall was of *him*. The cop
wasn't having any of that. As it can always be, one word and an attitude
and a show of power and a refusal to be bullied mixed themselves up
rather quickly and Davis was soon struggling with the cop to keep him
from using his billy club. There was a furor in the street as patrons ran up
the stairs from Birdland when they heard the trumpeter was in a tussle;
clubs started emptying and there was soon a large crowd.

Freddie Hubbard, who had come to New York in 1958, was going to
hear Davis for the first time in person:

> I lived in Brooklyn and was coming up out of the subway on
> 50th and Broadway. I walked up to Birdland, on 52nd and I saw all of
> these people standing outside the club. I looked in the circle and saw
> Miles Davis fighting with two cops, plain clothesmen. They were
> swinging blackjacks at Miles and he had a pretty, white Italian suit
> on. He was boxing them and hit one of the guys right on the jaw and
> I'll never forget that sound of his fist before the cop went through one
> of those thick windows and broke the glass in what they called a Ham
> and Egger. Everybody cheered, "Oh." But the other guy continued to
> beat Miles on the head and it amazed me to see all of the people
> standing around, Coltrane, Cannonball, and it might have been
> Wynton Kelly or Red Garland watching this man getting beaten.
> They did not jump in. More cops came and eventually arrested Miles
> and blood was streaming down his head. The amount of blows that
> he took must have had a damaging effect. They were trying to knock
> him out. I wanted to break in and help the brother, but people said,
> "Don't go in there." When I asked his band why they didn't jump in
> to help the man, they said, "We can't get involved in *that*."

The police took Davis to the precinct house on Fifty-fourth Street,
where he was to be booked for assault and resisting arrest. The crowd followed them to the police station, where two Negroes told the detective
who hit Davis over the head that if he thought he was so tough he could
step outside and find out what it felt like to get a *real* ass-whipping. Realizing that the wrong Negro had been roughed up this time, the cops in
charge interrupted the booking procedure and allowed Davis to get some

medical treatment, which resulted in ten stitches. The trumpeter spent the night in jail and made the front pages the next day, blood spattering his sporty one-button jacket with no lapels.

The incident was very shocking to the jazz world at large because Davis had seemed so untouchable. Within his universe, the violence toward Davis took everyone almost as off guard as Kennedy's assassination did the country a few years later. This was New York City, not the South. Oh, really?

The trumpeter eventually won a suit against the City of New York, but was forever after convinced that no matter how high he might ever rise, unless a white man looking for a Negro to bully knew *exactly* who he was, Miles Dewey Davis III might find out what demonic forces kept the battleship of racism afloat and ready for action. Until the end of his life, the incident could suddenly pop up in a conversation with Davis that seemed to have no bearing on race. It stuck. The stardom that brought him top club and concert salaries, the sales of hundreds of thousands of records, his Mercedes Gold Wing, the fine home converted from a Russian Orthodox church, the lines upon lines of women ready to drop their drawers at his request, the musicians imitating his dress, his manner, and his attitude, and the jazz polls showing that he was the man of the hour were all smudged blue with irony as far as he was concerned. The blood stopped flowing but the thuds of the blackjacks reverberated.

By the spring of 1961 other kinds of blood were being drawn. Ornette Coleman had arrived in New York fifteen months earlier and was at the center of a controversy about so-called free jazz, which dispensed with harmony in favor of a shifting, quirky, angular, simplistic, and gripping rendition of the demons and the dreams in the soul of the time— that discomfort with the drab order of suburban suffocation, that desire to return to some kind of primitive purity, that anger at the facelessness of the individual in the cheese dip of melded Americana, that terror of the end of the world that could be brought about by a small number of men with unprecedented weapons of incalculable destruction, that lonely-boy shriek and sob that Coleman conjured up through his white plastic saxophone with such determination that some felt as though they were not so much listening as watching bricks passionately but fruitlessly thrown through the endless windows of a factory intent on making humanity no more than a mechanistic extension of a constricted sense of order and production. Coltrane, considered by his least sympathetic listeners as no more than an incredibly long-winded and hysterical academic, went for the call of the wild, too, and the vastly intellectual blast furnace that he had brought to Davis's bandstand was now busy incinerating the distance between the academy and the outback—the blues cry jumbled up in all kinds of incantational rhythms, the simple but layered forms turning the piano and the bass into extensions of the scalding, polyrhythmic drums—with the saxophonist down on one knee, stripping himself nude musically and becoming a tireless native dancer whose auditory image took the listener deeper and deeper into the horrors and the magic of the rain forest.

What was cool Miles Davis going to do about all of that?

Well, he was going to let all concerned know the difference between him and everybody else under hot discussion. Davis would come from strength, pure, complex, and simple. What he always possessed as a hole card was a personal epistemology, an individual way of knowing, and that code of knowing was formed at its source by all the thinking he had done about the trumpet, the tone he had discovered within it, his understanding of how much distinct colors could add to the communicative power of notes, what improvised rhythms of swing and of floating song meant to momentum and how harmony and accent could work together, meaning that an unexpected note didn't need to be given heavy emphasis because the element of surprise created the *illusion* of emphasis.

Then there was the epistemology of the blues, which he had heard Charlie Parker play backwards and forwards, which Ellington gave extraordinary plasticity, which Monk bent and thumped into new conditions on the keyboard, which most white men didn't feel comfortable playing and which far too many Negroes understood best in its store-bought form of cliché, self-pity, and overstatement, not in its deep song context which met the same devil in the midnight crossroads that flamenco did. The Miles Davis blues, his gutbucket authority, had a Spanish streak of violence, tragedy, and transcendent disregard for unearned happiness, sometimes delivered with the arrogance of a matador heckling a bull, sometimes as quietly and as darkly as a dying person taking in the final breaths that are so near quiet it seems the animation of the life force is dissolving into a meager train of shriveling sighs.

There were also the epistemological boudoir discoveries Davis had made as an offstage romantic lead, as a pimp during his heroin days, as an experimenter in many shades of jade, as one whose teetering and tottering on the masculine-feminine line led to stories that were the gossip joy of his inferiors, especially those musicians who could not equal his success in any direction, on or off the bandstand. All of those two-heads-on-a-pillow experiences had taught him about frailty, about longing, about whispers and shouts, about giggles and cries, about smells and textures of skin, about all the forces and the shadings of translucent feeling that are liberated when the time is right or when the sun goes down and there's nobody else around. That density of romantic and erotic knowing gave his ballad renditions an intimacy that was laid on the air without the slightest tremor of apology. In a decidedly rowdy Negro club filled with hustlers and whores Davis could bring quiet with his Harmon mute stuck in the bell of his horn as some love song lay under his musical and emotional microscope. He had the power to make an audience briefly become better than itself.

At that very first Carnegie Hall concert of his, with a well-rehearsed large band of sixteen white and three black musicians looking over their music, and the central force the Negro men of his own quintet—Hank Mobley, Wynton Kelly, Paul Chambers, and Jimmy Cobb—prepared to set each note afire, Miles Davis had all intentions of being even better than himself. The inky prince of jazz had trained and sought all of the strength necessary to flex his feeling and his will on the people in the seats of Carnegie Hall. He had been working on his horn for stamina and range—playing long improvisations, squealing into the upper register, tackling avant-garde ideas about pitch and color, and inventing completely unpredictable rhythms—as the indispensable two volumes of *Miles Davis in Person* reveal, recorded a month earlier at San Francisco's Blackhawk. But there may have been more than preparation for the big concert on his mind when he was playing all of that mighty horn. Drummer Jimmy Cobb was in the band at the time and has another perspective:

As far as the way he was playing at the Blackhawk before we got to New York and did Carnegie Hall, all those long solos, and like that, they could have been because he was showing out for Marguerite Mays. He tried to tell her I couldn't play for looking at her but I told him to speak for himself, which is what he meant anyway. She was Willie Mays's wife. That woman was *as fine as possible*.

The trumpeter was introduced to that audience by the disc jockey Symphony Sid Torin, a Jewish hipster, pothead, huckster, knucklehead, lover of jazz and jazz musicians and the position over them his radio broadcasts and on-the-air interviews had given him. Torin and Miles went back to the days of Charlie Parker, who condescendingly referred to the self-described "all night, all frantic one" as "Symphonic Sidney." Svelte and superbly tailored in the Manhattan town largely tamed by robber barons who had built libraries, museums, and concert halls to honor themselves, the suave country boy from East St. Louis was ready to let it rip. He intended to whip it until it turned red. He wanted to seduce it and tease all its clothes off. He wanted to ruminate about it and shoot a tragically informed arrow of song into the air before he closed the door and painted his address blue. Miles Davis was not there to bullshit. But he *was* anxious. Everyone remembers him being that way, and so was Evans, of whom Jimmy Cobb recounts:

> Gil said that he was petrified. He was really scared to do that concert. So he was drinking corn whiskey he had brought down from 125th Street. He had never been in front of that many people before. Gil said he would rather do a lot of other things rather than go out on that stage. Miles was nervous, too. It was a big deal for all of us. It was a social event. This guy named Pete Long who worked in promotion up in Harlem at the Apollo was a friend of ours and he was kind of a promoter. I think he was part of that evening. I think it was his idea that every woman who came in got a rose. It was a high class event.

As a benefit for the African Medical Education and Research Foundation, it was also a political event. Not very long before the performance, a delegation of five or six people was brought to Davis's home by Max Roach, the great poetic genius of the drums and a close friend who had worked with the trumpeter in Charlie Parker's band. The delegation was convinced that the African Research Foundation was in cahoots with South Africa and other forces upholding colonialism. They were inclined to see race in broad, black nationalist terms that were rooted in the nineteenth century. Those conceptions ran through the Caribbean, and were, due to W.E.B. Du Bois, given the name Pan-Africanism, a politics of color based on the idea that a sin committed against any black person at any point on the globe by a representative of any kind of white racism or colonial power was a sin against all blue-black to bone-colored people anywhere. Race and its relationship to racism precluded all else. The men Max Roach brought to Davis's home urged him not to perform. Davis said, rather oddly, given what had happened to him not yet two years ago in front of Birdland, that if you had enough money you could buy your freedom. He was going to play. They left, he went about his business.

Davis had been interested for a while in having a concert at Carnegie Hall but didn't know exactly how to go about doing it, especially if such an event involved him approaching anybody. He wanted to be the one approached. Jean Bach became aware of this and made that information available to Dr. Tom Rees, whom she had known since 1945. Rees was one of the surgeons who had founded the Flying Doctors of East Africa, which was a division of the African Medical Education and Research Foundation. Begun in 1957, the Flying Doctors started building what is now a medical force of over four thousand people, more than 90 percent of them black Africans. At that time, Rees and his people needed a benefit in New York to help further the work they were doing. The doctor went to see the trumpet player. He had a surprise for Davis:

> When I was studying medicine I was a jazz musician, earning my way through school. I knew a white trumpeter, who played in the same band, named Doug Mettome, who ended up playing in the Billy Eckstine Band, in which Miles played. In fact, Doug was the only white player in the band. He and Miles became very close. As you know, Miles was not very fond of white people. He was *not* fond

of white people. But he loved Doug because, whenever they traveled in the South, the band, of course, in those days, had to stay in rickety hotels and stuff. Doug, being white, could have stayed in a nicer place, but he didn't choose to; he stayed with the band.

When I went to see Miles at his house he was very suspicious, almost antagonistic. What did I want? What was I doing there? I broke the ice by telling him I had been a pal of Doug Mettome. That melted him right away. He really loved Doug. I talked to him straight. You had to; that was how he talked. I told him that this organization was doing good for Africans, who had, otherwise, no medical care and we were devoted to providing medical training and teaching in Africa. I told him that our organization in New York was a mixed organization, that we had several black people as well as whites on our board. After several meetings and conversations with him, he finally thought it might be a pretty good idea. We spoke to Gil Evans about it and Gil thought it was a great idea. Along comes the night. We had a beautiful audience, about half white and half black audience. Everybody was dressed up. It was really quite a scene.

As the recording shows, Davis was in particularly powerful form. He had brought his own brand of virtuosity to high profile. There was nothing in his distinct style that he could not do on that night. Cobb remembers Evans being so nervous that the orchestral introduction to the first piece, "So What," began more slowly than it should have, meandering along, which meant nothing and even provided a fine contrast to the explosion of the quintet moving into position. Davis immediately let everyone know how much swing they were going to have to handle. As usual, there was his characteristic phrasing flotation, which made it possible for the hard groove of Negro muscularity to coexist with reflection. So we heard the optimum achievement of jazz—getting the triangle of the meat, the mind, and the emotions together; no separation. In a player like Davis, that sort of perfection was outstanding because his lyrical gifts and his freedom of line could carry along even the intelligent listener who had no comprehension of jazz. By keeping that song going on he could "call the children home" just as effectively for his time as Buddy Bolden had when jazz rose from the womb of the gutbucket around the turn of the century in good old funky-butt New Orleans.

Tenor saxophonist Hank Mobley was also aflame, though a more conventional player than Davis, and Wynton Kelly laid out some of the greatest improvised rhythm ever captured as his feature on "So What" preceded the ending of the tune. Davis then performed with the large ensemble, his "Spring Is Here" defined by a confident beauty based in the weight that his tone could give whatever note he played. Next he and the quintet did "Teo," a flamenco-influenced waltz with an Afro beat that found the trumpeter leaving no doubt that he was at the forefront of new sonic directions and new materials for his instrument, nearly shrieking into the upper register with repeated exclamations of a force the audience that night found shocking. After his second feature on the piece, Davis let Kelly dissolve the waltz before, almost suddenly, starting "Walkin'," now a fast blues that found him exhibiting some of the red hot playing much more expected of someone like Roy Eldridge, emotion and drive pulling the rhythm section instead of being driven by it. Mobley, nobody's second-string bluesman, pushed his bell right into the cut of the groove; Kelly, never to be outswung, laid down swing upon swing, his final chords as percussive as Monk's; Chambers bowed his bass feature with no loss of momentum, and Davis and Cobb then took turns pitching and smacking back each other's balls of fire.

Davis turned another corner of feeling. He then stood in the middle of the Evans arrangements using his horn to create a different texture of intimacy on "The Meaning of the Blues" and "Lament" before prancing into the jaunty arrangement of pianist Ahmad Jamal's "New Rhumba." That Jamal number is a tribute to one of the trumpeter's signal influences. Every statement, each exchange with the orchestra, the shapes of his lines, the dramatic ascents into the upper register, the nuances of his rhythm are very nearly perfect. The first half of the concert concluded, Miles Davis had brought the cool and the hot into alignment, successfully daring to be the aesthetic link between extremes. He had it all going on, and everyone there knew it.

The audience during intermission was ecstatic. Then the second half began. On the recording a tune starts then ends mysteriously. Jimmy Cobb recalls:

> Miles was playing "Someday My Prince Will Come." Then he suddenly took the tune out and walked off. I didn't know what was going on at first until the harp player asked me, "Is he supposed to be there?" I asked who she meant. And there was Max Roach squatted like an Indian holding up a sign saying "Africa for Africans." Then a stagehand came out and ushered Max off.

Some remember Roach being lifted and carried off, though the drummer says he walked off the stage and when he got into the wings, Davis told the stagehands, "Don't touch him." Tom Rees says that he went backstage to see what was happening because everyone was out front but there was no Miles Davis. The trumpeter's wife of six months, dancer Frances Taylor, and Gil Evans talked to Rees. They told him that Davis was finished for the night. He was going home. They couldn't convince him to do otherwise but Evans was willing to go out and get the job done with the orchestra. Rees found Davis seething behind a curtain, feeling that he had been set up and lied to by the doctor. When Rees said the opposite of anything racist was going on and that the proof was clearly the audience itself, black and white people in attendance come to hear him together, Davis peeked out but said that Max Roach was his friend and he couldn't go against someone he had known that long.

Rees got Davis to go outside with him, where they found Roach picketing with members of the delegation that had come to the trumpeter's home in an attempt to stop him from playing the benefit. As Rees talked with Roach, it became clear that neither he nor anyone else knew exactly what the Flying Doctors of East Africa actually did. There had been wrong information. Rees told the drummer that if there was anything racist about the organization he would be in protest against it as well. The doctor summarized what he and his team did. Rees also wanted to know why Roach almost destroyed the trumpeter's concert and so angered him that he would not go back on, which would lead to his being pulverized by the papers the next morning. It could unnecessarily hurt the career of Miles Davis. Finally, Roach relented and began to say that maybe there was a misunderstanding and that Davis should finish the concert. All the facts could be sorted out later. Davis was not immediately ready to go back out there. Perhaps his mood had been so jangled that he didn't want to try and recapture the concentration he would need to maintain the level of the first half. Upon considering that Gil Evans would have to pick up the slack and face the disappointment of the audience alone, Miles Davis, loyal to his best buddy, took his horn and went back on.

On the recording it's clear that his playing is not as consistently good as it was in the first half, though the rest of the band maintains the same standards of groove, stank, and swing they had set before intermission. Davis's "Oleo" is as strong as a Gillespie set of razors run through the "I Got Rhythm" chord changes, but "No Blues" falls back on some pat material from the Blackhawk recordings. He sounds professional but distracted and may well have still wanted to go home. Then, with "I Thought About You," he recovers and the ballad artistry that had no trumpet equals since the arrival of Charlie Parker turns down the lights in the hall to the point where whispers get their best hearing. As a finale, Davis plays an excerpt from "Concierto de Aranjuez" with Evans and the orchestra. The piece has little to do with jazz and the arrangement is nothing of serious import for the idiom but there is a fascinating contrast between what the ensemble sounds like and how the blues knowledge that Davis imparts with such swing remakes the entire context every time he blows a note, either written or improvised. Even his far-from-subtle mistakes don't mar the overall effect of his aesthetic individuality. By the last note, the trumpeter has reasserted himself as an ordering conqueror of the present, which is what all jazz musicians aspire to, whether playing the music as written or as they think it ought to be.

The concert received a standing ovation, which was deserved. But it also represented, with the craft on the bandstand and the cooperation of the races, what was to be destroyed when the Civil Rights Movement was overrun by the forces of Black Power. Neither Miles Davis nor Max Roach, each man a genius, could have imagined just how clearly the

events of that evening summed up much of the music and the social texture that had come into being since they both performed with Charlie
Parker on Fifty-second Street fifteen years earlier. Triumph and doom
were in the air that night, the former symbolized later by the 1963 March
on Washington, the latter by the Birmingham bombing murders of four
little girls a few weeks later, then the assassination of Jack Kennedy two
months following that Sunday morning explosion. From that point on,
the destination was set and no one, regardless of how much money he or
she possessed, would be able to buy any kind of freedom from all that. Not
even Miles Davis.

PART NINE

Shout-Chorus
on the Way Out:

How Dare We Do

All the Things

We Dare to Do?

Blues to Be Redefined*

Do not blaspheme. It is the gods who weep. They have watched us killing each other since the beginning of time. They cannot save us from ourselves.

RAN, Akira Kurosawa's variation on *King Lear*

1. How You Like Me Now?

A Long Overture in Black and White,
In Seared Flesh and Spilled Blood

Things have become so chaotic, or so apparently chaotic, that we might sometimes think that we live not in the United States but in France. Sleaze mongers, from the world of politics all the way over to the public entertainments, symbolize our national ills and our difficulties with perceiving ourselves as a whole nation, the many who make the one, the rich set of improvisations and traditions that are so easily recognized as American by anyone from outside of this country. The very complex interplay between politics and society, each influencing the

*Delivered on March 7, 1996, at Adelphi University as part of a conference entitled "Rethinking the Western Tradition."

other only as fast as attitudes become digestible, demands that we address something about speed and our sensibility. Once ideas have become platitudes or slogans that soak up enough emotion to affect what happens in voting booths, we see how things too often work in our society.

"Don't Tread on Me," "Remember the Alamo," "Tippecanoe and Tyler, too" have evolved into what we now call the sound bite. One of our most serious problems, however, is that our difficulties are far too complicated to fit into an era demanding that all messages take no longer than a commercial break, far too intricate to be explained clearly to an audience interested in hearing little more than two or three sentences that are supposed to function like some sort of auditory baling wire capable of holding the protean heap of American blues in place long enough for the mythic garbage trucks of our nation to haul them away. But swirling through the rancid fumes of all of this political and intellectual fast food is a set of manifestations that says much about the condition of the American soul as it relates to the issue of rethinking the Western tradition in terms of politics and society in our world. I would first like to look at some of them and then turn to what I consider our perpetual American reserves, those evergreen ideas and impulses that have allowed us to make it this far and will surely help us to get beyond where we are now.

We find ourselves looking at a terrain on which Louis Farrakhan comes close to draining all political, social, and moral seriousness from Afro-American affairs as he stands in Washington, D.C., before perhaps a million men, to whom he explains what the icons and numbers on dollar bills supposedly mean, the multitudinous audience for his lunatic numerology and incoherence made possible by an organizing apparatus extending so far outside of his racist cult that it includes churches and sororities. The exceeding bulk of that network of organizations was probably introduced to Farrakhan by Benjamin Chavis, a skirt-chasing minister and sanctimonious hustler whose Christianity took a backseat to his affection for demagoguery, and whose fumblings *and* fondlings during his brief tenure as executive director of the NAACP nearly brought the organization to ruin, its concern for integration almost incinerated by racial animus. Our American press, ever paternalistic and given to treating Negro Americans as though they are never more than savages pitifully shaking hoodoo dolls at the heavens, looked upon the Million Man March as some sort of grand moment, or at least one that could be condescended to with the kind of talk about unity and self-esteem that was reminiscent of the antebellum barrels of molasses passed out to the slaves at the end of a good season. But there is something amiss in our country when so many fairly well-off black people, seeking some sort of unity as an answer to the ravages of urban life, gather around the ineloquent brier patch of Farrakhan's lingo, which can include stories about his own space travel and claims from his minions that the Nation of Islam has developed a cure for AIDS—*Star Trek*, snake oil, and racial paranoia in one package.

At the other end of the field, but actually right next to Farrakhan, is Patrick J. Buchanan, who is trying to become the Tom Watson of his time, a vulgar populist whose appeal is to every veiled and unveiled form of xenophobia troubling the soul of our country. It is equally true, as one writer said of Buchanan, that he is part of a phenomenon that has spread its bile across the stretch of our mass communications network, substituting shock for substance, rage for reason, threat for thorough assessment. In this time, we observe politicians whose material parallels the Hollywood car chases, gunfights, explosions, and mutilations of the action-trash genre. Such politicians realize that the drama of political insight is much harder to achieve than the voluminous insults that draw whoops and cheers from the audience members, all of these diatribes on the stump fusing into a talk television spear jammed into the side of the body politic, itself already crucified with spikes of simplemindedness and wearing a thorny crown of omnidirectional fear and bitterness. When Buchanan walked down an Arizona street in a cowboy hat carrying an automatic rifle horizontally held over his head with both hands, his face contorted into that smile that makes him look like an Asian mask of demonic glee, we saw the spiritual mirror of Louis Farrakhan at those times when the presence of the boss of the Nation of Islam at the center of attention— and his confidence man recognition of the imbecility behind the eyes of those looking on in awe—strikes the mean, mean minister himself as some cosmic joke of gargantuan proportions.

In the horror of the bombing of the World Trade Center by Arab extremists and the greatest act of mass murder in American history, the Oklahoma City bombing, we are able to see two variations on the politics of rage. As Martin Peretz has pointed out, the explosions at the World

Trade Center detonated our traditional idea of immigrants, whether, I might add, that idea was hostile or tolerant. Previously, even if we resented them, we thought of immigrants as people who came to America for something better than what they were getting where they were born. The point was to move ahead, to take advantage of the public school system, the medical expertise, the job market, and the freedom to invent a way for yourself. Now we wonder if we might also be confronted with a small or large number of indoctrinated immigrants who see America as "the Great Satan" and find it perfectly reasonable to consider or go about committing terrorist acts that bring about death, destruction, and chaos. If the many blown to bloody shreds and parts of bodies in that federal building in Oklahoma City met eternity at the hands of rebel groups who feel that they have a score to settle with the federal government, either getting revenge for the massacre at Waco or giving murderous form to an anger built on blaming Washington for what are thought of as satanic infringements on freedom, then we have felt once again the horror and the heartbreak wrought by some amorphous monster within, a beast whose ancestry is traceable at least back to the anarchic forces of the Natchez Traces of 200 years ago, or the various badlands that moved farther and farther west, where law was always seen as the enemy. Further, these violent immigrants and native-born Americans are truly statements of our age, where all is capable of being magnified, for, whether these people arrive from outside of the country or are homegrown, they are made ominous because the nature of destructive contemporary technology is such that those with small, porous minds can surely create large, large disasters.

These sorts of people and their ruthless actions also make it as hard as it has ever been for us to get beyond the surface distinctions our democratic contract is intended to supplant. This happened during the Civil Rights Movement, when the Southern accent rising off of a white person's tongue was heard at too many educated social gatherings in the North as an automatic mark of shame, a connection to social gremlins, an inflection that could rally condescension or insulting presumptions. We most recently observed this very same tendency when so many people assumed, following the arrests connected to the World Trade Center bombing, that the Oklahoma City tragedy must surely have been the work of Middle Eastern extremists. This prejudice, given the way media influences us, is also fed by the factual actions of Hamas as it goes about its war against all Israelis—men, women, children—making no distinctions between civilians and soldiers. Yet we cannot realize ourselves within the grand scheme of our social contract if we allow attitudes toward entire groups of immigrants or native-born people to be determined by the worst actions of individuals from certain religious, geographical, and cultural categories. This pollutes our politics and our society, even when the loudest voices from those groups sometimes *demand* that we look at them in a special way!

There can be no greater gathering of pollutants than what we have come to accept, or gather to witness, in our popular entertainments, from television to film, in our advertisements for clothing, for perfumes, for automobiles. As the controversy surrounding the content of popular entertainment proves, I am far from alone in believing that such things have a debilitating effect on the spirit of the society, on race relations, on sexual trends, on manners themselves. Such material reduces what originally arrived as a kind of democratic spunk, which became internationally famous on the charismatic basis of its unpretentious disdain for unearned privilege and for its very own expression of deadpan compassion and lyrical flippancy. We are surely surrounded at this moment by the crass combination of cynicism and whorishness that seeks to replace the stimulation of originality with the shocking affront that is either self-righteous or contemptuous. Exploiting variations played to the tune of what the jazz musician Roland Kirk called "volunteered slavery" stretch across our electronic means of communication, of documentation, of creating products. In other words, money is no longer seen as the root of all evil but is now recognized as the justification for personal or collective debasement, the worst sort of capitalism, the dark world of profit in which the quality of the product is only as significant as the public is gullible.

We cannot, in a time as uncivil as ours, fail to contemplate how bad manners have become and how we often find ourselves more alienated from others than we can easily recall because there now seems to be no basic idea of the treatment of strangers that will allow us to feel at ease among those whom we do not know. We expect abuse in public places and often get it, from foul-mouthed children to excessively rude adults. An old Greek tale told by one who was perhaps a blind slave fits in this. One of the central themes of *The Odyssey* is how civilization reveals itself to the vulnerable stranger. With Odysseus, we recognize, in situation after situation, that those who are truly civilized do not take advantage of the wandering stranger and show hospitality to this new arrival. This sort of hospitality, which assumes kinship, seems to foreshadow the democratic legal idea that one is innocent until proven guilty.

Sometimes I feel that part of our trouble in the area of civility arrives from both the horror stories of slavery that we have heard over the last thirty years and from an idea that we have seen evolve into monstrous behavior since the middle 1950s, which is that we prove ourselves most individual when we make sure that we don't give a damn what anybody else thinks about us. What the horrifying stories of humiliation during slavery have done, it seems to me, is lead to a confusion between service and subservience, which results in people of all races giving you bad service in order to prove that they aren't inferior to you. I think the simplistic idea of not giving a damn is also an example of how our American pursuit of individuality and our nose-thumbing attitudes toward excessive and pretentious convention have been distorted. Moreover, this cavalier rudeness submits to the facelessness of the metropolis in which the kind of hideous behavior that would be chastised in the small community is possible because it is so easy to disappear inside the vast population or move so swiftly—as the terrible stranger—from one part of town to another.

We cannot forget how much sheer ignorance we are witnessing as well. These people are either too poorly educated or too naive or too willing to exhibit their low-down versions of the worst upper-class behavior that they are all the way outside of the rituals of fundamental etiquette. Not having any sense of all the stages meat must go through in order to arrive on their favorite fast-food griddle, or how tapping rubber trees is the beginning of their Air Jordans, or what it takes to make the cotton clothes they wear or the wool or any tools or weapons or audio toys that result from precision engineering, these people feel that they exist on a lane separate from everyone else and that in that lane they can speak whatever foul words they know at whatever volumes they choose no matter who else is around. In a certain sense, they are saying that what they do makes no difference in the larger picture, just as what they feel has no effect on the course of life either. They have surrendered to aggressive gloom. In this mix of battered civility we should forget neither the obnoxious trash aristocracy of rock and rap nor the millionaire athletes who have replaced sportsmanship with the thin-skinned pugnaciousness of thugs playing and fighting in the street.

Included in the repulsive tone of public affairs are the news media, which promote glum cynicism and reduce almost all issues to arm-wrestling between opponents, "rather than our collective efforts to solve collective problems," as James Fallows writes in *Breaking the News,* wherein he also observes that when journalists ask questions "they often do so with a discourtesy and rancor, as at the typical White House news conference, that represents the public's views much less than it reflects the modern journalist's belief that being independent boils down to act-ing hostile." Then, as the body counts, the maimed, and the traumatized bear witness to, there are so many who make lower-class communities into gauntlets of perpetual threat, reminding us of what Shakespeare meant in *Henry V* when he wrote:

> And as our vineyards, fallows, meads, and hedges,
> Defective in their natures, grow to wildness,
> Even so our houses, and ourselves, and children,
> Have lost, or do not learn, for want of time,
> The sciences that should become our country;
> But grow like savages, as soldiers will,
> That nothing do but meditate on blood,
> To swearing, and stern looks, diffused attire,
> And everything that seems unnatural.

Great googamooga: We sure the hell got us a long hard way to go.

2. Moving Back to the Outskirts of History

Since our story is about the ongoing conflict between our aspirations and our discontents, the fundamental fact of our develop-ment is, essentially, redefinition. We have inherited every great idea that has come out of the Western world, especially the various ways in which the

New Testament rejected the tribalism of the Old Testament, laying the foundation for what was to evolve into the secular ideas of the Enlightenment, when the conception of our common humanity was to slowly override all distinctions of national boundary, religion, and politics. As we know, this was seen as a rational rejection of xenophobia. The deep, imperishable condition was humanity; the rest was what we might now call cultural evening clothes for the infinite *bal masque*. Perhaps fanciful, elegant or terrifying, but those cultural evening clothes are not what we recognize when the other stands naked before us. Though most of our great arguments have to do with the relationships of style, taste, and belief to results, the Enlightenment opened the way for us to understand rationally that humanity is the essence that precedes the existence of the culturally unique.

In our own democracy, an innovative sense of freedom was invented based on the rights of life, liberty, and the pursuit of happiness. The intention was that we would be judged by our deeds, not by our backgrounds. Yet we have long been trading blows with the refinement of the tribal idea as it appears in the proposition of an aristocracy. That is because our various prejudices on the planes of race, religion, class, and sex have appeared over and over, almost always as stubborn versions of aristocratic privilege, which keep us from easily realizing the grandest ideals of our democracy. This explains why our story, our evolution, is about the discontented passion that rises into action whenever our aspirations are limited by presumptions that do not hold sacred the democratic vision of no aristocracies other than those of merit. So redefinition in our nation always arrives at the point of struggle against the ideas that both deny human commonality and have been written into law, determining how we relate to one another, both on the federal and the local levels.

Today, right now, is a period of protean turmoil. The increasingly technological world is a merry-go-round moving at an ever faster clip and we now seem to find ourselves only bruising or breaking our fingers if we try to snatch the brass ring. Discontent is thick in the air but our aspirations may not really be, at least for now, up to the democratic vision that would ennoble them and further the strengths of the society. That is because our present moment is one of excessive narcissism, and exaggerated self-involvement is always at odds with democracy as a form of social order and social understanding. That narcissism shows itself in special-interest groups of one distinction or another, almost all of them so hypnotized by their own mirrors that they cannot see themselves in relationship to the society at large, particularly in any way that we might call profound. So the pace of the world, the intimidating velocity that attends the machines which we hate as much as we love, and the need for a democratic vision of interconnection are what challenge us no end. As in every dark period of our history, when the sun seems to be on leave, the fog thick as an elephant's hide, and doom grooming itself to take the society out, there are those who will tell you that they know exactly which of us are to blame for all of this and just what should be done about them.

But ours is a dark period that arrives in a very unusual form. In a number of ways, we have more than we have ever had—better health, better wages, longer life spans, finer living conditions—but we are either cynical or angry about how poorly we have handled the demons of crime, ignorance, and prejudice. Our cities are now looked upon in the popular imagination as they were by hayseeds over a hundred years ago—Sodoms of violence, sexual plague, and potential catastrophe. The post–World War II tendency to get away, to move on out into the suburbs, has reversed the motion from the rural to the urban that historically brought so much surging vitality to each metropolis that helped define the culture and the sophistication of the country. Where the blues singer might once have sung of how the bright lights of the big city stole his baby from home, the contemporary blues of urban life weighs upon those who no longer believe in the mythic city that musicals and elegant jazz big bands made into an enormous steel, concrete, and glass ballroom large enough for the whole society to enter, each person bringing his or her vision of romance, of community, of effervescence. Crass concerns have taken over.

Those who have made their getaways from the cities angrily worry about being taxed to support what they consider incompetent bureaucracies that never get anything of value done about the cauldron of gummy social slop that has boiled over, melting away much of what is good while scalding the sensibility into a grotesque condition. The poor of the cities believe that they and their children are cursed by the contempt and the neglect of the more fortunate. If those poor are defined as so-called minorities, their gripes are connected to the raw and seamy aspects of our racial history. In the interest of truly collective problems we notice that, across the classes, our children bounce from the mass media fantasies of hedonism to those characterized by levels of violence unprecedented in their reach across the society and around the world.

Our problems now call for a redefinition in the direction of democratic consciousness, but a consciousness that must reassert, it seems to me, the unusual combination of tragic recognition and optimism that underlies the deepest meanings of our social contract. In *The All-American Skin Game*, I make the point that our society is organized on principles that accept the perpetual struggle between problems of power and the ideals pushed into the world by the Founding Fathers. Those men, because of their scorn for aristocratic privilege and because of their belief in the abilities of elected officials and those whom they represent, had insights into the nature of humanity as it makes itself felt in social terms. Their tragic sense was that we have to be able to reassert our ideals whenever the lower sides of humanity appear in the four forms I am sure bedevil all societies and economic structures—folly, corruption, mediocrity, and incompetence. Those lower sides have nothing to do with democracy itself; they are built, mysteriously, into the species. The naive among us are those who assess democracy—or capitalism or both—by the shortcomings of humanity itself, while failing to recognize that our essential social vision, as expressed through our governmental structures, provides the latitude for us to perpetually redress those things we find lacking.

We have the difficult freedom to redefine our aspirations when we become discontented, when we discover that something we might have thought was correct, or that our predecessors might have believed was fundamentally true, is found to be—or thought to be—all wrong. Essential to our social contract is the belief that we can, eventually, handle the abuses of power, that we can move beyond our prejudices, that we can redeem our society by improvising into policy those ideas that we find to be true, those ideas that take us closer and closer to our ideals and may, finally, go far beyond what the Founding Fathers themselves thought about the world. Yet the tragic consciousness founded in the perpetual possibility of readjusting our policies acknowledges that these problems will forever appear in different forms, mutating like those insects, rodents, and diseases that have prevailed beyond previous poisons and cures so that they can, once again, challenge the quality of our world and our health.

A relatively recent hindrance to our reasserting that tragic optimism comes into form as those who have entrenched themselves in one position or another make much of the prejudices of the Founding Fathers and of the fact that they weren't thinking about women or so-called minorities when they drew up those documents that have had such extraordinary impact on the nation and world. This creates a dangerous kind of cynicism and disillusionment in our young. It is a vision that appeals to kids because it is a very immature way of assessing American history, one that fails to recognize that the form of our government, as I just observed, allows us to redeem ourselves. It is because our social contract allows us to extend the human meanings of democracy beyond a single color or sex that it is of no consequence at this point what those brilliant men may have thought about the opposite sex or about people whose racial ingredients made them look somewhat different from all whose bloodlines led back to Europe. Their gift to this nation and the world wove together a social philosophy and a governmental form that could rediscover itself as prejudices that were once thought of as fact were found to be no more than superstition, which is xenophobia's foundation of fear, loathing, and condescension. What might have seemed an essentially poetic vision of humanity was actually structured in a way that would allow us to make the most of the rational as our beliefs were empirically and scientifically adjusted.

It is important to always realize that we have a very special relationship to the poetic and the rational, since the conception of rights is itself a poetic thing, while the social organization of law arrived at through debate, or adjusted through one version or another of the amendment, presumes the eventual victory of reason over limited vision. The very idea of rights moves away from the absolutes of force that we observe in the natural world, where pecking orders are almost always established by strength. The vision of rights is one of compassion and is what has led our nation to make the difficult changes that tend to allow the weak as much access to the benefits of our society as possible. Following that, it seems to me that one of the highest points in all of Western history was the development of the Abolition Movement, which arrived at a time when there were none of the scientific discoveries in place that now so easily knock down racial prejudice through our knowledge of the brain, of blood, of organ transplants, and so on. In the Abolitionists, we have a group of people who grew larger and larger and who were able to see more and more clearly through the superficial differences in skin color, physiognomy, and hair texture, recognizing that a portion of humanity was immorally bought and sold through the institution of bondage.

In a very real way that poetic vision of rights and of humanity anticipated scientific truth. As that movement grew, the debate over slavery became one of the most dramatic in our history and led, finally, to the bloodiest war this nation has ever fought. That very war between the states shows us another tragic aspect of our history and proves out the fact that however much we may be committed to the rational winning out over the irrational, we must also accept the cruel truth that sometimes there is no other way to deal with the irrational outside of literal war—the killing, dismembering, wounding, and maiming of the opposition in the interests of greater freedom. It is highly doubtful that the Founding Fathers ever foresaw such a bloody conflict over the issue of slavery, but since the very existence of the United States could only arrive through those same means, it was a logical evolution of the values for which they themselves had shed blood. Men like George Washington knew the literal meanings of blood, sweat, and tears. They had heard the cries of battle and the cries afterward. They knew that a man who has the stomach for fighting in war may someday find himself dazed and trying to push his intestines back into his body. The road to freedom is slick and sticky with blood and flesh.

A close examination of the Abolition Movement itself reveals that only a small group within it was actually committed to universal humanity and that Negro Americans had to struggle within the movement itself for recognition of their entire humanity. That is but another example of how our finest ideas are not always fully appreciated by those who think that they are speaking for the best kind of social evolution. At the same time, we have to recognize—let me say this one more once—that ideas within our nation are things that evolve on the basis of concerned engagement and unflinching debate. We rarely have anything delivered to us in a perfect form and find our fate one that is the result of our arguing toward the richest meanings of those ideas, our pushing what might not be thoroughly thought out—or thoroughly accepted—toward its grandest applications. If we are lucky.

That is why we find ourselves in such a mess. We are always struggling toward extending the very highest aspects of the Enlightenment. Our job is one of constantly fighting our way beyond every prejudicial sense of the world, whether it comes from within or without. This is the reason that race and gender have remained such complex problems in our society. We all have had to deal with the idea that white skin means something far more important than a color; we all have had to deal with the idea that being born a male means more than being born a female. We have also had to deal with the variety of class prejudices that sweeps aside the idea that quality can arrive from any class within the society. While the follies and corruptions of Marxist societies are now obvious the world over, it is also ice cold fact, as I say in an essay entitled "Melting Down the Iron Suits of History," that "We in the United States, which is the most successful commercial culture in the history of the world, maintain a running battle with the most corrupt manifestations of capitalism. American citizens are familiar with scandals involving government contracts, price-fixing, insider trading, the willful sale of dangerously shoddy products, money laundering, hell-for-leather pollution, and the rest of it." That is one of our great virtues, that we seek out the most civilized version of capitalism, which means bringing together morality, ethics, and the profit motive. But our American story is the story of working toward an understanding of universal potential, of coming to terms with all the representatives of humanity at large who find themselves players of one sort or another in the national tale. Perhaps, because the realization of our ideals is such a difficult job, we have forgotten exactly what our society truly means. Perhaps, because we have had so many failures in social policy, we are willing to sink down into this or that version of tribalism.

3. Wrong Way Wretched of the Earth Breakdown

What did Max Weber, whose definition of politics as the use of power you were riffing on, say: Only those who realize how aw-

> *ful and self-destructive and so on people can be and still pay dues*
> *for the privilege of administering their affairs truly have talent for*
> *politics. Something like that.*
>
> Albert Murray, *South to a Very Old Place*

Our politics have been influenced by our virtues as well as our tragic exemplifications of the lower inclinations of humanity. It is quite easy, therefore, to celebrate our most noble visions while denying our shortcomings. It is also easy to emphasize our shortcomings while denying our most noble traditions. All of this is the result of the fact that we too often fail to understand the complexity of what we find ourselves in the middle of, refusing to see just how hard it is to realize a democratic sense of life and society. That is why I believe that we periodically slump into the kind of Balkanized rage that expresses itself across race, sex, and class in our time. We are then retreating to a stance that falls short of a true democratic sensibility.

In our time, I would say that this is a version of what Arthur Schlesinger calls "the cycles of American history." In the terms of this discussion, we must look closely at those who so adamantly see themselves as so far outside of American privilege that they have embraced the idea of exclusion and have created a political vision in which the majority is all wrong and the minority is all right. (That includes a purely American sleight-of-hand in which women, who are the majority, become a minority at will and demand whatever minority privileges exist. Blackstone and Houdini would have appreciated that one.) This phenomenon is something I trace in our recent history to the emergence of Black Power, which spurned the conceptions of the Civil Rights Movement in the interests of a politics not based on the achievement of equality, but one rooted in racial hostility and highly inaccurate colonial metaphors.

Owing to the popularity and eventual canonization of Malcolm X, there was a very strong separatist feeling in the radical air of the middle 1960s and discussion was dominated by assertions of the Negro's alienation from America at large and the supposed fact that the Negro shared a common fate with colonials the world over, almost all of whom were in revolt against the Western world and capitalism. I choose to investigate this aspect of our recent history because it was an essential part of what led to the ethnic and sexual narcissism that presently hampers our ability to speak to one another across categories. It is also another telling example of the difference between what Americans come to believe about themselves and what their actual experience and history are.

What the Caribbean or African colonial often feels, as revealed by so much of the writing on the subject, whether fictional or polemical or both, is far removed from the American experience. The most obvious differences in the way things have shaken down are found in issues that pivot, from the beginning, on geographical and historical relationships to those who dominate politically and economically. The colonial knows that his or her people had essentially nothing to do with the creation of what gives uniqueness of style and attitude to the mother country, which is far, far away. The colonial provided no more than the subjugated labor that prepared the exported raw materials destined to fuel some part of the engine of modern life in the Western mother countries—no body of ideas, no technological innovations or refinements, no high position in the moral and social discourse, no deep aesthetic impact, no presence in the sense of humor and so on.

In terms of the Negro American, the problem was very different. Negroes were not like Africans trying to take back land that had been appropriated through imperial means; they were not dislocated colonials who grew up in countries where economics rotated around a few cash crops; Negroes were central to the development of all that we consider American. As participants or as representatives of issues, they had been on the front line at almost every important turning point in the history of the United States, from the true moment of colonial liberation in the Revolutionary War to the arguments over the way slavery repudiated both democratic purity and Christian morality, to the Civil War, to the winning of the West, to the world wars, to the evolution of a national music, a national sense of humor, a national body of dances, and a twentieth-century way of living in urban situations. So whenever Negroes began thinking of themselves as a "black colony" within America, they hadn't had their eyes opened; they had accepted a blindfold.

Right now, I would say that the blindfold has been accepted by many of those in categories outside of the province of race. One group after another seems to have done its own variations on Black Power alienation, perceiving itself, whether because of its sex or its sexual preferences or its age or its class, as some variation on a colony at odds with the United States, feeling good or safe or understood only within its special interest group, convinced that, in a nearly conspiratorial way, either the government or the rich or the poor or the men or the women or the immigrants or the foreigners or some unknown somebodies are out to get them—lying in wait to take almost all that they own or give them less than they deserve, for sins as simple as either having done a hard day's work or having lasted long enough to get some retirement benefits or, the most basic sin of all: having done no more than pop out of a normally or artificially inseminated womb on American soil.

So many have accepted the blindfold, in fact, that we are back to the blind feeling up the elephant, the donkey, and the marketplace. Almost every shape that they touch either frightens them or seems much less than they have been promised by politicians since the end of World War II. It is sometimes hot where they expected it to be cool, rough where they thought it smooth, sharp where they figured on something that wouldn't cut, and so on. Where they wanted the sensation of paradise, those knotting their own blindfolds ever tighter find themselves mad as hell and tired of being misled. As Robert J. Samuelson observes in *The Good Life and Its Discontents: The American Dream in the Age of Entitlement 1945–1995*, such people suffer from what he calls "the politics of overpromise."

That brings us to my conclusion, which is based on the need for a reiteration of the tragic optimism I earlier described as basic to our social contract, our form through which we do our best against folly, corruption, mediocrity, and incompetence. I believe the reiteration of that feeling and understanding is the mark to which our politicians have to rise. In what George Will calls "our therapeutic culture," reiterating that vision of tragic optimism is far from easy to bring off, primarily because we believe that through either humiliating ourselves publicly or giving vent to our "true feelings," we will be on the road to health, or at least on the way to the pharmacy with the right prescription. The various strains of anger and xenophobia that we find in just about every place we travel to in our land are not unreal; they are misguided and they are vented either loudly or in whispers. Many of these strains are the results of having been given the impression that, some day, life was going to be a crystal stair leading to some sort of utopia, which is another point Samuelson makes. But the conception of a utopia is a conception that has no time for tragic facts and is a revolt against the harsh and unpredictable nature of the world.

On one front we are susceptible to utopian thinking because our quite successful handling of so many natural threats to our lives has reduced a good number of the kinds of deaths that were depressingly normal before the arrival of penicillin and other "wonder drugs." I'm talking about the way it was when large families often expected the deaths of children, when pictures of the coffin business almost always included stacks of small ones that seemed not much larger than lunch pails. These are the kinds of developments in human health—and every other arena of creature comfort we now take for granted—that have set us up as chumps ready to wallow in a cult level of belief, anxious to follow whomever will most passionately guarantee us that we will make it to heaven on earth. Heaven, of course, is nowhere to be found. We just happen to have gotten closer to it as a nation than any other country in history.

I do not believe that we can handle our problems of race, class, sex, the environment, and so on until we accept our limitations and understand that there are problems that will not be finished at the same velocity that information presently travels through our technology. On one level, our political commentators will have to learn how to rethink what they do, which is the point James Fallows makes in a number of ways in *Breaking the News*. Fallows knows that seeing our national policy suggestions and battles as connected to the reality of life in our nation, as good, bad, or middling ways of handling everything from fair and effective law to public education, will demand more than sneering. Sure, politicians want to be reelected and they want their parties to triumph, but what they put into policy and fund or defund has many different tiers of effect on the protean complexities of American life. When the elected blow it, they should be chastised, but when they do something honorable it shouldn't be almost universally regarded throughout our media as no more than another strategic ploy. Uncompromising and sophisticated changes of perspective are important because we have so much to do and will have to invest quite a bit of time in doing it. Serious reporting will give us a more thorough perspective and it just might supply us with the morale necessary to truly engage our ever shifting whirlwind of troubles. We had better hope so.

As Senator Daniel Patrick Moynihan said a few years ago about our social ills, "Well, look at it this way: It took us thirty years to get into this mess and it'll probably take us about thirty years to get out of it." We should take heed of his observation, however daunting it might seem to those in an understandable rush to get every crimp immediately straightened. Unfortunately, howling oneself into despair because the right things aren't done in a jiffy parallels what Duke Ellington called "a complaint with no future." The most nuanced story of life is always a tale unavoidably focused on the *length* of the journey from a revelatory conception to its execution—in form and substance—which may be short this time, long the next. As members of an improvising democracy, we might do better to shape our vision on the form of the soap opera, not the sound bite. However melodramatic and topical, the soap opera makes it clear that problems go *on* and *on* and *on*. We are in a time when we have to redefine our aspirations and discover when our discontents are rational and when they are not. It is perhaps most necessary that we have leaders, regardless of party, regardless of right, middle, or left, who have the patience and the courage and the eloquence to come forward with a convincing sense of humanity that will allow us to acknowledge ourselves not only as what we are but as what we can be—adults fully aware of how fundamental human shortcomings and mistakes are to all eras, yet a people ready to face the lumps we must take in order to get as much of this stuff right as we can. Such leadership, from the local to the national level, should eventually draw those disengaged millions back into the political process. One never knows. As ever, our story is one everybody on the face of the earth follows. Our society has been the dark horse and it has been the Triple Crown winner. Perhaps that is how we have to see ourselves, as democratic jockeys moving in and out of the light with our mounts, winning, losing, improvising, learning, making great jumps, taking horrible falls, but always refusing to give an ear to anything less than the tragic optimism of the blues to be redefined.

Index

Aberdeen Training Center, 105
Abolition Movement, 337–39
Adelphi University, 327n
adoption, race and, 27–28
Advertisements for Myself (Mailer), 5
advertising, 15
affirmative action, 16–17
Africa, slavery in, 206–8
African American Review, 172
"Afro-Carib Zionism," 139–40
"Age of Redefinition," 14, 102
AIDS, 31
All-American Skin Game, The
    (Crouch), 3, 15, 336
Allen, Ray, 257
Allen, Woody, 75
Allgood, Sara, 275

Ambrose, Stephen, 257
American Academy of the Arts,
    138
American Dilemma, An (Myrdal),
    150
American Enterprise, 239
American Enterprise Institute, 13n
American Heritage, 159
American Indians, 27–28, 85, 134,
    141, 224, 281–83
American Irish Historical Society,
    272n
American Werewolf in London, An,
    241
Anti-Memoirs (Malraux), 147, 148n
anti-Semitism, 195
Anti-Slavery Society, 206

Armstrong, Louis, 47, 48, 54, 63,
   160, 161, 166, 273, 278–80,
   288, 292, 306, 311, 312
assimilation, 15, 81–89, 144–45,
   180–81, 223, 226
atomic bombs, 197–99, 200
Australia, 206
"authenticity," race and, 75, 83, 85,
   146, 149
Avakian, George, 309–10, 311

Babs, Alice, 64
Bach, Jean, 302–3, 308, 319
backwoodsmen, 141, 223
Bailey, F. Lee, 76, 87
Baker, Chet, 309
Baldwin, James, 5, 6, 57, 144, 243,
   303, 307
Basie, Count, 63
   autobiography of, 137, 159,
      160–61
bass, bassists, 60, 132–33, 166–67
Bearden, Romare, 161
Beatty, Warren, 253–58
Bechet, Sidney, 48, 52, 54, 63
Beckett, Samuel, 260, 261
Beer Can by the Highway (Kouwen-
   hoven), 39, 167–68
Belafonte, Harry, 298
Belgium, 203–5
Benin, 206
Benito Cereno (Melville), 117,
   123
Benjamin, Playthell, 59
Berger, David, 62
Bernstein, Leonard, 75
Bible, 120, 121
Bigard, Barney, 52, 61
Big Woods (Faulkner), 119
Birmingham, Ala., 94–96
Birth of a Nation, 290, 291
Black and Tan Fantasy, 60n
Black Boy (Wright), 114–16
"black identity," 225
Black Panther Party, 89, 114

Black Power, 4, 15, 81, 86, 139, 247,
   323, 340, 341
blacks, see middle class blacks; race;
   racism; slavery, slaves
Black Yankees (Piersen), 14
Blakely, Art, 313
Blanton, Jimmy, 60, 166
blaxploitation movies, 242–43
Blue Devils of Nada, The (Murray),
   138, 161
blues, 108, 114, 225, 277, 285, 307,
   316, 323, 335
   contemporary blacks and, 161
   Ellington and, 44, 47, 48, 49, 50,
      56, 59, 273, 274
   Murray and, 137, 159–62
Blues and Trouble (Piazza), 128–31
Bosnia, 212–15
Boston Globe, 136
Boston Phoenix, 163
Boyz N the Hood, 244
Branagh, Kenneth, 260
Braud, Wellman, 52
Bravender–Coyle, Paul, 206
Brawley, Tawana, 24
Breaking the News (Fallows), 333,
   343
Brennan, Walter, 276
Broken Blossoms, 290
Brooklyn Dodgers, 161
Brooks, Cleanth, 118
Brown, Clifford, 311, 312
Brown, James, 18, 247
Brown, Lawrence, 55, 64
Brown, Ron, 227–31
Brown, Tina, 192
Broyard, Anatole, 179–87
Buchanan, Pat, 31, 329
Bugliosi, Vincent, 78, 82, 92
Bulworth, 253, 254
Burke, Kenneth, 142, 159, 169
Burkina Faso, 207

Cagney, James, 244, 245
California, 16

Campanella, Roy, Jr., 161
Campanella, Roy, Sr., 161
capital punishment, 250–52
Capote, Truman, 148
Carisi, Johnny, 306
Carmichael, Stokely, 139
Carney, Harry, 51, 55, 64
Carolina Shout, 46
Carradine, John, 55
Carson, Warren, 172
Carter, Benny, 54, 307
Census Bureau, U.S., 226
Chambers, Paul, 310, 313, 317, 321
Chang, Michael, 223
Chavis, Benjamin, 328
Cheadle, Don, 244
Cheyenne Autumn, 285, 288
children:
    sex crimes against, 203–5
    slavery and, 206–8
China, People's Republic of, 201
Christianity, 120
City College of New York, 27
Civil Rights Movement, 94, 98,
    158, 296, 323, 330, 340
Claremont-McKenna College, 132n
Clark, Kenneth, 144
Clark, Marcia, 72, 76, 80, 87
Clarke, Kenny, 312–13
"Clean, Well-Lighted Place, A"
    (Hemingway), 171
Clinton, Bill, 30, 31, 32, 34, 102,
    105, 228, 230
Clockers, 241–42, 247–49
Cobb, Jimmy, 317, 318, 320, 321,
    322
Cochran, Johnnie, 69, 73, 76–77,
    85, 87, 88, 91
Cole, Nat, 298
Coleman, Ornette, 315
Collins, Addie Mae, 95, 96
Coltrane, John, 5–6, 47, 54, 64, 65,
    268, 310, 313, 316
Coming to America, 270
Communists, 115, 140

Connell, Evan, 7
Constitution, U.S., 95, 98, 119
Cook, Will Marion, 53–54
Cooper, James Fenimore, 223
Copland, Aaron, 256, 258
Cosby, Bill, 270, 311
Cotton Club, 58
crime:
    gangster rap and, 24–26
    and punishment, 34–36, 250–52
    race and, 23–24
    sexual, 203–5
    Smith case, 22–24
    social history and, 89–91
Crisis of the Negro Intellectual, The
    (Cruse), 27
Crisp, Donald, 55, 275–76, 290
Croatia, 229
Cruse, Harold, 27
Cult Baseball Players (Seymour), 161
cultural miscegenation, 220, 224
cultural relativism, 81
culture, race and, 15–16, 140–41,
    149–51, 180–87, 219–26
Cuomo, Mario, 74
Curtis, Ken, 287
Custer, George Armstrong, 78–79,
    80, 93

Darden, Christopher, 5, 72, 76,
    78–93
Davis, Kay, 64
Davis, Miles, 43, 46, 295–324
    as bandleader, 301, 306
    drugs and, 300–1, 308, 311
    Gillespie and, 304, 306
    Parker and, 303–4, 305, 306
Davis, Vernon, 305, 313
"Day of the Dead," 160
Dead Man Walking, 250–52, 290
Dead Presidents, 242, 245–47
Def Comedy Jam, 270
Defeat of the Mind, The (Finkiel-
    kraut), 139, 162
de Keyser, David, 266

Democratic Party, 228, 230
    1996 convention of, 32–34
Designated Mourner, The, 259–68
Devil in a Blue Dress, 242, 243–44,
    258
Diana, Princess of Wales, 191–93
Disuniting of America, The
    (Schlesinger), 82–83
Dole, Robert, 34
Donahue, Phil, 28–30
Douglass, Frederick, 151–52, 153,
    156, 157, 166
Drums Along the Mohawk, 282
Dubliners (Joyce), 119
Du Bois, W. E. B., 319
Dunbar, Paul Laurence, 53, 303
Dvořák, Antonín, 53, 54
"dynamics of confrontation," 159

Early, Gerald, 5
East L.A., 225
Eckstine, Billy, 298, 304, 307,
    308
Eldridge, Roy, 302, 321
Eliot, T. S., 170
Ellington, Duke, 5, 8, 43–66, 160,
    161, 162, 166–67, 171, 173,
    219, 273, 296, 297, 307, 316,
    344
    as bandleader, 48, 49, 52, 54–55,
        58–59, 60–61, 63–65
    as composer, 47–53, 55–58, 59–
        66
    early years of, 46–47
    Ford compared with, 45, 55, 274,
        285–88, 292
    four major elements in music of,
        47
    as pianist, 46–47, 65
    women and, 57–58
Ellington, Mercer, 55
Ellison, Fanny, 39
Ellison, Ralph, 6, 57, 71, 126, 132,
    140, 141, 150, 154, 222, 225,
    232, 247

influence and importance of,
    37–40
    Wright compared with, 114–16
Enlightenment, 334, 339
Epitaph of a Small Winner (Machado
    de Assis), 265
ethnicity, 140
evangelical humanism, 210–11
Evans, Gil, 299, 306, 309, 311, 312,
    318, 320, 322, 323
Evers, Medgar, 98, 99
Evers-William, Myrlie, 97–101

Fallows, James, 333, 343
families, single-parent, 143
Fargo, 20, 220, 290
Farrakhan, Louis, 34, 81, 100,
    328–29
Farrow, Mia, 75
fascism, 108, 109, 194–96
Faulkner, William, 5, 44, 117–27,
    130, 135, 148, 151, 169, 184,
    285
Feeney, Mark, 136
female mutilation, 207
Fetchit, Stepin, 284
"field slaves," 145
film reviews, 235–92
Finkielkraut, Alain, 139, 162
Fisher, Mary, 31
Flinn, Kelly, 104, 105
Flying Doctors of East Africa,
    295–96, 319, 322
Fonda, Henry, 55, 287
Ford, John, 5, 8, 246, 272–92
    democracy and, 288–91
    Ellington compared with, 45, 55,
        274, 285–88, 292
    jazz and, 272–73, 276–80,
        285–87, 292
    stock acting company of, 286
    westerns of, 280–85
"Forgotten Girl-Slaves of West
    Africa, The," 206–7
Fort Apache, 282, 284, 287

Founding Fathers, 336, 337
Frady, Marshall, 33
Franklin, Carl, 242, 243–44, 258
Fugitive, The, 291
Fuhrman, Mark, 74, 76, 80, 225
Fung, Dennis, 76

Gallagher, Tag, 287
gangster rap, 24–26
Garland, Red, 310, 313
Garrow, David, 100
Gary, Charles, 89
Gates, Henry "Skip," 37, 180
Germany, Nazi, 194–96
Ghana, 206
ghettos, 144–45
Gillespie, Dizzy, 54, 63, 298, 304,
     308, 311, 312, 323
Gingrich, Newt, 115–16
Ginsburg, Ruth Bader, 20
girls, slavery and, 206–8
Godfather, The, 238
Godfather, The, Part II, 238
Go Down, Moses (Faulkner),
     117–27, 130
Goethe, Johann Wolfgang von, 140
Golding, Susan, 31
Goldman, Ronald, 70, 77, 80, 93
Gonsalves, Paul, 55, 64
Good Life and Its Discontents, The
     (Samuelson), 342
Goodman, Benny, 224, 306
Good Morning Blues (Basie and Mur-
     ray), 137, 159, 160–61
Gorbachev, Mikhail, 201
Grapes of Wrath, The, 287
Greece, ancient, 120
Greenberg, Clement, 180–81
Greer, Sonny, 47
Griffith, D. W., 44, 273, 290
Grodin, Charles, 79
Gromyko, Andre, 267

Hamas, 331
Hamilton, Jimmy, 55, 61, 64

Hamilton, Jug, 154, 169–70
Hamlet, 260
Hare, David, 259, 260, 266
Harlem, 46, 57, 62
Harper, Michael, 233
Harper's, 148
Harriman, Pamela, 230
Harrison, Max, 51
"Harvard Blues," 295
Hawkins, Coleman, 46, 54
Heat, 238
He Got Game, 253–58
Helgesen, Sally, 220
Hemingway, Ernest, 7, 44, 119, 130,
     151, 161, 171, 174, 175, 184
Henderson, Horace, 54
Henry, John, 256, 258
Henry V (Shakespeare), 333
Hero and the Blues, The (Murray),
     54, 137, 142, 159, 160, 163
Hill Street Blues, 238
Hiroshima, 197–99, 200
history, race and, 339–44
Hitler, Adolf, 109, 195
Hodges, Johnny, 48, 50, 54, 55, 63,
     64, 65
Hodges, Linda, 27–28
Holiday, Billie, 306
Home (Jones), 5–6
homosexuals, 226
"house niggers," 145
Howe, Irving, 115
How Green Was My Valley, 274,
     292
Hubbard, Freddie, 303, 314
Huckleberry Finn (Twain), 286
Hughes, Allen and Albert, 242,
     244–47, 248
Hughes, Howard, 108
Hughes, Langston, 307
humanism:
     evangelical, 210–11
     universal, 207–8
Hyman, Stanley Edgar, 115
Hynes, Joe, 76

immigrants, 294
In Contempt (Darden), 78, 84
Indians, American, 27–28, 85, 134, 141, 224, 281–83
"ingrained cultural memory," 28
In Our Time (Hemingway), 119, 121, 130
intellectuals, 183–84, 185
In the American Grain (Williams), 5, 55
Intruder in the Dust (Faulkner), 285
Invisible Man (Ellison), 115, 132, 140, 154
Ishlon, Debbie, 310–11
Ito, Lance, 75–76, 77, 80

Jackson, Jesse, 32–34, 228, 230
Jackson, Jesse, Jr., 34
Jackson, Mahalia, 64
Jackson, Michael, 5, 106–10
Jamal, Ahmad, 321
James, Henry, 5, 6, 184
James, Michael, 59, 137
Japan, 197–202
   atomic bombing of, 197–99, 200
   World War II aggression of, 200–202
Japanese-Americans, 195
jazz, 108–9, 132–33, 180–81, 231, 295, 306–7, 311, 312, 315, 317, 320–21, 323, 335
   Ford and, 272–73, 276–80, 285–87, 292
   Murray and, 137, 159–62
   see also Ellington, Duke; Davis, Miles
Jeffries, Leonard, 27
Jeremiah, 117
Jesse (Frady), 33
Jesus Christ, 213
Jews, 72, 75, 144–45, 183, 185, 224
John Ford (McBride and Wilmington), 284
John Ford (Stowell), 277, 278, 280–81

John Ford: The Man and His Films (Gallagher), 287
Johnson, Ben, 55
Johnson, Charles, 207
Johnson, J. J., 311
Johnson, James P., 46, 54
Johnson, Lyndon B., 156, 258
Jones, Jimmy, 63
Jones, LeRoi, 5–6, 167, 268
Jones, Paula, 102, 105
Jones, Philly Joe, 301, 310, 313
Jordan, Michael, 15, 16, 92, 223
Joyce, James, 119, 151, 164, 166, 168, 175
Jung, Carl, 224
"junk justice," 204

Kafka Was the Rage (Broyard), 179–87
Kauffmann, Stanley, 259
Keaton, Buster, 279
Kelly, Wynton, 317, 321
Kemp, Jack, 31
Kemper, Walter, 276
Kennedy, Edward M. "Ted," 228
Kennedy, Jacqueline, 98
Kennedy, John F., 95, 229, 296, 324
King, B. B., 191
King, Coretta Scott, 97–101
King, Dexter, 100
King, Martin Luther, Jr., 33, 34, 95, 98, 99, 100, 229
Kirk, Roland, 331
Kouwenhoven, John A., 39, 148, 167–68
Kurosawa, Akira, 327
Kuwait, 209

Lambiet, Jose, 203–4
LaMotta, Vicki, 21
Last Hurrah, The, 290–91
Lee, Henry, 76
Lee, Spike, 15, 241–42, 247–49, 253–58
Leguizamo, John, 247

lesbians, 226
Lewis, John, 306, 311
Lewis, R.W.B., 36–37
Lewis and Clark Expedition, 19
liberals, 99
    racism of, 25, 26–28
*Life and Times of Frederick Douglass,
    The* (Douglass), 151–52, 156
Lincoln, Abraham, 305
"Little Man at Chehaw Station,
    The" (Ellison), 222, 225
Lonesome Dove, 238
Lopez, Rosa, 76
Lott, Trent, 104

McBride, Joseph, 280
MacDonald, Dwight, 180
McDormand, Frances, 20
Machado de Assis, Joaquim Maria,
    265
McKinney, Laura Hart, 80
McLaughlin, Victor, 55
McLean, Jackie, 299, 308, 312
McLuhan, Marshall, 185
McNair, Denise, 95, 96
Madonna, 21
Mailer, Norman, 5, 157
Malcolm X, 15, 85, 98, 99, 100, 101,
    145, 183, 340
Malraux, André, 147, 148n, 151,
    166
Mandela, Nelson, 207
Manhattan, 224–25
Mann, Thomas, 166
Mao Zedong, 201
Marsalis, Wynton, 57, 161, 231
Martin Luther King Center for
    Non-Violent Social Change,
    100
"Melting Down the Iron Suits of
    History" (Crouch), 15
Melville, Herman, 7, 44, 117, 122,
    123, 125, 170, 265–66,
    286
Menace II Society, 245, 246, 248

Mexican-Americans, 225
Mfume, Kweise, 100, 230
middle class blacks, 145, 228
Middle East, 209
Middle Passage (Johnson), 207
Miles, Vera, 282–83
Miley, Bubber, 48–49, 62
military:
    desegregation of, 157–58
    sexual harrassment in, 18, 102–5
military academies, women in, 18,
    20
Milken, Michael, 36
Miller, Dennis, 79
Million Dollar Movie, 291
Million Man March, 34, 328–29
Mingus, Charles, 48, 54
Mix, Tom, 149
Mobley, Hank, 317, 321
Moby Dick (Melville), 5, 170,
    265–66, 286
Monk, Thelonious, 46, 296, 306,
    309, 316, 321
Morris, Willie, 148
Morton, Jelly Roll, 52–53
Mosley, Walter, 243
Moveable Feast, A (Hemingway), 7
movie reviews, 235–92
Moynihan, Daniel Patrick, 344
Moynihan Report, 143
Muhammad, Elijah, 99
Mulligan, Gerry, 306, 309
Murphy, Eddie, 269–71
Murray, Albert, 5, 6, 19, 45, 54, 56,
    97, 132–78, 273, 339–40
    American Academy of the Arts
        induction of, 138
    blues and, 137
    obscurity of, 138
    output of, 136–38
    race and, 135–36, 137, 138–46,
        147–58
    "Scooter Novels" of, 137, 160,
        162–78
    South and, 133–35

music, *see* blues; jazz; popular music
Music Is My Mistress (Ellington), 58
My Darling Clementine, 276, 282, 287
Myrdal, Gunnar, 150

NAACP, 100, 105, 328
Nagasaki, 197–99, 200
Nance, Ray, 50, 55, 64
Nation, 161
National Book Award, 207
Nation of Islam, 76, 85, 99, 100, 329
Newport Jazz Festival, 296, 309
New School for Social Research, 183, 184
Newton, Huey, 89
New York *Daily News*, 8, 13, 203
New Yorker, 180, 192
New York Police Department, 21
New York Times, 27, 75, 179
Nichols, Mike, 266–67
Nigeria, 206
Nike, 15
Nixon, Richard M., 290
"non-fiction novels," 148
Noonan, Peggy, 223
North to Alaska, 288
Notes of a Hanging Judge (Crouch), 3, 4, 14
Nuremburg trials, 201
Nutty Professor, The, 270–71

O'Connor, Flannery, 135
O'Connor, Sandra Day, 20
Odyssey, The (Homer), 331–32
O'Hara, Maureen, 55, 275
Oklahoma City bombing, 94, 96, 330
O'Leary, Hazel, 20
Oliver, King, 48, 53
Olson, Charles, 6
Olympic Games of 1984, 223
Omni-Americans, The (Murray), 19, 97, 136–37, 138–46, 150, 151, 157, 159, 162, 174, 176

One False Move, 243
Operation Push, 34
Outrage (Bugliosi), 78, 82, 92–93

"Pantaloon in Black" (Faulkner), 169
Parker, Charlie, 46, 54, 296, 297, 303–4, 305, 308, 311, 313, 316, 318, 323, 324
Partisan Review, 181
"passing for white," 180
Pataki, George, 250
Patterson, Orlando, 201
Penn, Sean, 251
Peretz, Martin, 329–30
Phifer, Mekhi, 248
Philosophy of Literary Form, The (Burke), 142, 169
Piazza, Tom, 63, 128–31, 163
Piersen, William D., 14, 281
pioneer women, 19–20
Playboy, 20–22
Poitier, Sidney, 298
popular music, 106–10
pornography, 181–82
"Portrait of a Hipster" (Broyard), 181
Portrait of the Artist as a Young Man, A (Joyce), 168
Pound, Ezra, 6, 176
Powell, Adam Clayton, 228
Powell, Colin, 31–32, 34, 92, 223
Price, Richard, 248
Procope, Russell, 64
Pryor, Richard, 270
Public Enemy, 244
Public Enemy, 256
Pulp Fiction, 290

race:
    adoption and, 27–28
    assimilation and, 15, 81–89, 144–45, 180–81, 223, 226
    "authenticity" and, 75, 83, 85, 146, 149

Broyard and, 179–87
crime and, 22–24
culture and, 15–16, 140–41,
    149–51, 180–87, 219–26
diminishing importance of, 16,
    219–26
Ellington and, 58, 60
Ellison and, 114–16, 222
Faulkner and, 117–27
Ford and, 280–85
history and, 339–44
movies and, 239–40, 241–49,
    253–58, 280–85
Murray and, 135–36, 137,
    138–46, 147–58
Simpson trial and, 69–77, 78–93
Wright and Ellison and, 114–16
racism, 195, 282–83, 313–15
    of Hemingway, 161
    institutional, 89
    liberal, 25, 26–28
    Nation of Islam and, 99
    "uppityness" and, 74–75, 81
Ran, 327
Raw, 270
Ray, James Earl, 100
Reagan, Ronald, 31, 223
Redman, Don, 54
Reed, Ishmael, 241
Reed, Ralph, 31
Rees, Tom, 319–20, 322
Republican Party, 1996 convention
    of, 30–32, 223
Richards, Ann, 20
Richardson, Miranda, 266
Rio Bravo, 288
Rivera, Geraldo, 79
Roach, Max, 54, 319, 322, 323
Roaring Twenties, The, 245
Robbins, Tim, 252–54
Robertson, Carole, 95, 96
Robinson, Jackie, 161
Robinson, Sugar Ray, 296–97,
    300
Rogers, Will, 277–80, 291

Roker, Al, 269
Rollins, Sonny, 308, 313
Rome, ancient, 120
Roosevelt, Franklin D., 289
Roots, 86
Rourke, Constance, 141, 282
Rushing, Jimmy, 63
Russia, 194–95, 196, 198, 201

Sacagawea, 19
Saddam Hussein, 209
Safire, William, 75
St. Louis Blues, The, 50
Samuelson, Robert J., 342
Sarajevo, 212–15
Sarandon, Susan, 251
Saturday Night Live, 270
Scheck, Barry, 76
Schlesinger, Arthur, Jr., 82–83, 340
Schroeder, Patricia, 104
Schwartz, Delmore, 180–81, 184,
    185
Scott, Nathan and Charlotte, 232–
    34
Seabrook, Larry, 17
Searchers, The, 282–83, 287–88,
    289
Seattle Times, 206
segregation, 27, 32, 95, 148, 157
Sergeant Rutledge, 283–84
Seven League Boots (Murray), 160,
    164–67, 169, 171, 172–78
sex, 16, 186–87
sex crimes against children, 203–5
sexual harrassment in military, 18,
    102–5
Seymour, Gene, 161
Shabazz, Betty, 97–101
Shabazz, Malcolm, 100–101
Shabazz, Qubilah, 100, 101
Shadow and Act (Ellison), 114–16,
    140, 150
Shakespeare, William, 333
Shakur, Tupac, 5, 24–26
Shapiro, Robert, 73

Shawn, Wallace, 259, 260, 261, 264, 265, 268
Shaya, Carol, 20–22
She Wore a Yellow Ribbon, 286, 288
Shoenberg, Loren, 49, 306
Silver, Horace, 312
Silvia, Queen of Sweden, 204
Simmons, Russell, 270–71
Simpson, Nicole Brown, 70, 76, 77, 80, 93
Simpson, O. J., 5, 69–77, 78–93
single-parent families, 143
Sixteenth Street Baptist Church, 94–96
slavery, slaves, 19, 86, 145, 337–38
    in Africa, 206–8
Smart Hearts for the City (Solomon), 185, 221
Smith, Susan, 22–24
Smith, Willie "the Lion," 54
Solomon, Barbara Probst, 185, 221, 223
Son of the Morning Star (Connell), 7
Sontag, Susan, 75, 265
South, 232
    Faulkner and, 117–27, 135
    Murray and, 133–35, 146–58, 164–67
Southern Christian Leadership Conference, 95
South to a Very Old Place (Murray), 137, 138, 146–58, 163, 167, 169, 172, 178, 339–40
Soviet Union, 194–95, 196, 198, 201
Sprague, Morteza, 154, 157
Spyglass Tree, The (Murray), 137, 164, 169–72, 175, 176, 177
Stalin, Joseph, 195, 196
Stallone, Sylvester, 75
Steamboat Round the Bend, 284
Steiner, George, 30
Stewart, James, 287
Stomping the Blues (Murray), 137, 138, 159, 160, 273

Stowell, Peter, 277, 278, 280–81, 291
Strayhorn, Billy, 50, 61, 63, 65
stride piano, 46, 54
Strode, Woody, 283–84
Stuart, Charles, 23
Sullivan's Travels, 247
Supreme Court, U.S., 18, 20, 102
Sutton, Percy, 228
System of Dante's Hell, The (Jones), 167

Tagore, Rabindranath, 109
Taiwan, 201
Tate, Larenz, 246–47
Taylor, Art, 308
Taylor, Frances, 298, 322
television, 238
television talk shows, 28–30, 79–80
Temperley, Joe, 51
Terry, Clark, 63, 161
Texaco, 16, 17, 18
Thurmond, Strom, 32
Thurow, Lester, 16
"timbral harmony," 49–52
Time, 75
Togo, 206
Torin, Symphony Sid, 318
Tracy, Spencer, 290
Train Whistle Guitar (Murray), 137, 164, 168, 169, 170, 171, 172
tribalism, 226
True Grit, 288
Tubman, Harriet, 19, 97, 98
Tuskegee Institute, 153–56, 157, 165
Twister, 38–39
Two Rode Together, 287
Tynes, Margaret, 64

Ulysses (Joyce), 5, 164
United Nations Human Rights Committee, 206

United States:
    four elements in making of, 141
    international role of, 209–11
universal humanism, 207–8

Village Voice, 207
"volunteered slavery," 331

Wagon Master, 276
Wallace, George, 95
Waller, Fats, 54
Warren, Robert Penn, 135
Washington, Booker T., 153
Washington, Denzel, 243, 244,
    257–58
Washington, George, 338
Wayne, John, 55, 273, 286, 288–
    89
Webb, Chick, 53
Webster, Ben, 50, 60
Wee Willie Winkie, 284
Wesley, Cynthia, 95, 96
White, Jack E., 75
white-collar crime, 34, 36
"white trash," 124
Whitman, Christine Todd, 20, 31,
    223
Widmark, Richard, 287
Will, George, 342
Williams, Cootie, 64
Williams, William Carlos, 5, 6, 55
Wilmington, Michael, 284
Wilson, Edmund, 119

Winfrey, Oprah, 29, 92
Wings of Eagles, The, 288–89
Winters, Jonathan, 270
WLIB radio, 228
women, 15, 18–24, 31
    crime and race and, 22–24
    in Ford's movies, 275, 282–83
    genital mutilation of, 207
    King, Evers-Williams, and
        Shabazz, 97–101
    in military, 102–5
    in military academies, 18, 20
    pioneer, 19–20
    in *Playboy* photo spreads, 20–22
    sexual harrassment of, 18
    slavery and, 206–8
Woods, Tiger, 15
World Congress Against Commer-
    cial Sexual Exploitation of
    Children, 204
World Trade Center bombing, 330
World War II, 194–96, 197–99
Wright, Richard, 114–16, 135

Xenakis, Stephen N., 104

Yamamoto, Mike, 77
Yankees, 141
Young, Andrew, 33
Young, Lester, 306, 308
Young Mr. Lincoln, 281, 287, 291

Zigo, Gayla, 104

Permissions Acknowledgments

Many of the essays in this work include material that has been previously published, often under different titles: "Blues for Tomorrow: A Gathering of Commentaries on Our American Condition" includes a series of eight columns originally published in *The Daily News*.

"Duke Ellington: Transcontinental Swing" from "The Duke's Blues," originally published in *The New Yorker*, April 29 & May 6, 1996.

"Truth Crushed to Earth" from "The Good News," originally published in *Esquire* (Volume 124, No. 6, 12/95); "The Dardenilla Dilemma: Selling Hostile Chocolate and Vanilla Animus," originally published in *The Darden Dilemma*, edited by Ellis Cose (New York, HarperPerennial, 1997), "The Dream Was Not in Place" and "The King of Narcissism," originally published in *The Daily News*.

"Two on the Money" and "Somebody Knew," originally published in *The Daily News*; "Bible Belt Greco-Roman Blues: The Shadow of the Negro," originally published as the Introduction to *Go Down, Moses* by William Faulkner (New York, Modern Library, 1995); "The Blues Is the Accompaniment," originally published as the Foreword to *Blues and Trouble* by Tom Piazza (New York, St. Martin's Press, 1996).

"World War II at Fifty," "Hiroshima, Mon Amour," "Who's Sorry Now?," "Patty Cake with Blood," "Forgotten Girl-Slave Blues," "Whose Business Is Our Business?," originally published in *The Daily News*.

"Who Will Enjoy the Shadow of Whom?" from "Race Is Over: Black, White, Red, Yellow—Same Difference," originally published in *The New York Times* Magazine, September 29, 1996; "Meditation on Ron Brown, in Two Parts," "Spirits Spun in Gold," originally published as three columns in *The Daily News*.

"Two Out of Three: Reinventing Americana," originally published in *The Los Angeles Times*; "Blues at the Gallow Pole" and "*The Nutty Professor*," originally published in *The Daily News*; "John Henry Versus the Minstrel Machine," originally published as "Beatty, Lee, and Their Worlds of Blackness" in *The Los Angeles Times*; "Bull Feeney Plays the Blues: John Ford and the Meaning of Democracy," originally published in *The Recorder* (Volume 9, No. 2, Fall 1996).

"Blues to be Redefined," originally published in the *Partisan Review*.

Grateful acknowledgment is made to the following for permission to reprint previously published material: Carol Southern Books: Excerpts from *Kafka Was the Rage* by Anatole Broyard. Copyright © 1993 by Alexandra Broyard. Reprinted by permission of Carol Southern Books, an imprint of Clarkson N. Potter, a division of Crown Publishers, Inc.

HarperCollins Publishers, Inc.: Excerpts from *In Contempt* by Christopher Darden. Copyright © 1996 by Christopher Darden. Reprinted by permission of HarperCollins Publishers, Inc.

Twayne Publishers: Excerpt from *John Ford* by Peter Stowell. Copyright © 1986 by G.K. Hall & Co. Reprinted by permission of Twayne Publishers, an imprint of Simon & Schuster Macmillan.

Warner Bros. Publications U.S. Inc.: Excerpt from "Harvard Blues" by Count Basie, George Frazier, and Tad Smith, copyright © 1942 (renewed) by WB Music Corp. All rights reserved. Reprinted by permission of Warner Bros. Publications U.S. Inc., Miami, FL 33014.

Printed in the United States
by Baker & Taylor Publisher Services